WOMEN
IN
AMERICAN POLITICS

Martin Gruberg
WISCONSIN STATE UNIVERSITY

WOMEN IN
AMERICAN POLITICS

An Assessment and Sourcebook

Academia Press

Women in American Politics

Academia Press

P.O. Box 125
Oshkosh, Wisconsin

Preface

In politics, American Women have been virtually invisible. Political scientists, mostly male, have tended to overlook this major group. For example, the standard work on party and pressure politics, V. O. Key's *Politics, Parties, and Pressure Groups,* ignores women completely except for a few pages about suffragettes. A basic book on pressure groups, Harmon Zeigler's *Interest Groups in American Society,* also omits mention of women; and most textbooks about American government make no references to female political activity. The same is true of books on state and local government. Clearly, this situation does not reflect an absence of discrimination, but rather shows that in our society women bear the stigma of belonging to a minority group even though they constitute a majority.

Where on the political power scale do women stand today as voters, as interest group members, as party members, as government officials? Do they have parity with men, competing as equals for any and all offices and objectives? Are there times and places at which they enjoy certain success, having a monopoly of rewards or exercising dominant authority?

To provide factual answers to questions such as these, this book attempts to present a comprehensive picture of the position of women in American political life since the nineteenth amendment (1920). It begins with a glance at the high hopes of the days prior to "equal suffrage," and follows with a description of female voting behavior from 1920 to the present. It also considers the variety, strengths and weaknesses of the organizations which represent women in the political process, and includes a survey of the progress women have made in politics and in government since suffrage.

Finally, an evaluation of this record is offered—an evaluation which will maintain that, by and large, women have been fated to dwell in relative obscurity, accused of a lack of political interest or drive, and rebuffed into almost complete ineffectiveness. Despite this evaluation, the author views with optimism certain future patterns in the participation of women in politics and government.

Although one person is finally responsible, a book like this reflects the contributions of many. I would like to express my thanks to each and every one, but a fallible memory may cause me to omit many who are deserving of praise.

A number of my students have given valuable service. Assisting me in fact-gathering were such diligent workers as James Ochiltree, Helen Hankwitz, Jerome Catlin, Robert Selk, Dale Seeling, David Koss, Anne Belongia, and Bonnie Krull.

A great debt is also owed to my colleagues. In addition to the members of my department who read and criticized portions of the manuscript, David Chang, Charles Goff, L. Larry Leonard, Ralph Norem, and Jeffry Radell, I owe thanks to Jarvis Bush, Hugo Hartig, Helen Wahoski and the staff of the Forrest R. Polk Library, and to the Wisconsin State University—Oshkosh grant committee for partially subsidizing my research.

Special thanks are due to Mary Kleinschmit and Ruth Walker, typists, and to Elizabeth Roos, Gloria Klein, Ellis Steiner, Robin Haase, Mary Byrne, and Barbara and Molly Wolf.

Numerous organizations, governmental agencies, and public and private libraries have gone out of their way in helping to find material. These include the Democratic and Republican Parties, the League of Women Voters, the Women's Bureau, the Governors' Commissions on the Status of Women, the National Council of Women, the Radcliffe Women's Archives, the Miriam Holden Library, and the New York Public Library.

Finally, I wish to thank the political activists, male and female, who have taken time for interviews or questionnaires. I dare not name some for fear of slighting others.

This book is dedicated to my mother, Mollie Gruberg. Not least among her achievements, she has demonstrated that a woman can have a career without neglecting her family.

Martin Gruberg

Oshkosh, Wisconsin
January 1968

Contents

Part I.
Women in Politics:
An Assessment

The Achievement of American Women In Politics Since 1920

1a. Suffrage Arguments and Their Aftermath

The uphill struggle for woman suffrage began inauspiciously in 1848 at a rights convention at Seneca Falls, New York, where Elizabeth Cady Stanton startled some of the delegates by proclaiming that among other rights, women should have the vote. No direct action resulted from this manifesto, but it takes a long time for some seeds to germinate.

In 1869 two women's suffrage organizations were founded, the National Woman Suffrage Association, headed by Mrs. Stanton and Susan B. Anthony, and the American Woman Suffrage Association, headed by Lucy Stone and Julia Ward Howe.[1] Also in 1869 Congress proposed to the states an amendment making it illegal to deny the vote to anyone on the basis of race, color, or previous condition of servitude. At the same time, suffragists urged members of Congress to grant women the right to vote. Senator Charles Sumner of Massachusetts is said to have replied, "We know how the

Negro will vote, but are not so sure of the women." Other congressional and government leaders took refuge in the words of Thomas Jefferson: "Were our state a pure democracy, there would still be excluded from our deliberations . . . women, who, to prevent depravation of morals and ambiguity of issues, should not mix promiscuously in gatherings of men." The Great Libertarian also said: "The appointment of a woman to office is an innovation for which the public is not prepared, nor am I." Similarly, Dr. L. P. Brockett published in 1869 his *Women's Rights, Wrongs, and Privileges,*[2] maintaining that women were well represented in politics by their husbands and fathers. And he prophesied darkly that once woman was given the vote, the sexes would be at war. He warned that political disagreements could lead to the breakup of marriage, that women were too emotional for political matters, and that exposure to politics would cause them to lose their charm.

Dr. Brockett's message failed to travel west. In the same year that it was broadcast, the territory of Wyoming gave women the suffrage, and Utah followed suit. The succeeding decade saw women's organizations appealing repeatedly to Congress for universal suffrage. Some encouragement was given by Senator A. A. Sargeant of California, who said, in introducing a suffrage amendment in 1878: "I believe that by bringing the intelligence, the virtue, the good intentions possessed by the women of America to the ballot-box, we may have better politics, better administration and government, less grog-shops, less hells of iniquity, and an improvement in every direction."[3] Opponents of the bill asserted that women would be corrupted by the political process. Senator George Vest of Missouri declared: "It will unsex our mothers, wives and sisters, who are to-day influencing by their gentle caress the action of their husbands toward the good and pure. It will turn our blessed country's domestic peace into ward assemblyrooms."

With few variations upon these themes, the issue gave rise to pompous and windy utterances for 50 years. It was argued that woman's place was in the home, that politics was man's business. And proponents of the suffrage answered that, since politics permeates even the home, both husband and wife should be concerned: "The ballot will give her prestige equal to that of the father in her boy's mind; and so it will actually lighten her task as chief family teacher."[4] Unfortunately for the cause, however, tradition-oriented women did not want women's rights: "They had husbands, thank God, to look after their interests, and they needed no new laws to protect their rights."[5]

Meanwhile, forces were at work to lure women into factories, stores, offices, and schools—even into the sacrosanct world of politics. Especially on the western frontier, women did not lead sheltered lives. Perhaps it was this frontier reality, together with recognition of women's contributions, and possibly a spirit of egalitarianism and chivalry, or even a desire to induce migration of eligible women to the Rocky Mountain West, that brought Colorado (1893) and Idaho (1896) to award the ballot to women. Fourteen years later Washington gave women the vote (1910), followed with band-wagon action by California (1911), Arizona (1912), Kansas (1912), and Oregon (1912).

Opposing the spread of feminism were the liquor interests and the political machines. Frances Willard, the leader of the Woman's Christian Temperance Union, had vigorously espoused women's suffrage as a means of increasing the temperance vote.[6] Saloon-keepers and liquor manufacturers were fearful that votes for women would lead to votes for prohibition. In addition, many Republican and Democratic leaders were "uncertain about their ability to control an addition to the electorate which seemed to them relatively unsusceptible to bribery, more militant, and bent on disturbing reforms ranging from better sewer control, to the abolition of child labor . . ."[7] Some even feared that women voters would combine against men.

The women contended that for some positions in government they were especially qualified. For example, who were better qualified to be inspectors of factories employing women and girls, to be judges in juvenile courts, to be administrators of institutions in which women and girls or young children were cared for? Moreover, the vote for women would end discrimination against them in public employment. Certainly, they asserted, the special and tender perspectives of women would enrich the work of legislative bodies, especially in the consideration of social welfare proposals.

Further impetus was given the movement when Montana and Nevada gave women the vote in 1914. Along with the usual jibes at

"Petticoat Politics" and "Pantry Politics," it was frequently asserted that women were perfectly contented with their lot; only a minority of unhappy spinsters and misfits were behind the agitation for the ballot. The belief in the contentment of most women was, however, rudely jolted by militant suffragettes in the nine states where women could vote, who urged the punishment of the party in power, the Democrats, for failing to propose a constitutional amendment granting women the suffrage. During the congressional elections of 1914, only 20 of 43 Democratic candidates in these states won,[8] and the fury of women scorned was fully demonstrated.

The bitter maneuvering of almost seven decades seemed finally at an end when both party platforms in 1916 advocated the granting of woman suffrage by state action. Speaking for most of the South, Governor James E. Ferguson of Texas submitted a minority report opposing the Democratic Resolutions Committee statement on female suffrage,[9] but the Southerners lost the vote on this plank in the Democratic platform.[10]

In 1917 the militants resorted to more aggressive tactics, picketing the White House, burning copies of the President's speeches, and going on hunger strikes when arrested. Meanwhile, the United States had entered a war to preserve democracy abroad, providing opportunity for suffrage supporters to stage parades urging their particular brand of domestic democracy.

New York acquiesced in 1917, and Michigan, Oklahoma, and South Dakota followed. Thus on the eve of the passage of the nineteenth amendment, nearly 18 million women had already been enfranchised. The amendment actually gave the vote to an additional nine and a half million women. [11]

All sorts of dire predictions were reiterated in 1920. But some of the suffrage leaders believed that the female vote would end graft and corruption, do away with war, and right all wrongs. The *Washington Herald* said that "reason is to count for more than it used to, and emotion less."[12] A *Yale Review* writer observed: "Women in politics means a never-ending agitation and a constant cry for reform; for women, popularly supposed to be the conservative sex, are biological rebels whose spirit of revolt is tempered only by their idealism." [13] Male politicians, seeing how effective the suffragist lobby had become, feared the creation of a women's bloc of votes: "Women feel this sex difference still more than men; while a man may vote for a woman because he thinks her a good candidate in spite of being a woman, for a long time many women will tend to vote for another woman as a demonstration of *esprit de corps.*" [14]

The political reality of this fear was shown when Alfred E. Smith, sensing that the newly enfranchised women of the Empire State would vote as a bloc, tried to get the Democrats to nominate a woman for lieutenant governor when he ran for governor in 1920. But Senator John Sharp Williams of Mississippi demonstrated particular astuteness when he claimed: "The practical results of the adoption or defeat of the suffrage amendment will amount to nothing." [15]

Some Democratic party managers did not feel as assured as Senator Williams. They hoped that women voters in 1920 would save the party from electoral defeat on the issue of the League of Nations. Women who could vote in 1916 were supposed to have endorsed Wilson for "keeping us out of war," [16] and, of course, it was Wilson who urged the participation of the United States in the League of Nations. Surely, women would not desert their political idol.

Both parties exploited the peace issue. Republicans contended that Wilson's type of League would drag America into war. Democrats replied that the League was the alternative to war. Republicans further exploited the issue of "the high cost of living"—and thus demonstrated an awareness of the feminine political mystique. Republicans also made the charge that Cox and his backers were "wets." Democrats, on the other hand, made much of the National Woman's Party [17] report that evaluated both Cox and Harding. The report said that Harding's suffrage record was "varied, evasive, and non-committal" until October, 1918, whereas Cox from the first had shown a favorable attitude. [18] Harding won the election, perhaps because—with predictable feminine unpredictability—only about one-quarter of eligible female voters cast their ballots. [19] Despite this demonstration of indifference, reluctance, or sheer political ignorance and hesitation, the leading sociologist Franklin H. Giddings expressed his belief in 1922 that the immediate effects of the influence of women as a group in public life would be harmful. He indicted women for lack of political experience and emotionalism. [20]

The new voters had to go to school, and the League of Women Voters, the successor to the National American Woman Suffrage Association, promoted citizenship training programs[21] to upgrade women's political sensitivity. Partly as a result of such efforts, women quickly recognized their political allies and enemies. In Mississippi, for example, Henry L. Whitfield, former president of Mississippi State College for Women, was elected governor in 1923, largely through the efforts of alumnae of the college. And women claimed to have defeated James E. Ferguson in Texas and Cole Blease in South Carolina.[22] Gifford Pinchot attributed his election as Governor of Pennsylvania in 1922 to the support of women—especially to Mrs. Barclay H. Warburton, daughter of merchant-politician John Wanamaker and vice chairman of the Republican State Committee, and to Mrs. Pinchot. He also was endorsed by the WCTU. A similar revolt in the same year by GOP women in Indiana gave Albert J. Beveridge the party nomination for the U.S. Senate.[23] Beveridge had been a friend of women's causes when he had been in the Senate.

Despite ridicule, obstructionist tactics, and political ingenuousness—not to belittle sympathetic aid by a few male politicians—women did gain some immediate practical benefits from political power. During the first decade of their suffrage, the proportion of women postmasters increased from about one-tenth to nearly one-fifth,[24] and many state laws equalized or at least improved the position of woman "with regard to guardianship of her children, jury duty, inheritance, property, citizenship, and many other legal rights."[25] In 1920, Virginia permitted women to qualify for the bar,[26] the last state to do so. Again, the Sheppard-Towner Maternity bill, which proposed grants to the states for child-care programs, had been before Congress for three years. In 1921 it was passed by both houses by an overwhelming vote. In the following year, a bill providing independent citizenship for married women, known as the Cable Act, was passed in the House by a vote of 206 to nine, and in the Senate without a dissenting vote.

Nevertheless, there was still some dissatisfaction with the political status of women. A letter to the *New Republic,* written by a woman, took issue with an article on suffrage which stated that "women are ready now, whether the office be justice of the peace, mayor of New York, member of Congress or of the Cabinet." The writer thought "it would be more exact to say, 'Unmarried women and widows are ready now,' but the chances are that most married women, however able and ambitious, would not be ready at all." [27] She felt that society would condemn a married woman for neglecting her home while pursuing a profession.

This, then, is a major part of the background. Women—often with the assistance of men—strove to achieve equal suffrage, but it may be questioned whether this equal voice led to equal rights and equal power. Did women assume the role of political reformers and teachers, and, consequently, "purify" politics? Or did their biological and cultural "inferiority" make them unfit for politics? Were they more emotional than men in their approach to government, or less so? Would women's new role in public affairs have an adverse effect upon the family and the home? The answers to such questions are not immediately apparent; they remain controversial.

1b. Women as Voters

Some people thought in 1920 that more women than men would get to the polls, because men are often unable to be absent from work. However, only about one-fourth of the eligible women cast ballots in the Harding-Cox presidential election. [1]

Voting statistics according to sex are, at best, only informed guesses. One observer of the 1920 election has estimated that women accounted for 37 per cent of the total vote, and that 43 per cent of the eligible women voted. In 1924—the next presidential election—only 35 per cent of the eligible women voted. [2]

A substantial upswing occurred in time. "Morality" issues, prohibition and religion, evidently produced a greatly increased female turnout in 1928. But only 49 per cent of the women citizens voted in 1940, compared to 68 per cent of the men. [3] And in 1948, 45 per cent of the eligible women voted. In 1952, 55 per cent of the women went to the polls, along with 73 per cent of the men.

The vote participation rate among women appears to be generally 10 per cent below that of men, according to the 1956 national samples of the Survey Research Center of the University of

Michigan. In 1960, George Gallup reported that 68.3 million votes were cast by 34.7 million men and 33.6 million women.[5]

When the nineteenth amendment was ratified, it was thought that women were in the majority only in the New England states. But the 1960 Census indicated that 40 states and the District of Columbia had more women than men of voting age. Yet, despite a surplus of 3.6 million women, there are still more male voters. In only a few communities do women outnumber, outregister, and outvote men. In 1960, one such place was Milwaukee.[6] On the other hand, New York State showed 570,000 more women than men of voting age; only 170,000 more women than men were registered. In Pennsylvania, despite a surplus of 330,000 women, men out-registered women by 13,000.

The 1964 election was the twelfth presidential contest held since the nineteenth amendment. For the first time, according to Gallup, as many women as men voted. Even so, the proportion of men who voted was slightly higher.[7]

The Delinquent Voter. About 22 million women of voting age failed to vote in 1964. Some three and a half million more women than men abstained. Why?

Numerous explanations have been offered since the disappointing turnouts of the 1920's.[8] It was said then, and is still being said,[9] that time alone will overcome the long-established attitude that voting is a man's job. Women have not functioned as citizens as long as men have and, therefore, are not as aware of their responsibilities. Voting is a habit that develops slowly. Also, politics has seemed rough, dirty, and unladylike to many.[10]

"The vote having been thrust on me, my first instinct was to refuse to use it," said a busy socialite in 1925.[11] Her husband told her it was her civic duty—her vote would offset the ignorant voter. But she felt that women of her class would no more go into a polling booth than they would go into a saloon. (One result of the suffrage was that schools and firehouses replaced saloons and barbershops as places of balloting).

"I did not believe," another opponent of suffrage stated, "that the average woman would accept responsibilities that go with active and direct participation in government, and was afraid the privilege would be exercised chiefly by a few zealots and a class of women whose qualification for responsible citizenship is too limited to make them seem desirable as factors in the conduct of the country's affairs."[12]

After the 1928 campaign, one observer thought that her sex had received the suffrage prematurely. She felt that women voters tended to base decisions on "personalities, prejudice, slander, and rancorous conservatism."[13] But today educated women have gotten over their revulsion to voting, if not to politics. Voting now is regarded by most women as a civic duty.

The lowest level of political participation among women is found in areas where sex-role differences are most marked, in the South and in rural areas.[14] Sex differences in political behavior are also greater among the poor and the poorly educated. Middle class women vote more frequently than working class women.[15] Negro women are less likely to vote than white women.[16] The wives of Republican husbands are more likely to vote than are the wives of Democratic husbands, apparently because Republican voters tend to be better educated and better off economically.[17] A Census Bureau study found that the voting percentage of college-educated women was higher than that of college-educated men (88.2 per cent to 87.0 per cent).[18]

The largest groups of female non-voters are those over 60 and young women who are not yet established in their communities. Married women vote much more frequently than do the unmarried, but the presence of young children requiring constant attention sometimes serves as a barrier to voting. Married couples tend to vote together, or abstain together.[19] The census study disclosed that among the younger voters 21 to 34 years of age, the voting percentage of women was about one point less than that of men. Although men vote more than women, some polltakers believe that when women say they intend to vote, they are more apt than men actually to do so.[20]

Main Characteristics of Women Voters. Only a few policy issues that persist over a period of time affect men and women differently. Women are about as likely as men to feel strong identification with a political party.[21] Women, however, tend to display a less sophisticated level of concept formation.[22] Seldom do issues arise which polarize the sexes.[23] Gallup has suggested that women are generally uncertain about issues because they are not well informed.[24]

Even before women received the vote, they began to receive some political education. The women's pages of newspapers and the "Good Citizenship" and "Public Affairs" sections of women's magazines were a means for their political education.[25] The messages combined exhortation and advice. "Want to make your children better citizens? Go into politics."[26] Other sources of inspiration were the activities of the League of Women Voters, radio,[27] and television.

A certain political innocence has led some women to complain about legislators who are absent from the floor of their chamber and to praise others who never miss a roll call vote. Women have taken the lead in promoting non-partisan elections, the direct primary, the initiative and the referendum. Advanced as measures to strengthen party responsibility to the voters, these recommendations have often resulted in the weakening of party structures.[28]

Women, less politicized than men, are less apt to follow class considerations in voting, but they do frequently vote in agreement with their husbands.[29] Women vote three to five per cent more Republican than men.[30] However, if we consider a large variety of other social characteristics such as the greater life expectancy among women, the tendency of older people toward conservatism, and the low turnout in the South and among low-educated voters, few residual differences in partisanship remain between men and women. Perhaps women are less inclined to vote for third parties, although an exception could be made for the moral crusades for prohibition and clean government.[31]

How ideologically conservative are women? In attitude, women are more politically conservative on labor, changes in government, religious, domestic, and moral issues. Yet they are more in favor of government intervention and government ownership.[32] One study concluded: "The greatest general change affected by the women's movement, and one to which little attention has been paid, was the impetus given the steady nurturing of the philosophy of the service state, as it surely displaces the doctrine of definitely limited state action."[33] Said one woman: "Motherhood stimulates what you call radical thinking. You men plan for the present day and generation, but mothers plan for the future and for the race. You men go into politics with your heads, but mothers go into politics with their hearts."[34]

Geoffrey Gorer, a British anthropologist, attributed to women voters "the numerous and concerted attempts to legislate men into sobriety, morality and economy." He also contended that the reluctance of the U.S. to pursue an aggressive defense policy was due to women's "negative political influence, to the fear on the part of male politicians of losing the women's vote."[35]

This view has been seconded by William S. White: "It is the women, in every campaign I can remember, who themselves first speak of—and go on interminably speaking of—the woman's vote."[36] White criticized the female habit of reducing politics to a morality play of Good Guy vs. Bad Guy, calling it an "irrational blend of morality and sentimentalism."

Studies of voting habits in the West and Midwest by William McPhee of the Bureau of Applied Social Research at Columbia showed a real divergence between the sexes on such issues as prohibition, legalized gambling, and horse racing.[37] Women were more "against sin."[38]

Women are also more security-oriented. They are more sensitive to peace and foreign policy crises than men. Rear Admiral Fiske in 1925 expressed apprehension at women's meddling and do-good bent: "No man respects and admires women more than I do, but some women have faults, and the fault most commonly found is a seemingly insatiable desire to interfere in matters they do not understand. War they understand least, and from it they instinctively recoil. There is danger in this situation. Women now have the vote and they outnumber the men. There must be some action by the men which will bring women to realize that it is for their comfort and protection that all wars are fought. It is to the interest of women that they permit men to obtain the necessary armament. Only in this way can they be assured of the comfort and protection they need. In spite of themselves, we must protect the ladies!"[39]

Women were less in favor of universal military training than men. They were more disturbed about the Korean War. Pollster Louis Harris reported in 1952 that men tended to think the U.N. force should take the offensive whereas women wanted less fighting and less bloodshed.[40] Women were more in favor of the 1963 nuclear test ban treaty than were men.[41]

It is at the local level that women come into their own domain. Said one woman voter: "Women can understand what's going on in our own precincts. Even in the city. Like graft, overcrowded schools, holes in the streets, curfews for the kids, and stuff like that. But when we listen to those people in Washington about what's going on outside the country and why we ought to agree that what they're doing about it is okay . . . well, it doesn't make sense. Straight talk in simple language. That's what we want."[42] Women's groups are usually active in campaigns for new schools, clean water, consolidated libraries, improved city charters, traffic lights, voting machines, parks and recreation areas, updated registration lists, public housing, mental health facilities, conservation, censorship of books and motion pictures, civil service reform, Americanization, and social legislation.

Women decide most of the school elections. They determine the fate of most bond issues for city improvement. The 1964 phenomenon of the "white backlash" (adverse reaction to Negro demands for civil rights), which had job security implications for men, reflected women's concern for the neighborhood school.

The Institution for Social Research of the University of Michigan disagrees with those who would give social welfare matters—education, health, pensions—a feminine label.[43] Women have not proved to be more concerned than men in this area. Many wives referred interviewers to their husbands as the one in the family who paid attention to politics.[44]

James March, a sociologist, asked members of an eastern suburban League of Women Voters organization and their husbands to rank the most and least appropriate policy areas for that group's agenda. He found striking agreement between the sexes, that women might discuss "local government" and "educational policy," and that they should pay less attention to "labor policy" and "tax policy."[45]

As one Republican official put it, "If I'm talking to women's clubs . . . I'll talk about education and health matters rather than about South Vietnam or the balance of payments."[46]

But where does talking to the concern of an audience end and talking down to the audience begin? Katie Louchheim told a group of senators addressing a women's gathering: "Today you are going to address us not as fluttery or featherbrained females, but as coequal voters. We are limiting each of you to sixty seconds of oratory, and five subjects will be strictly forbidden. You are not to talk about (a) motherhood, (b) how pretty we all are, (c) the Red, White and Blue, (d) what lovely hats we are wearing or (e) how nice our chairman is." [47]

However, women apparently are less responsive to campaign issues than to the personalities of candidates. According to the Survey Research Center of the University of Michigan, women in a 1952 study were found to comprise only 39 per cent of those persons predominantly interested in issues. Of those primarily interested in candidates, 61 per cent were women.[48] On the basis of the 1952 vote, Louis Harris speculated on "the real possibility that in the future there will, in fact, be a 'women's vote' quite separate from the men's." [49]

Although early evidence is slim, many students of electoral behavior believe that the election of 1964 marked the first time since women were given the suffrage that they voted more Democratic in national elections than did the men. [50]

These findings have been echoed by Louis Harris.[51] Eisenhower was the feminine choice "partly because women didn't like Adlai Stevenson's divorce and partly because they saw a powerful force for peace in the former general."[52] Women also liked the image of a warm happy couple presented by the candidate and his wife.[53] And Nixon outpolled Kennedy among the ladies, partly because women feared a Catholic in the White House more than men did.[54]

Johnson's greater support from women in 1964 was explained by Gallup and Harris in terms of anxiety over questions of war and peace. By a majority of 53 per cent, women told Harris' *Newsweek* Poll that Goldwater as President would get the country into war; 55 per cent of the male voters disagreed. A second powerful issue motivating the women's vote more heavily toward Johnson was the issue of civil rights for Negroes. Significantly fewer women were influenced by the backlash sentiment. Men were more fearful than women about pressures and competition from Negroes in the job market, and more women than men tended to come under the influence of their churches, which were overwhelmingly for civil rights legislation.

1964 was also the year a woman, Margaret Chase Smith, ran for president. A recent Gallup poll found that 84 per cent of the population would vote for a qualified Catholic for president, 77 per cent for a qualified Jew, but only 55 per cent for a qualified woman.[55] Women themselves were more opposed to a woman president than were men, in the ratio of 45 per cent to 37 per cent.[56] One woman reporter concluded: "Women will continue to view a female politician in the same way they do women lawyers and doctors—distantly."[57] At the polls, women have shown no great enthusiasm for candidates of their own sex,[58] although Margaret Chase Smith credited her first Senate victory in 1948 to the support of women.

Harold W. Dodds, former president of Princeton University, asked women to recognize that there was a sexual division of labor in politics. "Large numbers of men go into politics to make a living or to get ahead in their business, rather than in response to an impulse to serve the public . . . Women's greatest contribution has been, heretofore, in the field of the formulation of issues and the building of opinion to be expressed through the ballot, rather than in the execution of policies through holding public office."[59]

Women, at last, are coming into their own as voters. They are as numerous as men at the polls, and their participation rate is approaching that of men. Sex differences, however, still figure in the pattern of voting. Women are more candidate-oriented than issue-oriented. They tend to favor conservative solutions. Women are less willing than men to support policies they perceive as warlike or aggressive. They have a greater moralistic orientation than men. They also seem to be less tolerant of political and religious non-conformity.[60]

Finally, women are less interested in the political process than are men. Finding a way to increase their participation is a continuing problem.

1c. Women's Indirect Political Influence

Perhaps comforting to the feminine mind is the myth that behind every great man is a woman who made him what he is.[1] One could say, with equal justification, that behind the great men are other men. Less comforting is the observation attributed to Mrs. Oliver Wendell Holmes that Washington is populated by successful men . . . and the women they married when they were young.[2]

Even before women received the vote, they possessed indirect influence. Some, like Cornelia Bryce Pinchot and Ruth Hanna McCormick, were their husbands' real political advisers and managers. Mrs. Pinchot was the daughter of a former U.S. minister to the Netherlands. Gifford Pinchot was credited with having drawn Jane Addams and Lillian Wald into Washington politics. In his early fight for forest conservation, he found unexpected backing among clubwomen and social workers. He counseled Theodore Roosevelt to draw in the social workers who furnished the luster in the Progressive Party.[3] His wife later ran twice unsuccessfully for Congress.

The Washington hostesses, according to former Chief Justice Fred Vinson, play the role of bringing Republicans and Democrats, senators and White House staff, civilians and military people together at social gatherings.[4] Among the renowned partygivers were Daisy Harriman, Mrs. John Henderson, Evalyn Walsh McLean, Eleanor "Cissy" Patterson, Perle Mesta, and Gwendolin Cafritz.[5]

Mrs. Alice Roosevelt Longworth, T. R.'s daughter and the wife of a speaker of the house, worked behind the scenes against such pet hates as the World Court, the League of Nations, and the London Naval Treaty.[6] The sister of Hoover's vice president, Charles Dawes, Mrs. Dolly Gann, was equally knowledgeable about politics.

In 1928 a presidential candidate's wife became an issue in the campaign. It was said that Al Smith's wife, Katie, "simply would not do in the White House."[7] Mrs. Florence T. Griswold, Republican national committeewoman for Texas, told a meeting of the WCTU in Houston: "Can you imagine an aristocratic foreign ambassador saying to Mrs. Al Smith, 'What a charming gown!' and the reply: 'You said a mouthful!' "[8]

Especially since women received the vote, the first ladies have been quite conspicuous in presidential campaigns. They have always figured in the social life of Washington. Some presidential wives have had an influence on their husband's decisions.

William Howard Taft's wife, Helen, attended every cabinet meeting with him. When the press accused her of influencing policy, she insisted that she went along to keep him awake.[9]

Woodrow Wilson's second wife, Edith, had had no experience or knowledge of politics. "Female independence, and traditional male rights such as voting, did not fit into her concept of a southern lady's proper behavior,"[10] Yet, for at least six weeks after Wilson's stroke, she was called by many the "Acting President."[11] She completely dictated his business schedule and transferred all messages to and from the President. She "insisted on referring to this period as her 'stewardship'—which implies management within delegated authority, but no assumption of independent policy-making authority."[12] Mrs. Wilson served as a sounding board for her husband's thoughts and turned him against his other advisers, House, Timulty, and Lansing. (Her feeling of dislike for them was reciprocated.) Lansing, the secretary of state, did not know the code which the President used to communicate with his emissaries abroad. In Washington, only the President, Mrs. Wilson, and Colonel House knew it. Decoding messages from the war front became one of her special duties. Ambassador to Berlin James Gerard was struck by the fact that she was present "and at times asked pertinent questions showing deep knowledge of foreign affairs" when he was called back to Washington to confer in late 1916.

Mrs. Florence Harding rewrote part of her husband's inaugural address, was consulted on major federal appointments, and chose which convicts should be given Christmas pardons. She was well informed on current governmental affairs and seemed to understand politics better than her husband.

Calvin Coolidge's wife, Grace, served as her husband's public relations officer. Mrs. Lou Henry Hoover was the first First Lady to make speeches, receive honorary degrees, and identify herself with public activities.

Mrs. Eleanor Roosevelt held press conferences, spoke out on political issues, took an active part in her husband's campaigns, and wrote a daily syndicated column. According to Dorothy Roe, "No First Lady, before or since, ever occasioned so much controversy, racked up as many headlines, or created as much general uproar as the inimitable Mrs. Franklin Delano Roosevelt."[14] Marianne Means felt that Mrs. Roosevelt was more New Deal than her husband.[15] "More than any other First Lady, she was a full partner in the tasks of the presidency, deeply involved in politics, in the operations of government agencies and in the conduct of public affairs." She was her husband's "eyes and ears," conscience and troubleshooter. (Edith Willkie was asked by reporters in 1940 whether she thought the First Lady should hold press conferences, write a column, and generally take part in public affairs. Mrs. Willkie replied, "Yes I do, if she is able to do it." This answer deflated the critics of Mrs. Roosevelt's activities.) Mrs. Roosevelt later became chairman of the United Nations Commission on Human Rights.

Mrs. Bess Truman discontinued Mrs. Roosevelt's practice of holding press conferences. Although she was a confidante and adviser to her husband on affairs of state, she shunned publicity. The next two First Ladies also preferred not to become involved in public affairs. Mrs. Eisenhower devoted herself to being helpful in such worthy causes as muscular dystrophy and the heart fund. She had never voted until 1952 when the General became a candidate for the presidency. She said, "When you are in the Army, you don't have any politics." Mrs. Jacqueline Kennedy regarded the position of First Lady as an intrusion into her private life. She used her position, though, for furthering the arts.

Michael Amrine, in his book about the first hundred days of Lyndon Johnson,[16] noted that no First Lady, not even Mrs. Eleanor Roosevelt, was as involved in public affairs as Lady Bird Johnson. Her business sense was largely responsible for the family fortune. When her husband became the first member of Congress to go on active duty in World War II, she took over the management of his Washington legislative office.[17] In 1960 she traveled 35,000 miles in 71 days, mostly in the South, campaigning for the Kennedy-Johnson ticket. Said Bobby Kennedy chivalrously: "Lady Bird carried Texas for us."[18] After her husband became president, she continued to travel around the country speaking about his Great Society program. In the 1964 campaign, Mrs. Johnson traveled 75,000 miles; she made 47 speeches in one four-day stint.[19] Hugh Sidey thought that "Mrs. Johnson in the years ahead will be identified with natural beauty in the way Jackie Kennedy is remembered for the restoration of the White House." Mrs. Johnson was one of a number of legislative wives "who took naturally to the rigors of campaigning . . . and are top-notch vote-getters besides."[20]

Often wives are not expected to talk politics, but just to attend coffee parties and socialize. Yet in the 1920's Mrs. Burton Wheeler went on the stump, making speeches for her senator husband, and Mrs. G. M. Pattangull became national committeewoman when her husband stood for governor of Maine. [21]

Mrs. Belle LaFollette, the first woman to be graduated from the University of Wisconsin Law School, handled her husband's congressional correspondence, attended debates in Congress, traveled around the country with him, and was a constant counsellor when important decisions were at hand. Yet she declined to seek his senate seat after he died, saying, "It would be against nature for me to undertake the responsibilities of political leadership." [22]

The wife of a present Wisconsin senator, Ellen Proxmire, has participated at every level of the Democratic Party, from precinct committeewoman to state executive secretary (the only full-time, paid position in the state organization). [23] Her father had worked for the U.S. Patent Office. She and William Proxmire became engaged during the 1956 Democratic Convention but did not announce it until after the election. He was running for governor and they felt that an announcement might prejudice the election by reminding the voters that they both had been divorced. [24]

Mrs. Proxmire is one of seven senators' wives who write newspaper columns. Together these columns appear in nearly 200 newspapers around the country. [25]

Other active senatorial wives of recent years who worked with their husbands on speeches, in the office, and in planning campaigns were Mrs. Robert A. Taft, [26] Mrs. Estes Kefauver, Mrs. Richard Nixon, Mrs. Paul Douglas (herself a former congresswoman), Mrs. Ernest Gruening, Mrs. Clair Engle, Mrs. Daniel Inouye, Mrs. Frank Church, Mrs. Vance Hartke, Mrs. Birch Bayh, Mrs. John Sherman Cooper, Mrs. Daniel Brewster, Mrs. Eugene McCarthy, Mrs. Lee Metcalf, Mrs. Alan Bible, Mrs. Tom McIntyre, Mrs. Wayne Morse, Mrs. Albert Gore, Mrs. Gale McGee, and Mrs. Wallace Bennett. [27]

There were talented wives on the Kennedy New Frontier. Mrs. Walt W. Rostow was the first woman professor at Massachusetts Institute of Technology and is an authority on diplomatic history and international relations. Antonia Chayes, wife of the state department legal adviser, is herself a lawyer. Mrs. Arthur Schlesinger, Jr., and Mrs. Arthur Goldberg are artists. Mrs. Chester Bowles is a specialist in Asian Affairs. Mrs. Eve Curie Labouisse is an author and former war correspondent. Mrs. Orville Freeman has done graduate work in public administration. Mrs. Stewart Udall is an authority on the American Indians of the Southwest and on the Colorado River.[28]

Not all wives are politically responsive. Sometimes, as in the cases of Adlai Stevenson and Pierre Salinger, the marriage breaks down under the strain of the husband's political activities. Senator Harry Byrd's wife, Anne, cared little for politics or Washington. She desired his retirement in 1958 but announced: "I do not believe my hopes should obstruct the judgment of those better informed who believe he can render valuable public service."[29]

1d. Women's Political Relationship to Men

Who are the men behind the women politicians? How have they contributed to or interfered with the women's success?

First can be listed the deceased incumbents whose widows got their start in politics "over their husband's dead body." They left to their widows at least two assets, their names, which had already been tried out before the voters, and the sympathy of people at a bereavement.

In the second category of "supportive males" are the parents, brothers, and other relatives whose example and connections have aided in nurturing and furthering political ambitions. Their encouragement and guidance may have given the woman a start. Their own political positions may have smoothed her way.[1]

Third are the husbands whose wives are active in politics during their lifetime. As in the case of the widows, some wives have profited politically because their husbands were well known.

How does a man feel whose wife is a successful politician? Very few have commented on this position. Except for the ex-husband of former Representative Coya Knudson, who cooperated with opposition politicians and proclaimed publicly "Coya, come home," the others appear to have been reconciled to their fate—at least in their public utterances. "More power to the little woman" is the gist of their remarks. But one wonders how they really feel about it.

One also wonders how the lady politicos feel about combining a career with a home. Is there a sense of guilt about deserting husband

and children, even briefly? What if she is more successful . . . rises higher, earns more money?[2] Will he develop ulcers, headaches, impotence? Will he, in the end, leave her?[3] At the least, fear of these consequences may cause a wife to limit her ambitions. Thus we often find the careerist who never leaves home before her husband and children have had their breakfast, who never accepts a promotion without talking it over with her spouse. In her book, *The Lady and the Vote,* Marion Sanders said that "while the two-job family can work very well . . . the two-ambition family cannot. Apart from the emotional tension that may be involved, it is not feasible for a family to follow two different sets of career opportunities."

Some husbands are sensitive to criticism of their politician-wives. They may leap too quickly to their wives' defense or they may feel that their own wisdom in selecting a marital partner has been questioned.

Usually, it would appear, the successful woman politician is married to a man who is not dependent on politics for a livelihood. If she is a judge, he may be a lawyer who more than makes up in income for his wife's prestige. Said one assemblywoman on the question of money-raising: "I have a husband who can afford me." She may be a legislator or administrator, but he often is a professor or businessman. It is easier for wives to take part in organizations if the husbands themselves are active in organizations.

Federal Judge Constance Baker Motley's husband is a real estate man. New York City Criminal Court Judge Joan O'Dwyer, who is the niece of a former mayor and former city councilman, is married to a lawyer who ran for state assemblyman in 1966. Frances Perkins' husband, Paul Wilson, was a financial statistician, who later became secretary and financial adviser to New York Mayor John Purroy Mitchell. The husband of one county vice chairman in Michigan was active in the local level of the Democratic Party and purchased for her a membership in the local Democratic Women's Club. He eventually came to regret his action. She was a capable volunteer and was given all sorts of assignments. He resented the time, effort and money she expended in party activities. Yet he was ambivalent. After her defeat for county treasurer in 1962, she announced that she would like to serve in the legislature. He said absolutely not. However, in 1964, he found himself working very hard putting up handbills and urging her on during her primary campaign. He objected strenuously to her continuing for another term as vice chairman, but she indicated that she was being pressured by the party to run.[4]

The mate of a state vice chairman at first thought her political work was wonderful, a way to keep busy. He himself was civic-minded although not active in politics. Then he became convinced that she might neglect their two boys. She turned down posts because she did not want to leave home. Her present position, however, is that of a full-time volunteer, requiring periodic trips around the state. He is too busy and uninterested to go along.[5]

Another husband, whose wife was a national committeewoman from Montana, had urged her to seek the office. He was, she said, unfailingly patient when political demands interfered with housekeeping. The husband was retired, "is an expert dishwasher, and on occasion even prepares a meal."[6]

One Minnesota woman was married to a man who had been elected secretary of a Young Democrats organization. She seemed to be doing most of his work and was drawn into party activities herself. He was an unsuccessful state legislative candidate and is the county chairman of the party. She is a district chairwoman.[7]

Hickman Price, Jr., allowed his wife, Margaret, to succeed him as Democratic delegate-at-large from Michigan to the 1952 convention.[8] She became the national committeewoman and, in time, assistant chairman of the Democratic Party. While he ran an automobile business in Sao Paulo, Brazil, she spent half her time in the U.S. Mr. Price, whose mother had been a suffragist, seemed resigned to her absence. He said: "I have but one wife to give to my party—and I'm damned proud of her!"[9]

Her predecessor, Mrs. Katie Louchheim, was married to a Washington investment consultant who used to quip that "home is just an extension of the Democratic National Committee." Mrs. Louchheim is now a deputy assistant secretary of state. She has always wanted to be a candidate for Congress but lives in Washington, D.C. "But had I lived in New Jersey or New York," she observed, "I would have had a husband and a family to consider." [10]

Mrs. Patricia Hutar resigned in 1965 as assistant chairman of the Republican Party because of what she called her "home situation," a husband and three-year-old daughter in Chicago. She was replaced by Mary Brooks, a widow.

Mrs. Gene Flatow, a district leader of the New York City Riverside Democrats, gave her husband much credit for her success. "Without my husband, I couldn't be the active, militant person I am in the first place. I represent no threat to his intelligence, or his masculinity. He's not a bit annoyed if I have to go to a meeting because he believes in what I'm doing." [11] Her husband, a professor of industrial engineering at New York University, joined the reform club at about the same time she did, and headed its housing committee.

Service in Congress by a wife puts quite a strain on family life. There is difficulty in rearing children. A man has his wife to take over the duties of entertaining, but in our society a woman cannot depend on a husband to do this even if she has a full-time job. At a conference on getting women into politics, one speaker queried: "If a woman runs for office, does her husband have to give coffee hours?" The wife relocates to suit her husband's career, rarely vice versa. An aide to Lyndon Johnson commented: "Most women just don't have movable husbands."

Mrs. Maurine Neuberger, who served beside her husband in the Oregon legislature,[12] terminated her political career to be a full-time U.S. senator's wife. Her husband, Richard, gave her credit for "putting me in the Senate."[13] Only after his death did she re-enter politics.

Congresswoman Catherine May's husband, a real estate and insurance broker who was active in civic and Republican causes, moved to Washington, D. C., and looked for a job there after her election. Clare Booth Luce and her husband were rarely separated for as long as three weeks at a time when she was a congresswoman or an ambassador. Her husband frequently commuted from their home in Connecticut to Washington in the course of his own business. Later his business often brought him to Rome where he had an office. Ambassador Patricia Harris was accompanied to Luxembourg by her husband, who closed his Washington law office. Another new ambassador, Carol C. Laise, married roving Ambassador Ellsworth Bunker. Congresswoman Martha Griffiths and her husband, Hicks, keep an apartment in Washington and also a home in Detroit.

Former Representative Iris Blitch lived with her son, a student at George Washington University Law School, in a home in Virginia across the river from Washington, while her husband tended to the family home in Homersville, Georgia, where he ran drug and timber businesses. They spent weekends and holidays together, with one or the other commuting. It had been her husband's idea that she run for office.

During her first two terms in Congress, Mrs. Cecil Harden and her husband, Frost, worked in different parts of the country. Then he retired from his own job and spent most of his time in Washington, with frequent visits home to Indiana to keep business interests going. When Congress was not in session, they were together in their home at Covington, Indiana.

Mr. John W. Pfost resigned from his job as chief engineer of an Idaho milk company to move to Washington to be with his wife. They spent eight months of the year in Washington and vacation times at their Idaho ranch. He campaigned for her and assisted in her congressional offices in Washington and Idaho. He admired his wife's energy. "She was just as busy in the real estate business while she was in that," he said, "as she is now in Congress."

There is the same problem for husbands of women in the executive branch. Mrs. Ivy Baker Priest, President Eisenhower's treasurer of the U.S., was married to a man in the wholesale furniture business in Utah. He commuted by plane weekends to Washington to be with her. When Mrs. Virginia Mae Brown became a member of the Interstate Commerce Commission, her lawyer-husband, James, resettled in Washington.

Evidently, it takes an exceptional man to assist an exceptional woman in politics. As Mrs. Claire B. Williams, former Republican national assistant chariman put it: "No married woman can go into anything on a more or less full-time basis—whether it's Girl Scouting or politics or becoming president of the General Federation of Women's Clubs—unless her husband is generous in his support and understanding and approval and sympathy." [14]

The fourth type of man-behind-the-woman is the political sponsor. A woman who expects to hold political office needs such a patron to intercede in her behalf in what is primarily a man's world and to promote her to positions in the party and government. [15]

Some sponsors have favored women in general, for example, President Johnson, Mayors Wagner and La Guardia, Governors Romney, Rockefeller, Folsom and Lawrence, whereas others like Boss Hague and "Pa" Ferguson have assisted one or a few disciples.

A. A. Adee, second assistant secretary of state for many years, rewarded female talent. His assistants included Ruth Shipley, head of the Passport Office, and Margaret Hanna, chief of the Office of Coordination and Review.

A woman looking for sponsorship has to do the same job of salesmanship with the sponsor as with the voters. Often, though, the man discerns aptitudes which the woman herself may not have discerned, aptitudes which she might, without his encouragement, consider it pretentious to claim.

1e. The Political Impotence of American Women

Have women achieved political equality? The answer is no. There is no denying that women have made progress politically, and that a number of exceptional women have attained very high positions. The question is: Has there been enough progress to justify a prediction of eventual equality? One might also ask: Does either sex really want equality?

Certainly, the nation is undergoing a reassessment of its attitude toward women. The Commission on the Status of Women created by President Kennedy called for removal of barriers to meaningful participation of women in business, labor, politics, and community affairs. In its wake were created commissions in 48 states, two cities, and several territories, to apply recommendations to local situations. Betty Friedan's book, *The Feminine Mystique,* discussed the plight of women pressured into early marriage by the cult of Togetherness . . . settling in later years, after their children have grown up, for mere jobs rather than careers. Mrs. Friedan's book sold over 800,000 copies in paperback and is still quoted frequently by many women who are dismayed by the existing situation.

Margaret Chase Smith's candidacy for the presidency was a symbol of women's struggle for recognition. The Senator suggested, however, that there were two fundamental reasons why women have not had more success in politics. "These reasons," she said, "are (1) men, and (2) women—men because they vigorously oppose women's holding public office—and women because they haven't stood together and exercised their majority voting power."[1]

Do women have a future in politics? Will there be a political breakthrough? Before offering conclusions, it is necessary to investigate the depths of male and female conservatism.

Male Conservatism. From Paul[2] to Luther,[3] from Blackstone[4] to Freud,[5] men have been reluctant to acknowledge that "woman's position in society is not the creation of nature but of history, convention, and environment."[6]

Insecure men are made nervous by successful women. These men need women's weakness to prove their own masculinity.[7] When women are not submissive, there is a male "backlash." According to psychologist Erik H. Erickson: "Where dominant identities depend on being dominant, it is hard to grant real equality to the dominated. Where one feels exposed, threatened, or cornered, it is difficult to be judicious."[8]

For some men, a working wife is evidence of their own failure.[9] Most of the jobs held by women do not place them in basic competition for status with their husbands. "The majority of 'career' women whose occupational status is comparable with that of men in their own class," noted sociologist Talcott Parsons, "at least in the upper middle and upper classes, are unmarried; and in the small proportion of cases where they are married, the result is a profound alteration in family structure." [10]

When there are two employed members of the family, there is likely to be recurrent stress on the marriage because of the wife's employment. There may be a dramatic reshuffling of marital roles, most notably in the division of labor. Traditional household responsibilities may be replaced by overlapping performances.[11]

Many a man, though, takes pride in his wife's accomplishments, finding her a more interesting person than she otherwise would be. This is especially true if the husband is upwardly mobile; a competent mate is an asset to a self-assured male.[12]

The traditionalist emphasizes that someone has to be "boss" in the family, and that in our society, at least, it is the man. This reasoning often is used to justify male dominance in politics.[13]

It came as an unpleasant shock to many men in 1920 when male-dominated government was in jeopardy. The initial reaction of male politicians was fear of the power of organized feminisim. And even after it became evident that women would not vote as a bloc, the male hostility continued.[14] It was not until 1963 that the Washington State Legislature repealed an 1890 law that made it illegal for women to hold political office.[15] In 1967, California State Senator Clark Bradley treated the Senate Judiciary Committee to a dissertation on how women fighting for equal rights were the cause of most of the problems of the world including, but not limited to, the disintegration of the family structure, juvenile delinquency, and man's lack of authority in the home.[16]

A Woman who attended the 1964 Democratic Convention as a delegate reported that she was appalled at the hostility displayed by some of the 46 males in her delegation toward the seven women. Always before, men had gone as delegates and women as alternates.[17]

Another woman told how the men of her party had helped her to win a primary election against a man, although they would not work for her in the general election because she was a woman.[18] A woman running for the state legislature reported that she had received abusive anonymous telephone calls from men.[19]

When a female politician protested not being notified of a meeting where an important decision had been made, she was told that the men had gotten together informally in the chairman's bedroom at two a.m.[20] A man might think that it would have been uncomfortable for everyone if she had been present. Men just do not "talk shop" in a bar or hotel with a woman, especially if the woman is young and unmarried.[21] Said one male politician: "I can never be comfortable when a woman is mixed up in a political conference, for I can never forget she is a woman."[22]

One professional woman observed, "Polite as male coworkers are toward me, when, at lunch or a meeting, any one of them feels he has an especially bright idea, he invariably directs his conversation to the other men, not to me."[23]

Said Samuel Butler, "All sensible men are of the same opinion about women. And no sensible man ever says what that opinion is." That may explain why politicians don't acknowledge discrimination, and why husbands don't often speak out on how they feel about having wives in politics. Men put women on a pedestal . . . to look down on them.[24]

Of course, women do have a kind of dominance in the family. There is a joke in which the man tells his friends: "In my family I make all the big decisions. I decide if we'll go to war, who will be elected president, and if there'll be a tax cut. My wife makes the little decisions . . . whether we'll have another baby, whether we'll buy a new car, where we'll spend our vacation." [25]

Philip Wylie and other critics turn this joke into a nightmare picture: America, the Matriarchy, the land of the domineering woman.[26] But the picture is a distortion. In actuality, there is a sexual division of labor. Men dominate in the worlds of politics, production, and science, and women rule over the home, consumption and morals.[27] Men are trained, or disposed, toward an instrumental mode of behavior and women learn, or are born with, an expressive orientation. Although there is no necessary reason why man's style should be the style in politics, it always has been.[28]

Among the absurdities of our civilization is the pattern of mate selection. Women marry up and men marry down, in education, occupation, and income. Women are admired for their looks, not their ability. "Men seldom make passes at girls who wear glasses."[29]

There is a cultural lag in our stereotypes. "To be 'delightfully illogical' is no asset for a teacher, and 'cuteness' is not what an employer needs in a department store buyer."[30]

"I think," said a woman reporter at the 1924 Democratic Convention, "that I will report this convention the way the men did the women at Cleveland (the Republican Convention). I will describe the clothes of these men from all over America, the strange cuts of their coats, their unaesthetic figures, their shiny hair, their lack of 'it.' "[31]

The crowning insult is the treatment of women as if they were children or members of a different species. Often the women in Congress are asked to come together for a group picture. Why not all the redheads or six-footers?

Then there is the humbug treatment. Pat the little lady on the back; she is not smart enough to see through the deception. A *Ladies Home Journal* article in April 1922 was entitled "The Most Powerful Lobby in Washington." The Protectionists? The munitions manufacturers? The Prohibition Movement? None of these, but rather the

Women's Joint Congressional Committee![32] In January 1965, *This Week* magazine told its readers that it is difficult for a man to get a government job in the Great Society; the women have a monopoly!

There is a selective perception according to sex. Most men are oblivious to any problem involving the status of women.[33] Few men attend meetings discussing women's role.[34] Men's groups invite few female speakers, although women's organizations frequently have male lecturers. Articles about women in politics or in other pursuits are buried on the women's pages or in women's magazines.

Man's unfairness to the women occurs in fields of education and business, as well as in government.[35] Many graduate schools of medicine, business and law have unacknowledged quotas on the number of women they will admit, usually five to 10 per cent.[36]

Mirra Komarovsky found that in teaching, the average salary of men was 38 per cent higher than the salary of women, the average earnings of men lawyers and judges were 49 per cent higher than those of women in the same professional group; of men physicians and surgeons, 67 per cent higher than women, and so on.[37]

There is segregation in the "help wanted" columns. On the male side are listed such jobs as lawyer, chemist, editor, accountant, and administrative assistant. On the female pages are such poorer paying auxiliary positions as legal stenographer, laboratory assistant, researcher, bookkeeper and secretary. Most newspapers now avoid the appearance of discrimination by referring to "Jobs of Interest— Male," but the discrimination still remains.

An early study of women in public office noted: "Where salary and power are concerned, a man fills the office chair. Where there is dignity of office but little else, or where there is routine work, little glory, and low pay, the men prove willing to admit women to an equal share in the 'spoils of office.' " [38]

Women on the job are always on trial. "When a woman fails," Mrs. Roosevelt noted, "it is much more serious than when a man fails, because the average person attributes the failure not to the individual but to the fact that she is a woman." If the woman succeeds, she is called an exception. [39]

A study of life insurance offices, where 66 per cent of the employees in 1950 were women, revealed that 98 per cent of the officers were men. [40] One out of six union members is a woman, yet there are few women union leaders. The Amalgamated Clothing Workers, for example, has 75 per cent female membership, but male leadership. A whole catalogue of objections to women executives can be collected from employers and workers, both male and female. [41]

Many employers believe that the woman worker is too often an emotional problem, taking all criticism personally, sometimes bursting into tears. In a position of responsibility, they say, she is apt to be fussy, neurotic, personal and inclined to favoritism. [42]

Women are "damned if they do and damned if they don't." The female executive is charged with being "overemotional" when she has been simply enthusiastic, "cold and remote" when she has been reserved, "masculine and aggressive" when she has been firm, and "too, too feminine" when she has been tactfully gentle. [43] These criticisms may be true, to some extent, possibly because women have developed habits of subordination to men which are difficult to shed. [44]

Stereotypes may contain an iota of truth, but generally reflect cultural prejudices rather than absolute truths. Boys in our culture are punished for being sissies and for crying, and girls for being tomboys and fighting back.

In her article "Working Women," Esther Peterson put it: "There is no evidence to show that a woman cries more often than a man 'blows his stack.'" Men knife men—and so do women! Mrs. Peterson has also been impressed by the high quality of questions from women following her lectures. [45]

A well-known trial lawyer, in an evaluation of women as jurors, pointed out: "Women, like men . . . are soft-hearted, hard-headed or realistically self-disciplined. They are receptive to the judge's instruction of the law, or resistant to it. They are attentive even to dull testimony, or bored by it. They are easily swayed by emotional appeal, or repelled by demagoguery. It is the individual person the lawyer must analyze, and the sex of that person is only in the rarest instance a key to the mystery . . . "[46]

A favorite libel against women is that marriage and motherhood are incompatible with certain professional activities. Mrs. Eleanor L. Dulles thought that the slow progress of women in the U.S. State Department was due to a deep-seated belief that women will soon leave for marriage. "But," she noted, "they don't get terribly excited when men leave the State Department to get into law firms." [47]

Margaret Chase Smith made a similar point. "There are plenty of examples of women public officials who have successfully maintained their homes and reared their children. A man legislator's division of his professional time as a lawyer, oddly enough, is never challenged."[48]

The question, however, will never be resolved by an appeal to male reason. Basically, their conservatism is rooted in the subconscious. To achieve female equality "with all deliberate speed" will take an act of will and organization by the women. Are they disposed to show their strength and determination?[49]

Female Conservatism. The tendency of men to appoint only a token number of women to important positions would have changed long ago if it had met a determined feminine resistance. Equally certain is it that women would have held many more elective positions. The shackles of minority status that hamper women have been fastened on them by themselves as well as by men.[50]

Very frequently in the literature a comparison has been made between the treatment of Negroes and of women in our society. [51] Both are discriminated against.[52] According to Maurice Duverger: "There is no more an inferior sex than there are inferior races or inferior classes. But there is a sex, and there are classes and races, who have come to believe in their inferiority because they have been persuaded of it in justification of their subordinate position in society."[53]

Sometimes self-hatred is mixed with envy of the male. More women than men would like to be reborn a member of the other sex. A *Fortune* poll asked both sexes, "If you could be born over again, would you rather be a man or a woman?" Only 65.7 per cent of the women indicated that they would stick to their sex, as opposed to 91.5 per cent of the men. Gerda W. Bowman, after doing research on promotion practices in the New York metropolitan area, said: "Amazing as it may seem, the prejudice against women in positions of authority appears to be even more deeply rooted in our culture than the concept of white supremacy."[54]

Duverger notes that women seem to be more anti-feminist than men, and asks, "Why do women agree to specialize in family, household and education matters, while admitting that men can do anything?" Margaret Chase Smith, whose lifework has given the lie to this limitation, observed that "we often hear the comment that 'women are all right in their place.' But what is their place? The answer of practically all men and many women is The Home. You never hear the comment that 'men are all right in their place,' because their place has never been restricted. They are certainly not restricted to masculine fields, or more accurately stated, barred by prejudice from the normally regarded feminine and domestic pursuits."[55]

In a National Opinion Research Center sample of 33,783 college graduates, there were over 11,000 women who expected to follow careers in elementary and secondary education, but only 285 women who hoped to enter the combined fields of medicine, law and engineering.[56] There is vast female underemployment, with women working below capabilities at a job rather than a career. Negroes and women supply the low-paid labor in our economy.

Female politicians and other professionals are "marginal people."[57] They are no longer comfortable associating primarily with traditionalist women, but are unable to establish social ties among men. Such a person is confronted with the necessity of being disloyal to feminine-role values as she adopts the values of the group into which she is moving.

As has been noted in the behavior of certain minority ethnic groups, women often manifest an ambivalence toward the success of other women. They may be proud of the individual's success, but concerned lest she take upon herself an attitude of superiority toward those she has left behind.

David Riesman has suggested that women are their own worst enemies. "The evidence lies in the tacit league of educated housewives accusing working mothers of neglecting their families, or the preference of women college students for male teachers, or the dislike of women to be 'bossed' by other women."[58]

Dame Patricia Hornsby-Smith, a British M.P. and the first woman chairman of a British investment company, agreed. "The men don't have to fight us—we knock ourselves out," she said, noting that many women still preferred working for men rather than for women. Anna Rosenberg concurred: "Men bend backward, not giving women a chance. So if women don't give women a chance, it's bad."[59]

A state senator and national committeewoman observed, from personal experience, that women tend to vote against other women.[60] As early as 1921, one woman advised her sisters to do just that: "If you are a woman yourself, you had better vote for a man who is afraid of your tongue than for another woman who has a tongue of her own and the feminine capacity for betraying your political confidence in her."[61]

There is at least a grain of truth to the criticisms. It is only natural to expect to find among the careerists some of the same embroilment in personalities that is manifest among the rank-and-file antifeminists. One woman politician warned other women embarking on public affairs: "Don't go into an important meeting and throw your weight around." The same advice could be given to a man, However, a male *faux pas* is treated as an individual error, not as representative of a group's behavior.

The New York Governor's Committee on the Education and Employment of Women concluded: "When a woman learns to relax, learns to roll with the punches, learns to give as well as take, learns to carry her share of whatever trouble is going around, she increases her value to her department and her company. When a woman has to be handled with care, fuss-budgets about little things, finds it inconvenient to stay long hours when long hours are called for, or to go to extra trouble, when a woman talks too much and keeps on talking, talks out of turn and doesn't know she's doing it, she is not only hurting herself, but she is doing the whole cause of women in business a disservice."[62]

The pendulum has swung between feminism and "femininism" throughout the 20th Century. The first feminist phase produced the vote and the emancipated twenties. More conscious effort was made to achieve equal status when women first got the vote than is made today. The forties and fifties were a period when women were told that their destiny was love, marriage and the baby carriage. Only recently has there been a reawakening of feminism.

It is questionable, though, whether feminism has wide appeal. A review of Eve Merriam's feminist tract, *After Nora Slammed the Door: American Women in the 1960's—The Unfinished Revolution,* stated: "Despite the reformers, it is still a fact that many women are happy and fulfilled being 'just housewives.' "[63]

Women have their own internalized judgment of what is proper female behavior. Most still associate the career women with spinsterhood or widowhood. Lotte Bailyn perceived: "That a man will spend at least one-third of his adult life in gainful work is a premise on which the plans for his life are based. But for a woman, society creates not a decision but a necessity for choice." This choice is circumscribed "by the expectation of society and of women themselves that no matter what else they may do, they will also, ideally, have a family."[64]

Women have many alternatives to a failing career. Foremost is marriage. A close runner-up is the face-saving device, which women share with other subordinate group members, of saying, "It wasn't my fault." Margaret Mead noted that in our culture men are unsexed by failure, women by success. "The more successful a man is in his job, the more certain everyone is that he will make a desirable husband; the more successful a woman is, the more most people are afraid she may not be a successful wife."[65]

Insurance against the penalties of success is found in dabbling and dilettantism in education, employment, and politics. Mirra Komarovsky found that some 40 per cent of the women undergraduates at two colleges said they had occasionally "played dumb" on dates, concealed some academic honor, pretended ignorance of a subject, "threw" games, or played down certain skills in obedience to the unwritten law that the man must be superior in particular areas.[66] Sixty-five per cent of the coeds on a large western campus thought that to be outstanding in academic work was damaging to a girl's chances for dates.

Employment is also seen by most young women as something less than a commitment.[67] It is a way of marking time before marriage, or a place for meeting eligible men, a means of enriching the family budget, or an escape from humdrum housewifery.

Politics is also, in the popular mind, something not to be taken seriously by a woman. This psychological withdrawal is, in part, a product of discrimination.[68] After all, women receive inferior rewards. Many feel that politics is men's business and that it is rotten business.[69] Professor Frank Sander of the Harvard Law School, who worked on the 1963 Status of Women report, told the *Harvard Law*

Record: "I sometimes found myself more zealous to grant women rights than the women were to accept them!"[70]

"In politics, as in marriage and business," according to India Edwards, "women get pretty much the treatment they are willing to accept."[71] The American woman would like to have the best of both worlds. She is undecided whether to continue to enjoy the view from the pedestal or to kick it over and try to achieve equality with the men.[72]

Dr. Rosemary Park, president of Barnard College, observed: "In the background of a woman's mind there is traditionally the thought that someone will take care of her, that some man will supply her answers."[73]

Diana Trilling declared that "no woman—no reasonably normal woman—wants to assert superiority over men, let alone dominate them. On the contrary, women want to be cherished and protected by men and dependent on men's superior strength. It is by this that they are made to feel most feminine."[74]

Many talented women have to stoop intellectually all their lives in order not to appear "taller" than their husbands. A wife may refuse to compete with her not very successful husband for fear of emasculating him still further in his own eyes.

Mrs. Barbara Bates Gunderson, a U.S. Civil Service commissioner, found: "Some federal career women shun promotion not because they fear responsibility or masculine resentment in the office, but because it would put them in an income bracket superior to their husbands."[75]

Modern woman is usually a contented bird in a gilded cage. For every denunciation of the "feminine mystique," the defining of a woman solely in terms of her relation to man as wife, mother, and homemaker, there seem to be several paeans on the happily-ever-after-in-the-suburbs theme.[76] Ministers preach that God made woman to be a wife and mother. Even woman activists still announce for publication [77] that a "woman's place is in the home."[78]

Pity the career-minded woman who receives discouragement from her relatives and friends.[79] She is told that she will wind up an old maid if she does not get out more. Do not overdo that studying bit; your friends are all getting married. Who are you kidding? You will probably never look at a book a year out of school.

Besides . . . admit to yourself that you really would prefer to have a man make your decisions.

There she is, the queen of the home, in suburbia where "housewifery expands to fit the time available."[80] A routine of shopping, chauffeuring, using dishwashers and driers and electric mixers, gardening, waxing and polishing, helping with the children's homework, scout work, PTA, collecting for mental health, and doing thousands of little chores.[81] In this monotony of home life "it is easy to let yourself go."[82] Yet higher education has given many women interests that are not wholly satisfied by their domestic activities. Will they use their talents or wallow in guilt and self-doubt?[83]

They are reconciled to their lot by asserting that their sacrifice is made for their children. But is there a surfeit of "smother love?" Too much togetherness makes for neuroses rather than self-reliance.

Ours is a world of the children of blue and the children of pink. Ordinarily, the boy grows up in his father's image, rough and ready, rewarded for being aggressive. Girls are given fewer opportunities for independent action, and these come later than for boys. They have a certain diffidence which results from role training. Over-protectiveness of either sex will result in a faulty adjustment to later societal demands. Men sometimes have the problem of projecting a masculine image, women of being too submissive.[84]

Women tend to greater ambivalence than men. Should they be assertive or submissive; free agents, or depend on a man to protect them?[85]

Barbara Gunderson noted: "The pressures of rivalry between women for the approval of men; the desire of the coveted tribute 'truly feminine'; the years of effort to achieve a reputation for being cooperative and acceptable to men in the work situation stifle effectiveness in overcoming the handicaps the female sex labors under in the union, business, political, and governmental world."[86]

A male candidate would not hesitate to ask for votes, money, or campaign support, but a woman would hesitate. Said one male political leader: "Women make the mistake of expecting us to seek them out for office more or less in the same manner that they expect a man to ask their hand in marriage."[87]

At a conference commemorating the 100th anniversary of the

first woman's rights convention, Miss Mary Donlon contended that "the doormat of politics and government does not spell welcome to women. Too often we hesitate to force our way into the institutions of policy and government. Therefore, we continue to be dominated by men."[88]

A decade after the suffrage, women were told they would have to fight in order to succeed in politics. Otherwise they would remain ornaments.[89] What is needed are more women able to assume the professional role in a political situation, and the feminine role in a social one.

It is clear that the roots of the present subordinate status of women go deeply into our culture. Only a fundamental alteration in our socialization process would change this condition.

Will There Be a Breakthrough? President Johnson described the 1960's as the most important time for U.S. women since they won the right to vote in 1920.[90] Certainly, these have been years of advancement. Nearly all of the states have had commissions to promote the full partnership of men and women in national life. More Americans are becoming aware of women's frequently unused potential. Two women ran for the Senate, one for the presidency, and many for numerous state and local offices.[91] For the first time, more women voted in a national election than men. Does all this mean that a political breakthrough is at hand?

The evidence does not leave much room for optimism in this respect. A 1964 article on women in southern politics concluded: "The numbers of women in public life, in proportion to the population, are probably no more today than in 1925."[92] Outside the South the picture is not sufficiently different to warrant a recast verdict.[93] It is true that exceptional women have distinguished themselves. The president and some governors, mayors, and party leaders have recognized and promoted qualified women. Progress toward equal treatment is apparent along a number of fronts. But the problem is of such proportions that piecemeal tinkerings will not result in equality.

There are elements of fantasy in some feminist activities, in the crusade for the "equal rights" amendment and in the wishful thinking that somehow, someday, there will be a woman president. The President's Commission on the Status of Women found a number of factors contributing to women's low rate of participation in the national life. If ever there is to be a breakthrough, there will have to be a correction in these areas: First, women will have to enter the occupations which lead to a political career, law, public and business administration. Second, women will have to extend their concern beyond the home and family and into the community. The years of child-rearing must serve as a training period for political activity once home responsibilities lessen. And third, women must be willing to compete with men for policies and positions. [94]

Our society is changing and women ought to benefit from these changes. We have moved from a rural to an urban and suburban society. There is a per capita increase in education [95] and income. With these changes come more knowledge and more time for politics and government, and more self-confidence in playing a role in these areas. But middle-class attitudes, while they may make men more willing to accept women as partners in the home, may not make either sex willing to encourage women as leaders, especially as "bosses" of men. Public life may still be stigmatized as unfeminine.

The process of education, beginning in the home, has to be altered so as to nourish and not discourage the ambitions of women. At present, when our society inculcates the recognized and accepted role appropriate to the sexes, it encourages men and women to want different things. The world is the man's domain, the home is the woman's. [96] Little wonder that boys show consistent superiority in political knowledge and are much better informed about politics than girls. The absence of the likelihood of an interesting future in an occupation will discourage a girl from persevering and will encourage dilettantism.

The young woman needs female models who make the image of opportunity real and justify the educational effort required. As Betty Friedan put it: "We need more heroines in fiction as well as non-fiction. They exist in real life and should be projected by the media to give women the image of a heroine who is using herself to the fullest for some purpose or goal." [97]

During school years, girls should gain a many-faceted conception of their self-worth. There should be a raising of their level of aspiration and a preparation for competition and leadership responsibilities. [98] Both parents and teachers should refrain from saying: "You can't do that because you are a girl."

The remedy will still fall short unless the attitudes of both sexes are changed. If the boy grows up intolerant of female competition, if his self-esteem depends on looking down on women, if his conception of the proper role of women is limited to childkeeping and housekeeping, the woman is not going to be able to combine a career with a family.

The school curriculum at present includes subject matter on the peoples of other lands and the contributions of different groups to our own culture. There should also be significant studies on the changing role of women. [99]

An extraordinary campaign to seek out and interest capable girls in careers in government should also begin. It is national policy to raise the sights of disadvantaged minority groups in our society. Why not make the same effort for a majority group?

There already are several teen-age citizenship programs. The General Federation of Women's Clubs sponsors institutes in citizenship. Twenty thousand young people participate each year in the nationwide American Legion- and Auxiliary-sponsored boys' and girls' state sessions. The YMCA's "Youth and Government" plan brings high school boys and girls to their state capitals to take over for a day the reins of state government. Debate and student government activities of most schools are other opportunities for leadership training.

Aside from talent hunts for student leaders, there should also be activities in the schools addressed to all pupils. Women in politics could be invited to speak to young boys and girls. The boys will see that political women need not be battle-axes, and the girls will have models to emulate. School textbooks and readers should present women in civic and vocational activities, not just in stereotyped roles.

Continuing Education and Flexible Employment Patterns. The traditionalist will probably be thinking at this point: "Why attempt social engineering? Aren't most men and women contented with the status quo? Let the men wear the pants and the women push the carriages!"

One answer is that our economy is in need of talented people regardless of sex. Only a limited number of people have I.Q.'s over 120. Look at any help-wanted section and see the long columns advertising for computer specialists and engineers, social and natural scientists, business and public administrators. Most of the brains which are lost belong to women. [100] If we go in for head shrinking, it is at our own expense.[101]

Another fact is that American women today do not go through life just having children and tending house. They marry earlier and stop having children earlier. Housekeeping is not the chore it used to be, thanks to labor-saving gadgets and supermarket foods. Tedium alone may send the women back to work. [102] Keeping up with the Joneses, still a powerful motivation, means that one income usually is not enough for a young family to live on. [103] So the wife takes a job. Finally, some women, like some men, find satisfaction in a career. [104] They would like the opportunity, which our society unquestioningly accords to men, of having both a family and a vocation. [105]

At present, about 26 million women are in the labor force, a figure which represents more than one-third of all women of working age and more than one-third of the labor force itself. [106] Many, perhaps most, are working below their potential. They lack the education or motivation to better their lot. They are surrounded by male and female prejudice against career women.

There is a sense of impermanence. The young female worker or student expects to marry and leave the labor force. She does not consider that within 20 years she will again seek work and that later her lack of skills will limit her opportunities. [107] The "circular dilemma" is that the young woman does not invest in graduate work or special training because she fears it will be wasted in a hostile market, yet she has little chance to advance without this education or training. [108]

One of the recommendations of the national and state commissions on the status of women is that opportunities be made available for women with family responsibilities to develop skills. These opportunities include (1) accessible part-time education, including attendance at university extension and community colleges, and refresher courses for older women, [109] (2) educational and vocational guidance, (3) more part-time placement facilities, (4) greater willingness of employers, private and public, to employ part-time personnel, [110] (5) provision for added domestic and child care service for working mothers. [111]

The traditionalist would ask: How will the family survive as a social unit in a society where the woman is making a living? At the least, a cooperative husband is required. And if the media of education and communication would favor rather than discourage woman's autonomy, the internal and external pressures on the wife and mother would be much less. The effect on the child of a working mother could even be beneficial. [112]

With more women in the labor force, especially in professional careers, there may be more likelihood that they will participate in politics. Women, and men, will become accustomed to seeing women in leadership positions. There will be a larger pool from which to recruit women. And there will be apprentice-training for higher political positions.

Just as the career woman may be recruited into political activity, so, too, may the volunteer woman. Politics is a ready outlet for women who are not looking for jobs but who have talent for organization. Skills and contacts acquired in church and charity work, scout groups, the PTA, and women's organizations [113] are often convertible into political capital.

Although Robert E. Lane observed that "as the moral custodians of the family and the community, women now find that they must include citizenship among their other duties," he asked: "Would it be wise to reinforce the feminist movement, emphasizing politics on the women's page along with the garden club and bridge club news, and making ward politics something like volunteer work for the Red Cross or the hospital auxiliary?" [114] Those who favor the involvement of women in public life would probably answer yes.

Women as Leaders and Managers. Merely to have women among the employed, while it might make men and women more willing to acknowledge female competence outside the home, would not guarantee that women will emerge as leaders. Leaders in our society come largely from the ranks of businessmen and professionals. Unless women can attain importance in these feeder hierarchies, they will never amount to much in government.

Because of the odds against women's reaching a high position, those few that do are among the most capable. "Meet any woman in a top job," said Dorothy Roe, "and you know she has to be good or she wouldn't be there. Meet a man in a similar job, and sometimes you wonder how he made it." [115]

The North Carolina Commission on the Status of Women concurred: "Are men given administrative posts because they are good at administration, or do they learn to become good administrators by having experience in administrative posts? Are men given the opportunity to advance because they are ambitious, or are they ambitious because they have an opportunity to advance?" [116]

There is a need to restructure social attitudes toward professional women. The present stereotypes prejudge women as leaders. The North Carolina Commission discovered that an experience under a woman supervisor by both men and women reduced the preference for male supervision and increased the likelihood of their answering "no difference."

One of the half-truths about women executives is that they are inconsiderate of human relations. Margaret Cussler, a sociologist who studied women officials, conceded that "they have some difficulties in maintaining social contacts," but she felt that "they recognize increasingly that social activities may well leaven work." [117] Women managers may be more committed because they have sacrificed a home life to get to their position. [118] On the other hand, women are attracted to work which involves concern with people. [119] Successful female executives practice leadership by indirection, suggesting rather than commanding.

Few women are executives. Men predominate in administrative and managerial posts and women in secretarial and clerical positions. The only managerial-level job which is characterized by a high proportion of women is manager in retail trades. More than three-quarters of the women workers have jobs in which men get relatively low pay, as clerks, secretaries, factory operatives, service workers, and teachers. [120] The proportion of women professional workers in the labor force was the same in 1962 as in 1940. [121]

Fortune estimated that only 5,000 of about 250,000 "real" executives were women. [122] Fewer than 40,000 U.S. women earned more than $10,000 a year, less than O.2 per cent of all women who work for a living. This figure includes actresses, movie stars, buyers, and professional women, as well as executives.

Only a handful of women are on the boards of directors of large banks and corporations. On the other hand, there are now 1,800 women stock brokers, ten times as many as in 1946, and at least 600 women advertising executives. There are now about 80,000 female accountants and auditors, 17 per cent of the total, as against less than 20,000 in 1940, eight per cent of the total. Ten thousand women are bank officers, including two hundred who are presidents of banks. [123]

Dr. Cussler attributed many of the recent economic gains of women to the expansion of the economy. "It seems to be true that when men are scarce and top jobs plentiful, there is no objection to putting a woman at the boss's desk. In times of war or rapid social change, bias is necessarily forgotten; it is remembered when there is time for the luxury of discrimination." [124]

But a disproportionate number of college-educated women still elect to go into traditional fields such as teaching. [125] This could indicate a lack of information about new fields open to women. At the same time, men are invading some traditionally female fields, such as schools and libraries, and are walking off with the prizes. Margaret Cousins observed pessimistically: "Actually, the number of women in positions of responsibility is declining." [126] Women are losing ground in the awarding of such positions as head librarian, superintendent of schools, elementary school principal, [127] and professor in women's colleges and teachers' colleges. [128]

A number of state commissions on the status of women and women's organizations have urged the compilation of rosters of female candidates for high-level appointive office. This is a step forward, but from where will the pool of political talent come? Unless there are many more women college teachers, organization and business executives, attorneys, and other professionals, there will be a dearth of suitable candidates.

Consider the field of law. Ninety-seven per cent of those attending law schools are men. Few opportunities exist for the part-time study of law. Although the number of women lawyers has increased, the percentage of female attorneys has remained constant. [129] Yet two-thirds of our presidents, vice presidents, and cabinet members have been lawyers, as were over 55 per cent of our representatives and senators, over 50 per cent of our state governors and over 25 per cent of our state legislators. [130]

Those women who do choose law as a career generally have family connections with lawyers. Women are hired by law firms for the "non-visible" research and library work. [131]

The majority of women doctors are in pediatrics. Only 5.5 per cent of the practicing doctors in the U.S. are women. [132]

Will Political Equality Be Achieved? Even if it could be demonstrated beyond question that the unequal status of women is a drag on our civilization and a disadvantage in an era of cold war, there is no assurance that our society will act to raise the status of over 100 million second-class Americans. At the moment, there is no reason to believe that a breakthrough will occur. Despite some stirrings, women are, for the most part, apathetic, and the question is below the threshold of male interest. No doubt amelioration is bound to take place, given continued prosperity and universal education. Parity, however, seems likely to remain a will-o'-the-wisp.

Women as Political Party Members

Even prior to the nineteenth amendment, some women were prominent in party politics. Jane Addams seconded Theodore Roosevelt's nomination in 1912 and toured the country in his behalf as a vote-getter without equal. She was one of the leading members of the national committee of the short-lived Progressive Party. Lillian Wald was her counterpart in the New York State Democratic Party from 1912 to 1928.

Said one woman in 1920: "Eight years ago my husband was horrified when I suggested that I should accompany him to the national convention. Four years ago he let me go along to stay in his room and answer the telephone. This year I am a delegate at large and he accompanies me." [1] The female vote had doubled the potential membership of the political parties and the men had to adjust to the new situation.

Ida Tarbell, an opponent of women's suffrage, commented, ten years after women had obtained the vote: "Women have become the tools of party leaders, just as men have. They have thought of parties rather than of issues." [2]

Women were also warned against involvement in the two major parties by Mrs. O. H. P. Belmont, national president of the National Woman's Party, who said: "Our goal is a third party, a permanent political party. Women are one-half the population of this country, and we believe that half should have its own political organization to stand for its own aspirations, ideals and political beliefs. If, to meet this situation, the two principal parties should combine into one and enter the field against the Woman's Party, none would be better pleased than we."

However, most women activists have chosen to take their chances as Republicans or Democrats. What is the role they have played in the two parties, as footsoldiers and as officers? How have they been treated by the men? How do they regard one another? Are party careers open to talent or are they limited by sex?

The Rank and File

Many women feel, as does Mrs. Barbara Gunderson, former republican national committeewoman from South Dakota, that "the essence of significant existence (in politics) is to be partisan."

Different roads lead into party politics. Congresswoman Jessica Weis wrote: "I got into politics because of a deep-seated hatred for housework, because I was economically able to spend the time, and because I had a frightful amount of excess energy, but mainly because I wanted to make some contribution to good government."

Some seem to have politics in their blood. Mrs. Constance Armitage, a Republican state vice chairman in South Carolina, was the descendant of a first cousin of George Washington who had been an officeholder under the first president. Her great-grandfather was speaker of the California House. Both her grandfathers were in the state senate and her mother was a professional lobbyist.

Other women enlist in parties to further their husband's career or their own. Still others want to support actively the goals or leaders of a party. It is paradoxical that even though women have been shown to be more ignorant of political issues and ideologies, they are more apt to join and work for a political party because of a concern about issues. As one woman politician put it: "Men go into politics to make money, directly or indirectly. Women go in to fight for causes."

Participation may result from a feeling of good citizenship developed by exposure to messages of duty coming from the schools, women's organizations, such as the LWV and the NFBPWC, and the press. Mrs. Kitty Massenburg, president of the Maryland Federation of Republican Women, was inspired by an eighth-grade civics teacher. She went on to major in political science in college and to take graduate work. Election day frauds in 1946 prodded her into action. [8]

Some women are recruited into the party fold by male leaders. Other politicians, more traditional, do everything they can to discourage women.

Initially there was male hostility to admitting women to the clubhouses. These had been "hang-outs," places to play cards, chew tobacco, and drink. Some women have the disposition to fit into such masculine groups, and others have not. One of the former is the 22-year-old office manager of the Wisconsin Democratic Party. She said: "Being a woman seems to make no difference in politics. You're expected to work the same hours, listen to the same language, and drink the same amount of beer as the rest. And I love it that way. If they start treating me like a woman, I'd feel left out." [9]

Mrs. Emily Newell Blair, an early Democratic leader, was successful in politics because she did not seem a threat to the men. "Do I not know that one of my chief recommendations to the politicians when they first asked me to go on a committee was my gentle, yielding manner?" [10]

One Republican national committeewoman confided: "I believe the men respect me because they know that politics is not a social outlet for me, but a job that I believe is important." [11]

A number of male politicians share James Branch Cabell's opinion that "no lady can ever be a gentleman." Legislative contacts for suffrage had to be made by the "sweetly feminine" types; arch-feminists would have disturbed the male politicians. [12]

Even today there is the stereotype of the "battle axe." The young woman who visits a club for the sake of volunteering for the campaign may be treated with incredulity by the regulars. "What's a nice girl like you doing in a place like this?" they seem to be saying.

According to Caroline K. Simon and Aileen Ryan, two successful New York State politicians, "A lady in politics has to look like a woman, dress like a lady, eat like a bird so she'll have a figure like a girl, think like a man, have the constitution of a horse, work like a dog, and have the hide of a rhinoceros." [13]

Marion Sanders, a New York Democrat, and Jessica Weis, a New

York Republican, were in agreement about the extent of women's influence in the councils of their parties: "The grownups wait till we leave the room before discussing the things that really matter." "You have the feeling that your opinion does not carry the weight of a man's opinion." [14]

Male politicians deny any discrimination, and allege that, if anything, they are especially willing to give women opportunities. Colonel Edward M. House once asked whether women in politics were more jealous of one another than were men. A feminist replied: "Just ask Colonel House whether any two Senators from the same state are really fond of each other." [15]

Men accuse women in the parties of a tendency to avoid real responsibility. Women reply that there is a male disinclination to give them such responsibility. [16]

Often, though, the woman playing the male game of politics has feelings of ambivalence. She can not take herself seriously when male and female colleagues do not.

Women contemplating running for office sometimes encounter discouragement from women friends: "Do you think you can cope with politicians?" "Aren't you afraid that you will expose yourself to a possible smear campaign?" "It will be difficult to dislodge an incumbent." "So many good people have been sacrificed. It will cost you too much in time, energy, and money." [17]

Former Republican National Chairman Hugh Scott wrote: "Women are backward in demanding a greater place in party councils, or perhaps they prefer to have policy made by the male politicians." His view is shared by Maurice Duverger: "While women have, legally, ceased to be minors, they still have the mentality of minors in many fields and, particularly in politics, they usually accept paternalism on the part of men." [18]

A Republican national committeewoman urged that women "stop thinking of themselves as 'women in politics' and start being realistic about what the job is. They should forget about who gets the corsage, and give up luncheons and fashion shows in favor of good hard work." [19]

Women are often around as window dressing—forever seconding nominations, occupying figurehead offices, confined to the safe backwater of the women's auxiliary. They are the committed volunteers, unconcerned with recognition and rewards. Whereas, as a Democratic state vice chairman said, the man who devotes himself to his local club usually does so in the hope of something like a judgeship.

One feminist objected to working "to a frazzle getting an all-men ticket elected." Alice Curtice Moyer-Wing wanted to work "with" men, not "for" them. [20]

Twenty years later, another woman asked: "Why is it that the men in my community, not the women, were taking the initial steps to find qualified candidates? Are we still following the old system 'the boys will choose them—the women support them?' " [21]

A state vice chairman bitterly concluded: "To be listed on the ballot, a woman should belong to the wrong party in a one-party state, where being a candidate means work and expense with a very slim chance of election." [22]

Louise Young reminded women: "In the long development of democratic government, no privileged group has ever been observed to yield up its power willingly or even to share it except with extreme reluctance." [23]

Samuel Grafton told of two cases of women fighting for recognition in party councils and receiving it: (a) Women in the Democratic Party of Denver complained that they were not able to have either voice or vote on the party's city-wide executive committee, then an all-male organization. District captains, male, were automatically members of that committee. The women launched a drive for the right to be captains in the district in which they were already the actual, effective workers. After a bitter fight, the women won. (b) In 1961, women delegates to the Republican state convention in Hawaii requested that a woman be made vice chairman of the party. After their request was denied, the women caucused and carried the fight to the convention floor, where they won. [24]

The first step in scaling the mountain of political success is to serve an apprenticeship at the precinct level. According to Maude E. Ten Eyck, a four-term state legislator from New York, "Reaching even the first rung of the political ladder involves such drudgery that a woman must want to get into this field intensely to stick it out." This point is reiterated by a male politician: "Women will never succeed in politics until they are willing to play the game of practical precinct politics, and they must learn to play it as well as the men. They must do favors, buy tickets, organize clambakes and picnics." [25]

At the time when the last statement was written, women were just "a small cog in the men's machines."[26] Today, though, in many communities women constitute the only large remaining pool of political labor that can be tapped to fill the vanishing ranks of patronage mercenaries.[27] Paradoxically, the crusade by women's groups for civil service reform created vacancies in the ranks of party footsoldiers, caused by the desertion of the spoilsmen, which were filled by women.

John Fischer observed: "Note who actually does the political work in your community. Who is it that sells the tickets to the Annual Dinner, mails out the reminders to register, gives tea parties for the Peerless Leader, keeps minutes at the committee meetings, drives voters to the polls on election day? Nine times out of ten a woman."[28]

A woman delegate to the 1964 Republican national convention from Oklahoma who has worked for the party for 14 years explained, "Women have more time to give. I estimate I have given 20 hours a week the last five years. You need the leadership of men—but for free time it is the women that do most of the actual work."[29] Women are more conscientious in attending committee meetings. There is greater male absenteeism.

"If the rent is to be paid regularly," noted Marion Sanders, "the American male can afford to invest a large slice of his energies in politics only if the odds favor a substantial reward, such as a government job, legal reference or a reasonable chance of election to public office. For most men this is a poor gamble."

For the ambitious, energetic, financially well-off woman, the payoff on an investment of time and effort in politics may seem ample. "The relative opportunities are greater for women than for men to hold party office," concluded a recent study of party leadership, "because there are fewer women than men activists, at least at the middle and upper levels of county and state party organization."[30] There is no shortage of workers of either sex on the eve of elections. The real opportunities to move into positions of responsibility come to those who enlist in an off year.

The Democratic *Campaign Manual* for 1964 urged that women be considered for more than the traditional "women's activities" of addressing envelopes, making telephone calls, and having coffee parties. [31] As one party worker put it: "You have to know how to handle a good volunteer if you want to hang on to her. If you just tell her to ring the doorbells or stuff envelopes or do some phoning, she'll probably quit. After all, that's just what she's been doing for the Cancer Drive or the PTA." [32]

A woman Democrat from Iowa contended that the women who enter politics are better educated and more efficient than their male counterparts. [33] They have given a different tone to clubhouse activities. While there is still need for canvassers, [34] election inspectors, poll watchers, baby sitters, literature distributors, receptionists, money raisers, and mailing list preparers, [35] there is also work for women speakers, researchers, and campaign managers.

There are still women and men who are in politics for their livelihood. They expect to be rewarded for their efforts with jobs such as election inspector, school-crossing guard, meter maid, or school lunchroom attendant. Often there is a husband-wife or father-daughter arrangement. [36] The party looks after its own.

Hugh Scott had one complaint: "It is not generally understood by women, even by many women politicians, that their participation in the policy-making activities of the party of their choice will increase in proportion as their assistance to the party finances improves." [37] Often women contributors are fronts for husbands or other relatives who may be barred by the Hatch Act or Corrupt Practices Act from donating in their own name. Mrs. Caryl Kline, a candidate for Congress from New York in 1958, admitted that "the hardest part of a campaign, for a woman, is having to be a bit of a beggar. I hate calling on businessmen for money." [38]

Senator William Benton once heard the women's division described as a "conspiracy of the grandmothers." He felt this libel was sadly out of date. "Without these veterans, any political organization would risk collapse." [39]

The Women's Divisions

Each of the parties has had from the eve of the nineteenth amendment special divisions of, by, and for women. These have been means for the representation of the sex in the councils of the parties and for recruitment and utilization of female footsoldiers for "Jimmy Higgins" work. [40]

The political parties in 1920 regarded the women's divisions as "needed temporarily as an efficient instrument in the aid of complete amalgamation." [41] This system of separate but equal facilities continued into the 1950's despite criticisms by reform women of "auxiliarism." The feminists felt that the way to break taboos was not to organize women's groups, but to get in where the men were and to demand equal rights. [42]

The auxiliaries did give women a foot in the door. According to Marion Sanders, "Their programs have often been sensibly geared to the capacity, pace and leisure of the civic-minded housewife, and have met the need for a protected environment where the inexperienced could develop their skills in matters parliamentary and political. They have thrived, too, because many women, like men, enjoy the company of their own sex." [43]

There were frustrations aplenty. A woman trade unionist complained: "They are always having teas and I sometimes think telephone calls are wasted. They tend to have too many education projects as in school, and this does not go over with most adults." [44]

Another woman activist announced she was resigning from "female politics." She complained about "women's simon-pure political organizations . . . where women make of political organization a sublimated mah-jongg tea, church social or sewing circle, according again to the social status of the group and the taste of its leader." [45]

The Democrats established their Women's Bureau of the National Committee in 1916 to seek feminine votes in the 11 western states where women had the suffrage. Mrs. Elizabeth Bass, a former president of the General Federation of Women's Clubs, was named director by her school classmate, Senator Thomas Walsh, who was in charge of the campaign in the West.

Mrs. Bass was succeeded in 1922 by Mrs. Emily Newell Blair,

who was also first vice chairman of the Democratic National Committee. Mrs. Blair, a journalist, was a veteran of the suffrage movement. She worked closely with the Women's National Democratic Club which had been organized in 1923 by Mrs. J. Borden Harriman and other prominent Washington, D.C., women. Mrs. Blair later became president of the club. Her husband served as an assistant attorney general under F.D.R.

The Women's Division of the Republican Party was created in 1918. Mrs. Harriet Taylor Upton, for 15 years the treasurer of the National American Woman Suffrage Association, became its director, and also vice chairman of the Republican National Committee. Her father, a supporter of Women's Suffrage, had been an Ohio common pleas judge and congressman. She was from Marion, Ohio, where she was for 15 years a member of the board of education, and was loyal to her fellow Ohioans, Harding and Daugherty. [46]

The men on the GOP National Committee decided to have a woman vice president of the national committee. This post was given to Mrs. Leonard G. Wood, making her in effect superior to Mrs. Upton, the head of Women's Activities. After Mrs. Upton's resignation, Mrs. Sallie T. Hert was given both places. Mrs. Upton ran unsuccessfully for nomination to Congress in 1924.

From 1924 to 1936, Mrs. Alvin T. Hert was Republican vice chairman. During much of this time she was assisted by Mrs. Ellis A. Yost as director of the Women's Division. Mrs. Hert had inherited her late husband's place as a member of the National Committee from Kentucky, as well as his chair as head of the American Creosoting Company. In 1930 she was being mentioned for a post in Hoover's cabinet. [47]

Lenna Yost had been active in behalf of education, woman suffrage, and prohibition. She was Washington representative of the National Woman's Christian Temperance Union for many years and was the first woman member of the West Virginia State Board of Education.

Mrs. Emily Blair was succeeded as vice chairman of the Democratic National Committee in 1928 by Mrs. Nellie Tayloe Ross, who had served briefly as governor of Wyoming. The direction of the Women's Division in the Roosevelt years was by Mary W. Dewson. Miss Dewson had impressed James Farley, the national chairman, with her organizing activities for the Democrats in New York in 1928. Previously, she had done parole work in the Massachusetts girls' reform schools, had served as executive secretary of the Massachusetts Commission of Inquiry into industrial conditons, and had been an official of the National Consumers League. Miss Dewson was responsible for promoting the appointment of women to positions in the New Deal. Her decade of leadership of the Women's Division was conspicuous for accomplishment. [48]

In 1935, Mrs. Robert Lincoln Hoyal became director of the Republican Women's Division. She was the widow and partner of a prosperous Arizona jeweler, had taught high school, and had been president of the Arizona Federation of Business and Professional Women's Clubs and of the American Legion Auxiliary. In 1936 she was the first woman of either party to act as assistant chairman of a national convention.

From 1937 to 1947 the head of the GOP Women's Division was Marion Martin of Maine. Miss Martin, who had already served terms in both houses of the Maine legislature, instituted a program similar to that which Mary Dewson was using to build up the Women's Division of the Democrats. Attention was paid to raising and spending funds, preparing campaign literature, and training precinct workers.

Directing the Democratic Women's Division in the 1940's were Mrs. Charles W. Tillett, [49] Mrs. Chase G. Woodhouse, [50] and Mrs. India Edwards. [51] Mrs. Edwards, like Miss Dewson, worked to get women appointed to governmental positions. It was supposed to have taken almost a year to make National Committeewoman Eugenie Anderson an ambassador and less than an hour to make National Committeewoman Georgia N. Clark treasurer of the United States. [52]

In 1952, India Edwards was offered the chairmanship of the Democratic National Committee but declined the post "on the grounds that a moment when party affairs were so snarled that no man appeared to be available for the job, was not the moment for the first woman to hold it." She doubted that the men were ready for such a radical break with tradition.

National committeewomen were also appointed to governmental positions under the Eisenhower administration. Mrs. Ivy

Baker Priest became treasurer of the U.S., and her replacement as head of women's activities, [53] Miss Bertha S. Adkins, later became under secretary of Health, Education and Welfare. [54]

Both parties abolished their Women's Divisions after the 1952 election, largely as an economy move. [55] The work of the Democrats' unit was integrated into the research and publicity departments. There was still to be an Office of Women's Activities. Miss Adkins was named director of special activities for the Republicans, and her responsibilities included not only women but other special sections— agriculture, minorities, labor, veterans, nationalities, ethnic groups, Young Republicans, and Republican Clubs.

The directors of Democratic and Republican women's activities in the late 1950's were Mrs. Katie Louchheim and Mrs. Clare B. Williams. Mrs. Louchheim, like Mrs. Blair and Mrs. Edwards, had had journalistic experience. She was active in Washington, D.C. Democratic politics for 15 years and had also worked for the U.N. [56] Mrs. Williams was a former teacher and businesswoman who became active in G O P Florida politics after her husband's retirement there in 1948.

Mrs. Louchheim was succeeded in 1960 by Mrs. Margaret Price, whose appointment was allegedly a means of appeasing the "liberal" Governor G. Mennen Williams for the selection of the "conservative" Lyndon Johnson as Kennedy's running mate. [57] Mrs. Price had run twice for Michigan auditor general but lost. She was the first woman in Michigan politics to poll more than a million votes.

Her Republican counterpart, Mrs. Elly Peterson, was also from Michigan. She had previously served as administrative assistant to the Republican state chairman and as state vice chairman. Mrs. Peterson resigned in 1964 to run for U.S. senator from Michigan. Her place was taken by a Goldwater backer, Mrs. Patricia Hutar of Illinois. In the following year, when Ray Bliss became chairman, Mrs. Hutar was succeeded by Mary Brooks, a state senator from Idaho. Mrs. Brooks is the widow of a U.S. senator and daughter of a former senator.

Women's offices in both parties continue to work as channels for bringing women into party membership and for training them for meaningful activities. They prepare how-to-do-it literature, conduct workshops and conferences, provide guest speakers, films and recordings, and handle special projects. They also represent the claims of party women for recognition. [58]

The Republicans hold an annual Women's Conference each spring in Washington, D.C. Thousands of women from all parts of the U.S. gather for training sessions. The Democrats also hold political schools where women are trained to make speeches, deal with the newspapers, study their party's programs and traditions, and get out the vote. It is strange that such activities seem desirable for women but not for men. Perhaps it is assumed that men know these things instinctively. [59]

Republican women are also associated in the National Federation of Republican Women, which numbers 500,000 women in 4,000 clubs in 50 states, the District of Columbia, and Puerto Rico. The NFRW was organized in 1938 as a means for knitting together local Republican women's clubs. Its chairman is an ex-officio member of the Republican National Committee's executive committee. The NFRW's activities overlapped the Women's Division, and the two organizations were from time to time "incongruously competitive." [60] Between 1938 and the early 1950's, the two women's offices worked together smoothly. In the fifties, however, two NFRW presidents, the wife of a congressman and the sister of a senator, thought that their organization should be autonomous. A battle royal developed in the NFRW in 1967. Mrs. Phyllis Schlafly of Illinois, author of a 1964 pro-Goldwater campaign book, *A Choice, Not an Echo,* and a NFRW vice president, was denied the traditional elevation to the presidency in a two-day convention marked with charges of election illegalities and threats to form a breakaway rival GOP women's group. Mrs. Schlafly lost to Mrs. Gladys O'Donnell, a California businesswoman, airplane pilot, veteran of Republican politics who has been a delegate to national GOP conventions since 1940. Mrs. O'Donnell, a less controversial conservative, announced that she wanted the Federation to represent the whole spectrum of Republican thinking.

The Democrats have no organization analogous to the NFRW. The Office of Women's Activities handles all matters pertaining to both club and regular party committee activities of Democratic women. There are local clubs, though, such as the Women's National Democratic Club of Washington, D.C., which has 1,155 members.

Women have also been closely involved in the 800 Young Republican and 600 Young Democratic clubs in cities and on campuses across the country. Often these clubs have reserved for a woman the post of co-chairman.

(1)   In 1964 Joanne Prevost, a member of Governor Peabody's personal staff, became the first female president of the Greater Boston Young Democrats.

(2)   Jean McKee joined the Young Republicans at Vassar. After college, she founded the Young Republican Club of Brooklyn Heights, N. Y. In 1964, she became the first woman ever to be elected president of the state Young Republicans. In 1966 Mrs. Mary Ann Krauss was chosen president of New York's Young GOP. She was re-elected in 1967.

(3)   From 1957 to 1959 Patsy Mink of Hawaii was vice president of the Young Democrats of America. She had organized the Oahu Young Democrats in 1954 and became the charter president of the Territorial Young Democrats in 1956. In 1964, she was elected to the U.S. Congress.

(4)   Mrs. Virginia Savell was elected president of the California Young Republicans in 1960.

(5)   Mrs. Ivy Baker Priest served as president of the Utah State Young Republicans Organization from 1934 to 1936.

(6)   Genevieve Blatt was president of the Young Democratic Clubs of Pennsylvania in 1946.

(7)   When the Young Republican national chairman resigned in 1952 to run for Congress, his co-chairman, Carol Arth, became the first women ever to serve as acting chairman of the Young Republican National Federation.

Women at the National Party Level

In 1900 each party had one woman delegate to the national convention. By 1920 there were 93 Democratic women delegates and 27 Republican. In 1964 there were 348 Democrats and 234 Republican.[61] On the surface, it would appear that women have come a long way in the two parties.

In fact, only one-sixth of the delegates are female. The proportion is greatest in the western states and least in the southern. [62] Honor, responsibility, and expense are attached to the job of convention delegate. Selection may reflect local circumstances. Florida law requires that half the delegates be women. New Hampshire has never had a woman delegate to a Republican convention. [63] Among the factors affecting selection of women delegates are the degree of conservatism in the social structure of the state, the extent of control of party organization by older-generation males, and the orientation of party leadership. Loose, disorganized, or insurgency-prone party organizations are more likely to admit women to their delegation. [64]

The only issue on which women delegates are likely to unite is the extent of recognition that should be accorded to women by the party. The 1952 Republican proposal to enlarge the national committee by adding state chairmen from the states carried by the party was criticized by the women for upsetting the balance between the sexes on the committee. Women campaigned in the 1950's for equal representation of men and women on all major committees, Credentials, Permanent Organization, Rules and Order of Business, and Platform and Resolutions, of the national conventions. [65]

Women are given honorary roles to play at the conventions. They escort a speaker or a candidate to the platform, second a nomination, or read a section of the platform. Often they are relegated to style shows or exclusive feminine luncheons, along with the wives of male delegates.

Marion Sanders voiced a familiar complaint when she said that the men with whom she served on the New York State Democratic platform committee allowed her to help draft planks on juvenile delinquency and mental health, but not on foreign affairs, where she had experience. [66]

Senator Margaret Chase Smith was invited by House Republican Leader Joseph Martin to be a speaker at the 1952 Republican Convention. As the time approached, she was informed that instead of the 20 minutes which had been planned for her address, there would only be time for a five-minute statement as a representative of a "minority." Mrs. Smith called the whole thing off. [67]

Senator Smith was not the first woman to receive support for president or vice president at a convention of a major party. In the hectic Democratic convention in 1924, three women received one or more votes for the presidential nomination and Mrs. Leroy Springs, chairman of the Credentials Committee, was formally nominated for vice president and received 38 votes. In 1928, Nellie Tayloe Ross received 31 votes on the first ballot for vice president. In 1952, Mrs. India Edwards and Judge Sarah Hughes were proposed for vice president at the Democratic convention, but there was no objection when it was moved that Senator J. Sparkman be nominated by acclamation. That same year, Clare Booth Luce was ready to nominate Mrs. Smith for the Republican vice presidential position, but both yielded to the tradition that the presidential candidate should be allowed to name his running mate. In 1964, though, Senator Smith was nominated for president and received about 30 votes.

The convention with its fireworks seems more a game for men than for women. [68] Emily Newell Blair thought that men accomplish their ends by competition with one another, while women accomplish their goals by systematic programming. "Women's conventions are given over to prearranged programs designed to inform the delegates on subjects in which they are interested. Much time is allotted to discussion methods, organization, publicity, and money raising; comparatively little to elections and resolutions." A woman said after the Democratic convention of 1924, "I've learned one thing: to make our planks worth while to the men, we must organize a fight over them." [69]

Part of the window-dressing [70] at the conventions is the secretary of the national committee. Since 1944 there has been a feminine voice calling the roll of the states. In that year, the Democrats named 27-year-old Mrs. Dorothy Vredenburgh to that duty. [71] Mrs. Vredenburgh, now Bush, [72] is still the secretary.

The Republicans did not lose much time in matching the Democrats. At a meeting of the national committee held January 22, 1945, Mrs. Dudley C. Hay was selected from among two men and two women in a secret ballot. [73] The Republican secretary from 1956 to the mid-sixties was Mrs. C. Douglas Buck, daughter-in-law of a former Delaware governor and U.S. senator.

Each state is represented on the national committee by one

woman and one man. [74] This 50-50 rule was conceived by Mrs.
George Bass, chairman of the Women's Bureau of the Democratic
National Committee in 1920. It provided a practical solution
affording women entrance into party politics.

According to Mrs. Eleanor Roosevelt, "fifty-fifty looks better
on paper than it has worked out in practice. Too often the vice
chairmen and the committeewomen are selected by the men, who
naturally pick women who will go along with them and not give
them any trouble. Thus they are apt to be mere stooges. . . Too often
the selection of a national committeewoman is based on her bank
account, social prestige, or party service rendered by a deceased
husband. And a state vice chairman, even if she has ability and a
mind of her own, finds herself frustrated by a kind of political
protocol under which she is not permitted to choose the women with
whom she is to work, but must accept those handed to her by the
masculine-dominated county committee." [75]

This view is seconded by Dr. Barbara Gunderson, a former
Republican national committeewoman: "If only we could say to
men in authority, 'When you do decide to recognize women, for
heaven's sake choose someone whose history, experience and
achievement satisfies the women. Don't look around for old Bill's
pretty little wife, Dotty, who always seems so pleasant at dinner
parties. That kind of appointment only infuriates the hard-working,
able women, and then they have the millstone of Dotty's performance record to contend with later on.' " [76]

In most cases it is necessary for a vice chairman or a
committeewoman to win the support of the male leader. This leader
may not himself occupy the position of chairman or committeeman.
Thus there are occasions where the female officeholder is more of a
power in the party than her male counterpart, who may be either
superannuated or an errand boy. One such heavyweight was Mrs.
Worthington Scranton, mother of the future governor of Pennsylvania, who was vice chairman of the Republican national
committee in 1940 and national committeewoman from 1928 to
1951, and was considered by many to be the most powerful woman
in the state's Republican party. [77]

Nearly one-third of the Republican national committeewomen
and nearly one-half of the Democratic were described in a recent

study as quite unimportant. Another six Republicans and nine Democrats were given a still lower rating by the informants, as completely unimportant. Cotter and Hennessy inferred from these replies that, if these women had little influence, then "no women have much influence in state political parties." [78] However, their table showed that 8.1 per cent of the Republican national committee-women and 0.7 per cent of the Democratic were rated among the top six in influence in their state parties.

Often the national committee position is the reward for a good job as state chairwoman. A number of vice chairmen have indicated that they hope to receive this promotion. After the exhausting routine of directing women's activities throughout the state, the national committee berth must seem a relief. There is both political and ceremonial work, mostly related to the quadrennial conventions. Usually, the national committees meet only twice a year. The committee members do advance planning and serve on the major committees. The Republican women are in charge of ticket arrange-ments, a task decentralized by the Democrats. The committeewomen are also responsible for "delegate cheeriness."

National committeewomen are more likely than committeemen to resign for reason of removal from their state. This reflects the tendency of women to defer to their husbands when there is the possibility of his job advancement through relocation. [79]

On the other hand, a committeewoman often began her political career through concern for her husband's political ambitions. Mrs. Jean Graham, Democratic national committeewoman from Colorado, decided to enter politics when her husband became a candidate for Congress. [80] She rose from precinct committeewoman to district captain to county registration and financial chairman to national committeewoman. Mrs. Earle Burwell's husband served as party co-chairman and was elected three times to the state legislature. Her 40 years in politics began by helping with his campaigns. Mrs. Bryant B. Brooks, who served for many years (1924-1937) as Republican national committeewoman for Wyoming, was the wife of a two-time governor. Mrs. John G. Pollard was the wife of a governor of Virginia and served as executive secretary to four successive governors before being asked in 1940 to be a candidate for the office of Democratic national committeewoman. She still held the post in 1964. Earle

Long's wife, Blanche, became Louisiana Democratic national committeewoman.

The record for continuous service is held by Mrs. Emma Guffey Miller, Democratic national committeewoman from Pennsylvania since 1932. She was sister of a U.S. senator, was one of eight vice chairmen of the Democratic national committee in 1936, and is national chairman of the National Woman's Party. Mrs. Miller never missed a meeting of a national committee.[81]

Often a whole family is engaged in politics. Mrs. Zelma Reeves Morrison, Democratic national committeewoman for Washington, is the daughter of a mother who served 15 years in the state legislature before becoming secretary of state and of a father who was minority leader in the legislature.[82] Mrs. Rose Bovaird, Republican national committeewoman for New Hampshire, is married to the moderator of her ward. Both her son and daughter are active in politics.[83] Mrs. Given Barnett, Idaho Republican national committeewoman, is married to a precinct committeeman. Her 16-year-old daughter is state committeewoman for the county teen-age Republicans.[84] Mrs. Geri Joseph's grain-merchant husband does not have time for politics; however, he regards her activities as Democratic national committeewoman for Minnesota as continuing his family's tradition of public service.[85]

In January, 1965, after a leadership fight, a Republican Policy Coordinating Committee was set up. Its announced membership did not include a single woman, suggestive of the unconscious way in which both national parties tend to ignore women when making decisions.[86]

Women at the State Party Level

Louis Harris asked in 1954: "Who ever heard of a woman campaign manager, or a woman county, state, or national chairman?"[87] Another decade has passed since then with but slight improvement in the picture.

Politics is largely man's preserve. For a woman to rise in the party, she usually needs a male sponsor. The male leaders tend to prefer docile females. According to Mrs. Roosevelt, [88] there are many county vice chairmen and state committeewomen who have been kept in office for years, doing nothing, by the male leaders who explain that they want to avoid a "hair-pulling contest." This often means they do not want to risk replacement by someone who might be harder to control.

It is fascinating to study the comments of the women who get appointed, by men, to the position of state vice chairman. When asked about the place women presently have in politics, one such leader replied: "To do the work that men do not have the time to do." She continued, "Women do not like to hear other women speak, and men do not like to hear women speak; and in order to run, one must." [89]

Another satellite said of her sex: "Women have a tendency to be carried away with themselves and their importance. And they just are not capable of making all the great decisions wisely. They aren't built to know all about farms, industries, highways, etc. Consequently, they get on men's nerves, and men don't have time to be bothered with them. I think the only place that they should have is to do the things that men cannot do—leg-work, organizational work among their own sex, etc." [90] As long as there are wise and capable men to run our government, this woman did not see any possibility of women's playing a greater political role.

Mrs. Ruth Watson of California, vice chairman of the Republican Central Committee, must deserve commendation from the men for her selflessness. She has made a point throughout her political career of never asking for any of the posts that she has held. Mrs. Watson does not accept expense reimbursements, not even for traveling. When asked how much her job cost her, she hesitated, and then said: "I have probably spent between ten and twenty thousand dollars in the last four years, traveling in the state and going to Washington." [91]

One state vice chairman complained that some male politicians "look around for the nearest woman every time there's drudgery to be done, but don't consult them otherwise." She was involved in all the hard and thankless chores for five years before getting the title of county secretary, and was promoted to county chairman only when no one else would take the job. Her party was in the minority. As state vice chairman, she felt left out of important deliberations. "Much of the discussion and give-and-take of decisions takes place where women may feel uncomfortable or unwelcome unless with husband or escort—in bars. When men adjourn to the bar after a heated discussion at a meeting, a woman goes home." [92]

Eleanor Clark French resigned as New York Democratic vice chairman in 1960, charging that she had been ignored on policy matters.

Some state co-chairmen do have political power behind them. One was encouraged to run with the man who became chairman so that he would get support from her district. [93] This is a case of being mutually dependent.

One of the most powerful women leaders was Mrs. Belle Moskowitz. She was Governor Al Smith's number one adviser on politics and social legislation. [94] Mrs. Moskowitz entered politics through welfare work and was an industrial counselor. [95] She served as secretary of a number of New York State committees. During the Democratic campaign of 1928, Mrs. Moskowitz ran the national headquarters, although technically she was only in charge of publicity. [96]

Genevieve Blatt, secretary of the Pennsylvania Democratic state committee, has been "the principal source of information concerning the political needs of the state and party for all the major state-wide candidates, including gubernatorial candidates Leader, Lawrence, and Dilworth." [97]

Many state laws and party constitutions provide that the vice chairman must be a woman. [98] These laws do not, however, specify that the chairman must be a man. There are very few instances, though, of a woman's becoming state chairman.

Mrs. William Maulsly of Iowa was temporarily elevated to state chairman of the Democratic Party in 1928. Two years later Mrs. Carl V. Rice became chairman of the Kansas Democratic Party for a few months. Other women have served as acting chairman. In 1934 Mrs. Frank E. Johnesse was elected Democratic state chairman in Idaho, after having served in that post for two years following the resignation of the gentleman who held it. She was an unsuccessful candidate for the Democratic nomination for Congress in 1938. Nadie Strayer, whose father was the dean of the Oregon state senate, became acting Democratic state chairman in 1937, to fill out an unexpired term. She went back to being vice chairman in 1938.

Congresswoman Mary Norton, a protege of boss Frank Hague, was elected chairman of the Democratic state committee of New Jersey in 1932. She served until 1935, and then went back to being vice chairman. She was again state chairman in 1943 and 1944.

Mrs. Elizabeth Snyder became chairman of the California Democratic state central committee in 1954 by defeating an assemblyman. She served until 1956. The Oregon Democrats currently have a woman chairman, Mrs. Martha Ann Adelsheim.

Mrs. Elly Peterson, Republican assistant national chairman and candidate for the U.S. senate, was governor George Romney's personal choice in 1965 for the post of Michigan state chairman.[99] Women are also conspicuous in the Michigan Democratic Party. A woman managed Governor G. Mennen Williams' campaign three times, and Governor John Swainson's campaign manager was a woman. Eight counties have women chairmen of their Democratic county committees.[100]

Often there are slots assigned to women by the parties. Symmetry, if nothing else, may require that there be a woman to manage the "woman's campaign."[101] A whole parallel organization may emerge, co-chairman, co-manager, co-leader, etc., with its own pattern of promotion.[102] In California, for example, every state-wide candidate has a woman co-campaign chairman.

How do women react to women in party positions? Sometimes the leaders are loyally supported. At other times, though, there is more rivalry and lack of trust than solidarity.[103] One state vice chairman acknowledged being referred to as "that woman." Since decision-making is monopolized by men, it is often assumed by women that female officials are yes-women.

Women at the Local Party Level

Quite logically, women have won their earliest and greatest acceptance at the local levels of politics. Michigan, with the coming of woman suffrage, changed the number of party state committee members elected from each congressional district from two to three, in order that a woman might be elected from each district, although that was not specified in the law. This resulted in 13 women members on the state committee, or one woman member from each congressional district. [104]

As early as 1918, Miss Mary Garrett Hay, who led the fight in New York in 1917 for women's suffrage, was named chairman of the Platform Committee of the state Republican convention, the most important position next to chairman of the convention. [105] She had the satisfaction of presiding over such enemies of the suffrage as Nicholas Murray Butler [106] and Senator James Wadsworth. Miss Hay resigned as chairman of the Women's Executive Committee of the Republican National Committee in 1920 rather than support Senator Wadsworth for re-election.

A Mrs. Halterman was considered a woman "boss" in Missouri in the late 1920's. Even today there are few women with that power. For 40 years Minnie Fisher Cunningham was very influential in Texas reform politics.

At present, 12 states adhere to the 50-50 principle providing for equal representation of men and women on all party committees. [107] Six additional states have the 50-50 rule in the Democratic Party, [108] and four have it in the Republican. [109] Eight southern states give much less than equal representation to women.

In 1956 there were less than 100 women county chairmen in the country's 3,072 counties, most of which had both Republican and Democratic organizations. [110] Most of the women chairmen were from New England states. Mrs. Katherine St. George, one of the select number, remembers a man's saying, "Well, I don't see how she can be county chairman. She won't be able to go into the saloons with the boys." [111]

Mrs. Marguerite Benson was the first woman ever elected, and re-elected, as Milwaukee County Democratic chairman. She later became state vice chairman and was appointed by Kennedy to be collector of customs for Wisconsin.

The path to local chairmanship is often by way of the role of understudy. Mrs. Margaret Schultz, the vice chairman, was elected to fill the post of Bingham County, Idaho, Democratic central committee chairman when the seat was vacated by the duly elected leader. [112] She felt that this recognition for her sex led to more women's becoming interested in party affairs and coming with their husbands to the meetings. "They don't feel now that it's dominated by men."

In November, 1964, the male leader of the New York County Democratic committee, known unofficially as "Tammany Hall," resigned. By virtue of her chairmanship of the county executive committee,[113] Mrs. Charlotte Spiegel became acting leader. Mrs. Spiegel's husband was a former state assemblyman who is a civil court judge. She had served as co-leader of her district for nine years. Although Mrs. Spiegel held the post of county leader for only a month, the attention paid to her temporary promotion led the city bar association's ethics committee to demand that either she retire from partisan politics or that her husband resign his judgeship. The committee said that the "intimate relationship between man and wife" creates suspicion "approaching that which would have been created if the judge himself had engaged" in politics.[114]

The first woman to be elected leader, not co-leader, of a political club in New York City was Dorothy Bell Lawrence. The male district leader had had her elected co-leader because she seemed young and innocent, a schoolteacher and Girl Scout leader fresh from Georgia. She soon discovered that he was inept, and succeeded in getting him replaced. The replacement was not much of an improvement. Mrs. Lawrence then did the unheard-of thing of getting herself selected as leader. It took a change in the county party's rules. She has been "boss" ever since. Her philosophy is that "a political machine is like an automobile; when you're driving, you can't take your hand off the wheel."[115] But there have not been many Mrs. Lawrences who were able to beat the men at their own game.

The reform clubs tend to give real opportunities for leadership to women. Many of these were attracted into politics by way of the 1952 Stevenson campaign. They resented being excluded from regular clubs or confined to an auxiliary organization.[116] They were accepted as equal partners, as comrades in arms, by the men of the new insurgent organizations.

One of these groups, the Village Independent Democrats, has been called a "matriarchy."[117] Its former president, Carol Greitzer, is now a Democratic district leader. The editor of the *Village Voice* said of her: "She is cool. She is feminine in appearance, and masculine in her way of thinking. She doesn't blow up or get hysterical." One Greenwich Village resident observed: "There are a lot of monuments around here to Carol Greitzer in the shape of stop lights, slow-down signs, and perhaps a little park bench in a corner." [118]

Another young reformer from the Village Independent Democrats, Sarah Schoenkopf, at 27 was able in 1960 to run against the chairman of the state Democratic Women's Division and defeat her for state committeewoman.

Another New York City reform club, the Riverside Democrats, has had two women presidents. The second president of the Riverside Democrats was Mrs. Barbara Palmore, a social worker and housewife. She was the first woman president of any Democratic club in the city. Miss Alice Sachs, a veteran of over 20 years in politics and leader of the Ninth Assembly District, became head of the caucus of reform district leaders. Ann P. Rode was leader of the Tenth Assembly District Democrats.

On several occasions the male and female leaders from reform clubs have taken opposite positions at meetings of the county executive committee. This would never happen in the old line clubs.[119] The co-leaders have even endorsed different candidates for the same office. Because the female leaders have their own base of strength within the organization, there is little or nothing the male leaders can do to discipline their colleagues.

It would seem that political success has not come to women solely because they have done good work for their political party. Why should they not be rewarded as men would be for similar activities? Is the blame to be placed on men or on women, or should it be shared? Why are women candidates often selected only in hopeless races or where the position seems to call for a woman? [120]

Why should it be the case that "every public speaker knows that an audience often likes to be vigorously exhorted and even thundered at by a man, but if the speaker is a woman, the same audience, though it may want eloquence, will want it flavored with far less denunciation and far more persuasion?" [121]

Women's Political Achievements
In Other Countries

To what extent is the subordinate political status of women in the United States the result of the fact that they are women? An answer may be implied in the limited extent to which women occupy high-level elective and appointive positions in lands with different cultures.

There have always been female dynasts of distinction, from Boadicea to Matilda, Elizabeth I, and Victoria, Cleopatra, Maria Theresa, and Catherine. [1] There have also been charismatic, legendary leaders like Joan of Arc. An accident of birth or crisis has often enabled a woman of ability to shine in a male society. Even in recent years, Elizabeth II of the United Kingdom, Wilhelmina and Juliana of the Netherlands, and Charlotte of Luxembourg have been chiefs of state in countries where few women achieve high governmental positions.

In a new country, where there are no incumbents to be dislodged and the political situation is fluid, women stand a better chance to attain office. In Weimar, Germany, where women got the vote at the same time as in the United States, the first Reichstag contained 41 women, [2] whereas only five women were elected to the U.S. Congress between 1916 and 1924.

In Canada in 1963, there were five women among the 265 elected members of the House of Commons and six women among the appointed members of the Senate. Women also held the posts of postmaster-general, civil service commissioner, and ambassador to Austria. [3]

Miss Agnes C. Macphail (Labor), the first woman member, entered the Canadian House of Commons in 1921 and was still there in 1940. She had been a teacher. The second woman in Commons, Mrs. George Black, did not arrive until 1935 when she succeeded her husband, a former speaker who had become ill.

It took considerable effort in the 1920's for women to win the right to sit in the Canadian Senate. Finally, in 1930, the women's organizations secured the appointment of Cairine Wilson. [4] Her father had been a senator and her husband a member of Parliament. Mrs. Wilson had large business interests in her own right and was honorary president of the National Federation of Liberal Women of Canada.

As in the United States, women found it easier to win office in the western region. Mrs. Mary Ellen Smith of British Columbia, the widow of a liberal labor leader, became the first widow to succeed to her husband's seat in the provincial legislature of British Columbia. She also became the first woman cabinet minister in the British Empire or on the North American continent and the first woman to serve as speaker of a legislative house. At the time of her death, Mrs. Smith was president of her provincial liberal party and of the Women's Liberal Clubs of Canada. Mrs. Nancy Hodges (Liberal) of British Columbia also became a speaker of the B.C. Legislature. Mrs. Hodges, a newspaperwoman, had been defeated for a house seat in 1939 but was victorious in 1941, 1945, and 1949.

The first woman to hold cabinet rank in the central government was Mrs. Ellen Fairclough, who was appointed secretary of state in 1957. The next year she became minister of Citizenship and Immigration. In 1963, Miss Judy La Marsh was named minister of National Health and Welfare. She played a major role in shaping important pension and welfare legislation and a bill to set up a new broadcasting commission. Miss La Marsh, a Liberal M. P. from

Niagara Falls, where she practiced law with her father, served until 1968 as secretary of state. She was good copy for the press, posing in a silly hat or saying "ministers and women in politics are far too pompous."

For much of the period since 1950, the civic affairs of Canada's capital city, Ottawa, were dominated by Miss Charlotte Whitton. She had been executive director of the Canadian Welfare Council when she entered politics to set an example for other women. She claimed that there were less than 200 women among the 25,000 members of the elective boards of the country. Miss Whitton attracted loyal female supporters and received the highest vote for the four-member Board of Control. She became deputy mayor. Some months after the election, she succeeded to the number one post on the mayor's death. In 1952 she campaigned successfully for a term of her own. She retired in 1956, but returned in 1960. In 1958 Miss Whitton was an unsuccessful candidate for Parliament. Six times she was named Canada's Woman of the Year. "Her Worship" was known for her battles with the masculine Board of Control. They accused her of being stubborn, intransigent, and "unreasonable beyond all getting along with." She crusaded against "that mess in City Hall" and promised honesty and hard work. Miss Whitton's motto was "What the Devil can't do, a woman can." She declared: "Whatever women do they must do twice as well as men to be thought half as good. Luckily, it is not difficult." She did feel, though, that a woman could not manage both a home and a job. "One or the other is shortchanged." In December 1964, Miss Whitton was defeated in a bid for a sixth term. [5]

Fourteen countries besides the United States gave women political rights about the time of World War I. Yet, according to a writer in 1947, the United States lagged behind in the percentage of women in 10 of 12 national legislatures. [6] These post-war events, however, were somewhat misleading. Sometimes, as in France, there was a new constitution and a desire for a fresh start after years of occupation and war. There may even have been an electoral feature, such as proportional representation or reserved seats, which made it easier for women to be selected. [7]

In one country, the United Kingdom, women held only three per cent of the seats in the House of Commons in the late 1940's. [8]

They now constitute four per cent of the total membership in the House of Commons, 28 out of 630. Seven of the 915 members of the House of Lords are women. One of the peeresses is Lady Gaitskell, widow of the Labor Party leader Hugh Gaitskell. She is also a delegate to the United Nations' social committee. There have been only about 80 women in Commons since Lady Astor blazed the way in 1919.

Lady Astor inherited a seat left by her husband when he moved to the House of Lords. Mrs. Lena Jeger and Mrs. Muriel Gammans succeeded their husbands. Lady Davidson, like Lady Astor, entered the House when her husband became a peer. Her father, grandfather, and great-grandfather had all been M.P.'s. Lady Davidson's father had been unsuccessful in his day in trying to get women admitted to the House of Lords. He also crusaded for women's suffrage and for women to sit on the county councils.

Lady Megan Lloyd George was the first daughter to sit in the same Parliament as her father. She served as a Liberal M.P. for 22 years and caused a political sensation in 1955 when she switched her allegiance to the Labor Party. Standing as a Laborite, she defeated a liberal challenger and held her seat until her death in 1966.

Between 1918 and 1928, only 11 women held seats in the Commons. In 1929, 14 women were elected. In 1931 there were 15. There were never more than 15 until 1945 when 87 women stood for Parliament and 24 were chosen, 21 Labor, one Conservative, one Liberal, and one Independent. In 1950 only 21 were successful.[9] Seventeen survived in 1951. Twenty-five were chosen in 1959. In 1964, 28 were elected, more than ever before.

As in the U.S., women are sometimes nominated to oppose female incumbents. Dame Irene Ward defeated Margaret Bondfield twice and later defeated an incumbent, Grace Colman. In 1955 Mrs. Judith Hart, a Laborite and a mother, was chosen to oppose Lady Tweedsmuir, a Conservative M.P. and a mother. The incumbent won, but Mrs. Hart captured a seat in 1959.

Women M.P.'s have been given less important ministerial posts. Only four women have attained cabinet rank. Three were Laborites: Minister of Labor Margaret Bondfield (1929-31), Minister of Education Ellen Wilkinson (1945-47), and Minister of Overseas Development Barbara Castle (1964-65). In December 1965, Mrs. Castle was named transportation minister. Miss Florence Horsbrugh, now Lady Horsbrugh, was named minister of Education in 1951, but was not included in the Conservative cabinet until September 1953. Dr. Edith Summerskill was minister of National Insurance in 1950, but was not part of the Labor cabinet. At present, there are six women holding non-cabinet portfolios. [10]

One of the female M.P.'s, Mrs. Eirene White, conceded that certain activities of male members were irritating, "such as when a woman has spoken from one side of the House and the Speaker then gallantly calls on a woman from the other side. It certainly reminds you that you're a woman." [11]

Some women members of Commons do their best to conceal the differences. Miss Joan Quennell relaxes by making parachute jumps. Lady Tweedsmuir was still speaking in the House in her seventh month of pregnancy, which was unknown even to her women colleagues. But the press referred to her, during her first campaign for parliament, as a "glamor girl" and "young widow," and when she walked down the center of the House of Commons to take her seat for the first time, some men emitted whistles.

In 1966 Elizabeth K. Lane became Britain's first woman High Court judge. The Lord Chancellor's office dubbed her "His Lordship, Mr. Justice Lane." After adverse public reaction, the Lord Chancellor's office reversed itself and referred to her as "Her Ladyship, Mrs. Justice Lane."

Women hold one-third of all seats at both Conservative and Labor Party conventions. There have been eight women chairmen of Conservative conventions, and six or seven at Labor conventions. [12]

Lady Violet Bonham-Carter, Herbert Asquith's daughter, was chairman of the British Liberal Party. Among the Labor chairmen were Miss Wilkinson and Mrs. Castle.

In local government, women's participation is particularly strong. Forty per cent of the members of the London County Council are women. However, women are much less numerous in other local councils. In 1951-52 no woman was a lord mayor or lord provost, though women had previously served as lord mayor of Liverpool, Manchester, Norwich, and Stoke-on-Trent. Only 30 women, about seven per cent of the total, were mayors in England, and in Scotland, just three of 106 provosts were women. [13]

A study of the status of British women concluded that "female social awareness is still too limited. . . .Apathy, diffidence and inhibitions . . . still handicap women after centuries of subjection. Only when a great band of women have learned to accept the challenge of responsibility, and from every class and neighborhood demand a share in policymaking as they once demanded the vote, is the proportion of men and women in politics likely to reach a reasonable equality." [14]

About 10 per cent of the legislative seats in Scandinavia are held by women. [15] These countries also have women ministers. Mrs. Nina Bang joined the Danish cabinet in 1924 and Muna Sillanpaa the Finnish cabinet in 1927. In 1963 Denmark had women as minister of Ecclesiastical Affairs, permanent under secretary to the Ministry of Education, justice of the Supreme Court, ambassador to Switzerland, and counselor of the Permanent Mission to the United Nations. Finland had a woman minister of Education, associate minister for Social Affairs, and ambassador to Norway. A vice president of the Norwegian Storting was a woman as were the minister for Family and Consumer Affairs and the director of the Central Bureau of Statistics. Mrs. Schweigard-Selmer became minister of Justice in 1966. In Sweden women were appointed minister without portfolio, first curator of the National Museum, ambassador to the United Nations, and ambassador at large. Mrs. Alva Myrdal, wife of the noted economist, Gunnar Myrdal, is head of the Swedish delegation to the 17-nation disarmament committee in Geneva. She has played a prominent part in U.N. arms debates and in negotiations for the nuclear test ban treaty. Mrs. Myrdal served five years as Sweden's ambassador to India.

In 1951 Mrs. Ingeborg Hansen became the first woman president of the Danish Parliament. Mrs. Inga Thorsson, the first woman to be elected to the Stockholm City Council, became mayor in 1959. Four years later, Mrs. Edel Saunte became the first female lord mayor of Copenhagen. That same year Miss Ragnhildur Helgadottir became Iceland's first woman speaker of Parliament.

Contrary to the popular impression, women are not numerous in the legislatures of Communist countries. In the Soviet Union in 1963, 10 of the 738 seats in the Council of Union were held by women, and 15 of the 640 places in the Council of Nationalities.

There were two women in the 33-member Presidium of the Supreme Soviet including Mme. Ekaterina A. Furtseva, the minister of Culture.[16] In 1957 Maria Kovrigina was minister of Health.

In Yugoslavia there were four women in the 587-member Federal People's Assembly. Six women held posts of under secretary, assisting secretary, acting secretary, and assistant director. Mrs. Mara Rodic spent four years as ambassador to Switzerland, represented her government on the executive committee of the U.N. Children's Fund, and became chairman of the U.N.'s Social Committee in 1967.

France had only five women in the Senate of 307 seats, and eight in the National Assembly of 552 posts in 1963. There were 33 women in the assembly which drafted the constitution of 1946. Twenty-two were elected in 1951, but only 19 in 1956. However, 402 local councils are headed by women mayors. A woman is a member of the Cour de Cassation, the Supreme Court, and another is director general of personnel.

In West Germany there were 44 women in the 499-member Bundestag in 1963, and 38 in 1966. There was also a female minister of Health and two women were justices on the High Court for Civil and Criminal Matters. In 1963 Italy had only three women senators of 249 and 25 deputies of 596. The first postwar Italian Parliament had 43 women. The only high post held by an Italian woman was under secretary of the Ministry of Public Education.[17] In the Netherlands five seats in the 75-member First Chamber were held by women and 15 in the 150-member Second Chamber. Miss Margaretha Klompe, the minister of Social Welfare, was the first woman to hold a Dutch cabinet post.

In Ireland, Mrs. Tom Clarke, widow of a Fenian leader executed by the British, became the first woman chairman of the Dublin County Council. The next woman to serve as Dublin's lord mayor, Mrs. Catherine Byrne, was chosen in 1958. Mrs. Josephine McNeil was Eire's minister to Switzerland, a masculine stronghold.

Of the Latin American countries, Brazil had only one woman in its 326-member Chamber of Deputies. Its ambassador to Costa Rica was a woman. Costa Rica had a single woman in its 57-member Legislative Assembly; its ambassador to the United Kingdom was a woman. Mexico did not have a single woman delegate in its Senate and had only six women among the 178 members of the Chamber of

Deputies. The under secretary of Cultural Affairs was a woman, as were a justice on the Supreme Court and the ambassador to Denmark. Mrs. Amalia de Castillo Ledon became the first woman to hold a ministerial post in the Mexican government when she became under secretary in the Department of Education in 1960. Two years later Mrs. M. C. Salmoran de Tamayo became the first woman appointed to the Mexican Supreme Court.

In 1966 President Joaquin Balaguer named a woman as governor of each of the Dominican Republic's 26 provinces. The governorships are more ceremonial than political.

The Venezuelan national Congress had five women among its 184 members in 1963. Venezuela also had a female ambassador to Uruguay. Sra. Josefina Valencia de Hubach, governor of Cauca Province in the neighboring country of Colombia, was named minister of Education in 1956.

A woman is mayor of a Latin American city of half a million. She is Dona Felisa Rincon de Gautier of San Juan, Puerto Rico, the oldest city under the American flag. In 1938 she became president of the San Juan Committee of the fledgling Popular Democratic Party. And in 1940 she married a lawyer, Jenero de Gautier, who became assistant attorney general in the insular Department of Justice. In 1940 and 1944 her husband forbade her acceptance of the mayoral nomination.[18] But she filled a vacancy in 1946 and won re-election in 1948, 1952, 1956, 1960, and 1964, by vote of the San Juan Board of Commissioners. She announced in 1964 that this was her last term. Her sister joined her in the city government as secretary of the capital and, on occasion, acting mayor. Senora de Gautier's main concerns are health, sanitation, housing, education, fiestas and celebrations, and acting as a goodwill ambassador. She is a champion of the poor. Another woman mayor in Latin America is Mrs. Anita Fernandini de Navanjo, who was elected mayor of Lima, Peru, in 1963, the first woman to occupy that position.

In the Middle East, Turkey had only two women in the 150-member Senate and three in the 450-member National Assembly. In 1954 Madama Malahat Ruacan became the first woman appointed judge of the Turkish Supreme Court. The next year she was joined by Nezakat Gorele. The United Arab Republic had a woman minister of Social Affairs. Israel had only one woman in the 120-member Knesset. She was the deputy speaker. Israel's minister for Foreign Affairs was Mrs. Golda Meir, who previously held the post of minister of Labor. She resigned in 1966 and became secretary general of the Mapai Party. Tel Aviv has a woman mayor.

In Asia, after the assassination of her husband in 1959, Mrs. Sirimavo Bandaranaike became prime minister of Ceylon, minister of Defense and External Affairs, and president of the Sri Lanka Freedom Party. From 1946 to 1960 she had been treasurer, vice president, and president of the Lanka Mahilu Samiti, the women's organization of the party. There were two women, including Mrs. Bandaranaike, in the 30-member Senate and two in the 157-member House of Representatives. Mrs. Bandaranaike's party lost control of the government in the 1965 election. She was not the first woman in the Ceylonese cabinet. Mrs. Vimala Wijeyewardene, who was appointed minister of Health in 1956 and minister of Housing and Local Government in 1959, had that honor.

India has 27 women in its legislative Upper House (out of 236) and 35 in its Lower House (out of 509). In the Shastri government were Mrs. Suchila Nayar, minister of Health, and Mrs. Indira Gandhi, Nehru's daughter, minister of Information. In 1959 Mrs. Gandhi was elected president of the Indian National Congress Party. After Shastri's death in January, 1966, Mrs. Gandhi became prime minister. Other women who have held high offices in India since independence are Mrs. Vijaya Lakshmi Pandit, Nehru's sister, who was Indian ambassador to the U.S.S.R., the U.S., and the U.K., and U.N. General Assembly president; Rajkumari Amrit Kaur, minister of Health; and Mrs. Sarojini Naidu, governor of the United Provinces. Mrs. Suchetra Kripalani was elected leader of the Congress legislative party (i.e., chief minister) in the Indian state of Uttar Pradesh (population 75 million) in 1963. She was the first woman to serve as a chief minister of an Indian state. Padmaja Naidu was governor of West Bengal.

Women have also held important posts in Indian local government. In 1956 Srimati Sulochana Modi became mayor of Bombay. Three years later Mrs. Aruna Asaf Ali was elected to her second term as mayor of Delhi. By law, every village council must have a woman member.

Pakistan has six seats reserved for women in its 156-member National Assembly. The minister for Education in West Pakistan, Begum Mahwooda Salim Khan, was the country's first female minister. Pakistan's ambassador to Italy was a woman. In 1964 Miss Fatima Jinnah, 71-year-old sister of the late Mohamed Ali Jinnah, father of his nation's independence, ran unsuccessfully for the presidency against the incumbent, Mohamed Ayub Khan.

In Australia, the Hon. Dame Annabella Rankin, D.B.E., minister for Housing since January 1966, is the first woman in Australian history to administer a federal department.

In 1965 Miss Kobra Noorzai was named Afghanistan's minister of Public Health to become the first woman cabinet member in Afghan history. The Indonesian minister of Social Affairs and minister to Belgium were women. So, too, was the Burmese ambassador to India and Nepal.

Seven members of the Japanese House of Representatives, out of 467, were women.[19] The minister of Science and Technology was a woman. The first Japanese woman to hold a cabinet position was Mrs. Masa Nakayama, who became minister of Welfare in 1960.

China has had several powerful women in recent years, including the sisters, Mme. Sun Yat Sen and Mme. Chiang Kai Shek. The latest to derive authority from her husband's image is the wife of Chairman Mao Tse Tung, Chiang Ching. This former actress and private secretary to the Communist leader emerged in August 1966, from years of obscurity, to assume a key role in the Great Proletarian Cultural Revolution. She was sole adviser to the People's Liberation Army purge group.[20]

There was one woman in the Philippine Senate, of 25 seats, and two in the House of Representatives, of 120. Women held the posts of social welfare administrator, under secretary of commerce, minister-counselor to Italy, and minister-counselor to the Federal Republic of Germany.

In Africa, Algeria's first 190-member Parliament had 10 women deputies. The September 1964 election cut the number to two, one of them the widow of the late Foreign Minister Mohammed Khemisti. Outside the major cities, the National Women's Union is nonexistent. On the local level, the ruling National Liberation Front discourages women from signing up as party members. When they are admitted, they are segregated. No women hold cabinet posts or membership on the 101-member party Central Committee.[21] Neighboring Tunisia has one woman in its 190-member National Assembly.

Ghana reserves 10 seats for women in its National Assembly of 104 members. There were also in 1963 two female deputy ministers and a woman high court judge, Mrs. Annie Jiagge, who was appointed in 1962 after serving as a circuit judge. More typical, though, of the status of women in tropical Africa is Nigeria's one woman in its 52-member Senate. Cameroon has one woman in its 100-member National Assembly; Chad has one in 85; Ethiopia one in 251; Mali one in 79; Sierra Leone one in 74; and Upper Volta one in 50. The president of the juvenile court of Tananarive, Malagasy Republic, is a woman, as is the mayor of Freetown, Sierra Leone.

Miss Angie Brooks, assistant secretary of state for Liberia, represented her country at the U.N. since 1954, most of the time in the Trusteeship Committee. In 1967 she advanced to the presidency of the Trusteeship Council.

A U.N. report has stated: "In most countries, as in the United States, the percentage of women in high-level official positions is not large in relation to the total number of women in the population."[22] Newly independent and some socially democratic countries have substantial female representation. Traditionalist cultures tend to have few women in prominent or responsible positions.

Part II.
Women in Politics:
A Sourcebook

A Survey of Women's Organizations In America

A common myth exaggerates the unseen power of women. Its source is the political maxim that "dominion follows property." Since American women buy 80 per cent of the consumer goods and are the chief beneficiaries of most estates, own 65 per cent of savings accounts, receive 80 per cent of the benefits of life insurance, own 75 per cent of all suburban homes as well as 40 per cent of all real estate, the theory holds that they must exercise secret influence over American political life. According to this view, men are the puppets, women pull the strings.

A more modest claim is that women, like men, influence the political process through the interest groups to which they belong. These groups are able to employ resources effectively in the decision-making arena. Such resources include the quality and quantity of their membership, the character of their leadership, the efficiency of their organization, access to money and other ingredients of power, friends in political positions, allies in organizations, and favorable public image.

America is a nation of joiners and women are as apt to associate as men. Men go into citizens' unions, taxpayers' associations, budget commissions, chambers of commerce, manufacturers' associations, trade unions, veterans' groups, specific trade interest groups, sports and hobby clubs, fraternal societies, and a host of other affiliations.

Women belong to work with church groups, labor organizations, social agencies, and organizations related to children. They are also members of alumnae associations, political parties, ethnic societies, neighborhood groups, and social clubs. They may affiliate with service groups, professional associations, self-improvement organizations, good-government leagues, or with a wide variety of similar organizations that serve women's interest.

A considerable number of women, like many men, do not belong to any organization. Their concerns are largely within their homes. Sometimes the press of household duties, outside employment or ill health militates against their assuming additional relationships. These non-joiners often lack both experience and skill in organization work. They tend to be in the low-income, low-education group, and consequently may feel that there is neither prestige nor profit to be gained from membership in an interest group.

A UNESCO study of the political role of women [3] distinguished five kinds of women's associations which may have political concerns. These included: (a) Civic associations, such as associations of women voters; (b) Defense associations, such as suffrage movements, feminist associations, and women's political parties; (c) Associations concerned with practical interests, such as housewives' leagues, mothers' leagues, professional associations; (d) Religious associations and (e) Co-ordinating associations, such as federations of women's societies. When groups such as these are considered in detail certain questions demand attention: How adequately do women's groups speak for women? How concerned are these groups with political goals? How effective are they in accomplishing their objectives? Is segregation by sex necessary for fair representation of women in the political process? How valuable are these groups as a training ground for more direct participation in political activities? To what extent do these groups encourage and develop female independence?

4a. Civic Groups

Lyndon Johnson once exclaimed: "I like women singly but I am scared of them in organizations." This view has been echoed by another veteran of the political wars: "A woman with a cause can be a fearsome thing." Damned as "sentimental busybodies,"[4] lauded for their selfless dedication to public well-being, the women's civic associations are conspicuous in most communities. Thanks to the weapon of the vote, when women complain to county commissioners or city officials about vice, vermin, or other blights, these officials respond.[5]

According to sociologist Arnold M. Rose, "There is one type of association that many women, but few men, join—the self-improvement or educational association."[6] Such groups are often devoted to discussing recent political events and to performing public service activities.[7]

The League of Women Voters. The League of Women Voters was founded in 1919 at the Jubilee Convention of the National American Woman Suffrage Association. It was supposed to be a temporary organization to compensate for the women's inferior political experience and knowledge. As such it was to inform the membership on techniques of voting, teach them the principles and structure of government, and help to catch up on neglected social legislation. These purposes—voter education, a voice for women in politics, and governmental reform—have remained the main aims of the LWV, along with the later goal of improving the electorate in general.

At first old-line politicians were suspicious of the organization. The Women's Republican Club of New York passed a resolution calling the League "a menace to our national life"—un-American in principle because it encourages dissension between men and women voters.[8]

The League still has its critics,[9] though it is no longer accused of fomenting a battle between the sexes. Some harassed politicians, however, call the group the "Plague of Women Voters." The LWV studiously avoids questions pertaining only to women and claims to be an organization to serve the entire community. It has deliberately avoided subjects in the "home and mother" category. Instead, it is

concerned with matters not normally considered "women's interests." Thus the LWV may be less appealing to many women than it
would be if it limited itself to traditionally feminine topics.

The League prides itself on taking considerable time to discuss
and study an issue before announcing support or opposition. The
goal is "to present all sides—to promote none." [10] Until 1944 the
LWV maintained the practice of studying questions of policy for a
minimum of two years before taking action. Once a decision is made,
the League has shown persistence in campaigning. The formula is:
Action after consensus. "Action without study is irresponsible and
study without action is frustrating." [11]

There is monthly discussion on programs at the grass-roots level
in local units meeting in homes. Each local league has at least four
general-membership meetings a year. Six months before the biennial
national convention, the local leagues submit recommendations for
the new national program. The National Board then prepares a
Proposed Program which is sent to the local league for a second
round of discussion. Final decisions are made by delegates at the
convention. A similar process of membership consultation is used to
arrive at state and local programs.

The first national president, Mrs. Maud Wood Park, reported in
1924: "All together, nearly two-thirds of our active federal program
has been written off by congressional enactment of 15 measures." In
addition, "420 bills supported by state leagues have become law in
these years; 64 bills opposed by state leagues have been defeated." [12]

One of the major achievements of the League was its campaign
for civil service reform. In two years (1934-36) the League's drive
was endorsed by 1,200 organizations in 20 states. A number of state
merit systems were initiated, and at the national level the Ramspeck
bill was passed. Lawrence Sullivan, writing in the *New York Times,*
called these civil service developments "the most significant stirrings
upon this issue on the national stage in perhaps a quarter-
century." [13]

The National LWV supported Constitutional Amendments 20,
23, and 24, and opposed the proposed Bricker and Liberty
Amendments. These would limit the executive's ability to make
non-treaty agreements with other countries and set a constitutional
limitation on tax rates. From 1928 to 1933, the League was

practically the only citizens' organization to campaign for the Tennessee Valley Authority.

The 1920 LWV Convention passed a resolution urging that the United States support the League of Nations with the least possible delay. In the words of an official history of the League, "the issue of U.S. membership in the League of Nations was soon caught up in a bitter partisan struggle and the League of Women Voters, while avidly studying the subject all the while, delayed until 1932 an all-out position to support U.S. membership in the League of Nations." [14] But the LWV was from the first a supporter of the United Nations. It distributed more than a million pieces of literature in support of U.S. ratification of the U.N. charter.

One of the current agenda proposals for 1964-66 was "support of U.S. policies which promote world economic development, maintain a sound U.S. economy, and further international and regional cooperation." The LWV legislative representative who testified before the House Committee on Foreign Affairs in behalf of the Foreign Assistance Bill of 1964 was asked about the military phase of the legislation. She declined to comment, pointing out that the League was not interested in military matters. [15]

The Convention resolutions are guidelines for the National Board, enabling it to support specific measures but not committing the organization on matters where League consensus is lacking.

The primary concern of the LWV is local government. A study by the Survey Research Center of the University of Michigan found that LWV members have the greatest interest in local current agenda items. These problems are close to home, where developments can be watched and members can see the results of their efforts firsthand. "Living without sewers is a daily problem while war may become real only when one's son goes off to fight." [16]

Among the League's state and local crusades through the years have been those for the city-manager plan, home rule, ballot and election reform, reapportionment, civil service reform, and equal opportunity in education and employment. There is always work to be done in such areas as county government, planning and zoning, education, health and welfare, libraries, housing, urban renewal, recreation, fiscal policy, parking, water resources, transportation, the judiciary, and civil rights. Assisting each local league in its study and action programs are at least 40 pieces of informational material which are sent each month from national and state headquarters.

Local leagues were responsible for attaining the New York City Charter of 1936 and the city manager plan of government for Cleveland, Cincinnati, Portland, Maine, and many smaller cities. [17]

The LWV had a 20-year drive to secure permanent personal registration for New York voters. The Georgia LWV was credited with the elimination of the poll tax in that state. Many leagues are involved in voter registration drives, sometimes with civil rights organizations. The LWV provides literature on topics such as how to vote.

The Michigan leagues obtained 209,000 of the 320,038 signatures on a petition to call a state constitutional convention in 1963. Three league members served as convention delegates and league-sponsored items were incorporated in the new constitution. When the proposed document finally came before the voters, the League helped distribute 38,000 booklets and 100,000 bumper stickers to support it. It was approved with only 10,000 votes to spare. [18]

The League was in the lead for years in the national campaign for legislative redistricting which culminated in the Supreme Court decisions calling for "one man, one vote." State leagues documented malapportionments, testified before legislative committees, urged state constitutional amendments, and backed legal suits.

Leagues prepare numerous educational publications, including the "Know Your Government" series of pamphlets: Know Your County, School System, Party, Town, Nation, etc., [19] and research pamphlets on current agenda items. [20]

The leagues also sponsor "Meet the Candidates" sessions. The NYC League has a "Direct Line" television program where people call in questions for candidates. Often a series of questions are asked in writing by the leagues of all the candidates and answers are distributed either in a Guide to Candidates or through the newspaper.

The League is a lobbying organization. [21] It asks its membership to participate in letter-writing campaigns and supplies them with background material so that they can write effectively. [22] It asks local leagues to hold meetings with legislators to discuss subjects in which the LWV has an interest. Informal coffee hours with legislators are also frequently conducted by LWV board members.

The LWV method is "wooing our legislators in a dignified and league-like manner." [23] This technique was attacked by a Kennedy administration aide for its gentility. "They never threaten reprisals. They never take sides in an election. They're so non-partisan they're completely useless. Why they're even chary about advertising to their members which congressmen voted with the League and which voted against it." [24]

The League from its beginning has been criticized for its "political virginity." Ernestine Evans called the LWV "a sort of water wings for women to use before they swim out a real distance from shore." [25] The leaders of the League acknowledge that it is not a substitute for political party. Members are encouraged to be active in the party of their choice. The League was begun as a training ground, yet some contend it continues as a "halfway house"—a refuge from the rough and tumble world of the activists.

No member of any league board can engage in partisan activity during her term of office. In some communities leagues feel they can not ask women whose husbands are active in politics to serve on their board. The Survey Research Center found that most LWV members wanted to permit league officers to be active in party politics, while board members and particularly presidents were reluctant to endorse this position. [26] The latter may have recognized that partisan political activity could compromise the League's reputation for neutrality and reduce its effectiveness.

The League reports an annual exodus of 300 of its officers and board members who shed their nonpartisanship to enter political parties. [27] Board membership is thus a springboard for entering a party. Mrs. Casper Whitney, a member of the LWV's National Board, did not run again for office when her term expired in April 1928. Instead, she became chairman of the Women's Independent Committee for Smith for President. Mrs. F. Lewis Slade, director of the New York State LWV, resigned her office to become chairman of the National Women's Committee for Hoover.

An example of political evolution is the career of Lavinia Engle. From 1913 to 1920 she was a field secretary of the National American Woman Suffrage Association. In 1920 she became director of the Maryland League. From 1929 to 1933 she served as a member of the Maryland House of Delegates (legislature) and in 1936 became an official in the Social Security Administration.

Eugenie Anderson and her sister, Elizabeth, were both active in the LWV in Red Wing, Minnesota. Mrs. Anderson became U.S. ambassador to Denmark and Bulgaria; her sister was elected to the City Council. Mrs. Samuel Lord, Jr., resigned as president of the Delaware League to run successfully as a Republican to the state senate. After serving as national first vice president of the League, Mrs. Harold A. Stone was elected a Democratic member of the Virginia House of Delegates. Maurine B. Neuberger's first active participation in anything political came as the result of an Oregon LWV reapportioning campaign. She went from this to the state legislature and the U.S. Senate.

Some LWV officers find it frustrating to enter political parties at the stuffing-and-stamping level. They may return to the security and fulfillment of the League after such a humbling experience.

League people are often chosen for local, state, and national government commissions. The League's reputation for nonpartisanship takes an issue "out of politics." To league members this is a way to get into politics through a back door. Past National President Phillips was named to commissions on Voter Registration and Trade. Past President Strauss was a member of the U.S. delegation to the United Nations.

In 1964 one out of every 38 League members in Illinois was participating in government at the policy level. [28] League members were in the state legislature, the state Commission on Human Relations, the state Board on Higher Education, the state Commission on Children, the Governor's Commission on the Status of Women, the state Fair Employment Practices Commission, the state Election Laws Commission, the Board of Mental Health Commissioners, the Northeast Illinois Metropolitan Area Planning Commission, the Chicago Transit Authority, the Chicago Commission on Human Relations, and on other local bodies. Over 80 per cent of these had served on their local League boards.

Surprisingly enough, there are only about 135,500 members of the League. They belong to 1,181 local leagues located in all 50 states and the District of Columbia. [29] A University of Michigan study found that 65 per cent of the members are wives of men in managerial or professional positions while fewer than 5 per cent were married to blue collar workers. Over 85 per cent of the League's active members are married, have children and have been to college. [30]

Sometimes a new program, for example, one on water resources, may bring in new members with special interests; but the League has never departed from its study emphasis merely for the sake of attracting large numbers of dues payers.

A study of the League's activities prior to 1941 noted that leadership at the national level came mainly from single women and widows. [31] The work involved in the national positions is too demanding to be handled by married women with family responsibilities.

The first president, Maud Wood Park, was a widow. The next three, from 1924 to 1950, were all unmarried. The pattern changed with the selection [32] of Mrs. John G. Lee. Her husband, an aeronautical engineer, encouraged her to accept the presidency. Often an accommodating husband supports and encourages the league member. He baby sits while she attends unit meetings. Mrs. Lee, who served for six years as president of the Connecticut LWV, was the daughter of a prominent suffragist.

The current president, Mrs. Robert J. Stuart, grew up in a political home. Her grandfather was a member of the Missouri House of Representatives and then served 24 years as an elected judge. Her father was also in politics.

The League pays a price for its homogeneity of membership. It is known to less than 10 per cent of the adult female population.[33] Among wives of semi-skilled and unskilled industrial workers, only about a third have heard of the LWV. [34]

From time to time, it has been proposed that the League become coeducational.[35] New York's former secretary of state, Caroline K. Simon, urged the League to become the "League of Voters" and to open its membership to men. [36] Sara B. Brumbaugh advocated the same policy and thought that women's special needs could be cared for by internal administrative arrangements. [37] League officers reply that there is something different in the participation of women when men are about. [38]

The League is unique and uniquely successful. It is a vital refutation of many libels against women in politics. Of League members it can be said: they do their homework. Not all political issues have to be partisan; good government needs dedicated, informed, impartial advocates.

The National Congress of Parents and Teachers. Women are influential in organizations such as the American Association for the United Nations, the Foreign Policy Association, the International Institute of Education, the American Red Cross, the National Education Association, the National Consumers League, and the National Congress of Parents and Teachers. The NCPT cannot be classified as a woman's organization, since it is open to parents, teachers and other citizens interested in the welfare of children and youth. From 1897 to 1924, though, it was named the National Congress of Mothers. More than one-third of the 12 million National Congress memberships are held by men. At the 1962 national convention of the NCPT, it was revealed that 32 per cent of the 46,457 PTA presidents were men. In certain states the percentage of male PTA heads was even higher, including New York, 33 per cent, Connecticut, 45 per cent, and Delaware, 80 per cent.[39]

Association policies are set at the annual national conventions. In the 1920's the organization adopted the "Six P's" program: Peace (through arms reduction, the World Court, and an association of nations), Prohibition, Protection of Women in Industry, Physical Education, Protection of the Home, and Public Schools. Its recurrent concern is for the well-being of the child. The partnership of parents and teachers has led the group to work for better schools, improved school tax structures, and freedom of thought.

Like the LWV, the PTA's and their officers abstain from partisan activities and discussions, including the endorsement of candidates for public office.

Patriotic Organizations. Two main types of women's patriotic organizations can be distinguished: those which are auxiliaries of male veterans' organizations[40] and those which are restricted to women who are descendants of early Americans.[41] All are sensitive to any allegation that they are engaging in "politics." Instead, they assert that their purposes are historical, educational, patriotic, benevolent, and social. Periodically, they feel the need to caution members to refrain from activity done in the name of the organization which might be construed as "political." [42]

The Daughters of the American Revolution (DAR) points out that it maintains no lobby at national, state or local government levels, contributes to no political party or candidates in any way, initiates no legislation, and does not even have any legislative chairman in its own internal setup.

Despite this disclaimer, the DAR, like some of the other patriotic groups, has from time to time been active in politics. These groups have promoted military preparedness, immigration restrictions, patriotic education, including, at times, censorship and loyalty oaths, protective tariffs, and veterans' benefits. Sometimes the goals of protecting America from subversive influences and activities and of defending national sovereignty have led to opposition to United Nations activities and support for restrictions on the President's treaty-making powers.

These organizations represent, for the most part, a minority voice among the women's groups. There is a paradox here. Women have been considered conservatives by disposition, yet most of the major women's groups are on the liberal portion of the political spectrum. [43]

In the 1920's the DAR lashed out at the liberal women's organizations and peace societies. Among those singled out for special attack were Jane Addams, head of the Women's International League for Peace and Freedom; Florence Kelley, secretary of the National Consumers League; and Rose Schneiderman, president of the Women's Trade Union League.

Peace Organizations. The patriotic organizations believe in peace-by-preparedness; the peace organizations promote peace by international agreement and disarmament. The work of the latter groups is manifestly political. They have legislative representatives and seek to mold public opinion on questions of public policy.

Mrs. Carrie Chapman Catt moved from the fight for women's suffrage into a campaign for world peace. In the twenties she originated a National Conference on the Cause and Cure of War. It supported the League of Nations, the World Court, disarmament conferences, and the Kellogg-Briand Pact to outlaw war. After the U.S. entered World War II, the organization became the Women's

Action Committee for Victory and Lasting Peace and eventually disbanded.

Elihu Root, whose wife was a leader of the anti-suffragists, found in 1929 that the support of women's organizations was significant in bringing public opinion to bear on the Senate to ratify the treaty providing for American adherence to the World Court. About 30 men's and women's peace organizations were brought together to form the National Peace Conference. [44]

One of the groups associated in the National Peace Conference was the U.S. section of the Women's International League for Peace and Freedom. This group was created in 1915 and Jane Addams, the social worker, was its first president. Its most notable campaign was for the Nye Senate investigation of the munitions industry. Among the WIL lobbyists was Elizabeth Wheeler, daughter of Senator Wheeler. Congresswoman Caroline O'Day was a member of the Board of the WIL. [45]

The program of the WIL, an organization claiming 50,000 members in 21 states and 34 different nations, has both international and domestic aspects. As might be expected, the League backs a strong United Nations and all steps leading to general and complete disarmament under U.N. supervision. It supports foreign economic aid, preferably multilateral, but opposes military assistance. The group has worked for the passage of an anti-lynching bill, an anti-poll tax bill, a permanent Fair Employment Practices Commission, and modification of the immigration laws.

Civic Organizations. Some civil rights organizations are women's groups. The largest of these is the National Council of Negro Women. It is a coordinating agency for 20 national organizations and 95 local councils with a total membership of nearly 850,000. Since 1935 it has sought the cooperation and membership of all races, and has worked for the integration of Negroes into the economic, social, cultural, civic, and political life of every community.

In recent years a number of ad hoc civil rights, and anti-civil rights, political action organizations have arisen whose membership is largely female. Among these were the National Committee for a Fair Employment Act, whose director was Dr. Anna Hedgeman; [46] Stop This Outrageous Purge, a group of Little Rock, Arkansas, moderates organized to conduct a school board election campaign; and Parents and Taxpayers, a New York City group opposed to the promotion of integration through modification of neighborhood school lines. [47]

Ad hoc committees spring up to deal with all sorts of local problems: zoning, especially those opposing the location of junk yards, housing projects, funeral parlors or airports, [48] fluoridation of drinking water, conservation, youth welfare and the like.

These committees also arise to reflect feeling on national and international problems. One of these is the Women's Strike for Peace. Its head, a modern-day Lysistrata, is a professional illustrator who said she is "just a housewife." Her followers insist that once atomic testing stops, they will stay happily at home with their children. [49]

Still another kind of female civic group are the women's city clubs. These outlets for idealism, the counterpart of male city clubs, enable the relatively well-to-do to work on projects for improving their communities. Sometimes, as in the case of New York City's Citizens Union, the sexes come together to formulate recommendations for making the metropolis a better place in which to live.

Alliances. It was only natural that the techniques learned in the fight for the suffrage would continue to be used after 1920. The Woman's Joint Congressional Committee, called informally the "Front Door Lobby" or the "Women's Lobby," [50] was created as a clearinghouse of national women's organizations which were interested in supporting or defeating bills presented to Congress. [51]

The initiative for the WJCC came from the National Women's Trade Union League. [52] It was also promoted by Florence Kelley of the National Consumers League and Maud Wood Park of the National League of Women Voters. Among the other organizations which from time to time were in WJCC were the American Association of University Women, The American Federation of Teachers, the National Board of the UWCA, the National Congress of Parents and Teachers, the National Council of Jewish Women, the National Education Association, the National Federation of Business and Professional Women's Clubs, the General Federation of Women's Clubs, and the Woman's Christian Temperance Union. [53]

When five member organizations endorsed a measure, a legislative subcommittee was created to plan a campaign for the bill. The WJCC never took action in its own name. Among the topics tackled by subcommittees were improved education, maternal and infant health, the Child Labor Amendment, social hygiene, independent citizenship for married women, reclassification of the civil service, prohibition enforcement, adequate funds for the Women's Bureau and Children's Bureau, the World Court, revision of the Food and Drug Acts, adequate support for the Office of Education, equal pay for equal work laws, opposition to the "Equal Rights" Amendment, national representation for the District of Columbia, unemployment insurance, and the arms embargo.

One commentator said that the Woman's Joint Congressional Committee indexed everything about a legislator from business, banking, and political affiliations to his taste in food, drink, and women. [54]

The lobbying for the 1921 Sheppard-Towner Maternity and Infancy Law, a program of federal grants-in-aid to encourage state programs, gave a liberal education in obstetrics to congressmen. [55] But by 1925 the legislators had gotten over their fears of woman power and refused to continue appropriations for infant and maternity aid. In order to get Congress to continue the Act beyond its initial six years, Senator Sheppard offered a compromise amendment by which the Maternity and Infancy Act, as well as the provisions for appropriations, would cease to be in effect after June 30, 1929. This termination bill became law in 1927.

The period of effectiveness of the WJCC, according to Eleanor Flexnor, was in the years immediately following the enfranchisement of women. [56] The organization still exists as an informal clearing-house of information for liberal-minded groups.

One of the questions which brought together like-minded groups in the 1960's was the issue of a school-aid bill. Proponents of Federal aid to education included the National Education Association, the American Federation of Teachers, the American Council on Education, the American Association of University Women, the American Association of School Administrators, the National Council of Jewish Women, the National Congress of Parents and Teachers, the National Farmers Union, Americans for Democratic Action, the American Civil Liberties Union, the American Library Association, the American Nurses Association, the American Vocational Association, the American Veterans Committee, and several industrial unions. Opposing them were the Chamber of Commerce of the

United States, the National Association of Manufacturers, the Investment Bankers Association of America, the American Farm Bureau Federation, the American Legion, the American Medical Association, the National Association of Real Estate Boards, and the National Catholic Welfare Conference. [57]

Every state in the 1920's had its equivalent of the WJCC, a legislative council of women's groups ranging from the Women's Trade Union League to the Methodist Home Missionary Council. Some have survived.

There are also confederations at the local level. One of the most successful is the Inter-Group Council of Milwaukee County, a group representing 35 women's service, philanthropic, business and professional clubs representing about 20,000 women, which since 1948 has endorsed qualified women for government boards and commissions. On the city level it has placed women on the Art, Christmas Tree, City Plan, City Service, Crime Prevention, Fourth of July, Motion Picture, Election, and Safety commissions, as well as on the Housing Authority, Museum Board of Trustees, Development Authority, and Board of Review. On the county level there are women on the Citizenship, Civil Service, Metropolitan Crime Prevention and Safety commissions, as well as on the Appeal Board of the Department of Air Pollution Control, the Special Commission of the Common Council on Radio and Television, the Water Policy Board, and the Election Commission. The group sends observers to meetings of city and county boards and commissions and invites members of these groups to speak at membership meetings.

4b. Women's Status Groups

A second category of women's groups includes those which seek to reduce female disadvantages in what they see as still largely a man's world. These defense organizations disagree, however, on whether the goal should be equal rights or compensatory treatment.

National Woman's Party. In 1913 Dr. Alice Paul formed the Congressional Union for Woman Suffrage, a militant suffrage organization based on the example of the British suffragettes. This was renamed the National Woman's Party in 1916 and campaigned against Wilson's re-election. It was intended to be the balance of power in the 12 states where women had the presidential vote. The NWP was reorganized in 1921 to work for equal rights.

The NWP has been dubbed a child of Mrs. Oliver H. P. Belmont's fortune and Dr. Alice Paul's brains.[58] Mrs. Belmont, the president of the NWP, urged her followers in 1920 to refrain from voting as a protest against man's failure to give women equal rights in the national councils of the parties.[59] By 1922 she was taking seriously the name of her group: "I do not want to see any woman elected to a man's party. I do not want to see any woman in the Senate as a Republican or a Democrat." [60]

The National Woman's Party supported Hoover in 1928 because of a speech made by Governor Smith attacking the enemies of special legislation protecting women.[61] The NWP was delighted that Hoover's running mate was Charles Curtis, the sponsor of their Equal Rights Amendment in the Senate.

Through the years the NWP has had many prominent women in its small membership: Edna St. Vincent Millay, Georgia O'Keefe, Eva Le Gallienne, Gloria Swanson, Amelia Earhart, Mrs. John J. Raskob, Mrs. Harvey Wiley, a national chairman of the NWP who was also a chairman of legislation of the General Federation of Women's Clubs, Mrs. Harriet Stanton-Blatch, daughter of Elizabeth Cady Stanton, and Perle Mesta. The average NWP member is a well-educated career woman, often a lawyer or writer. Burnita Matthews, now a federal judge, was counsel for the NWP. The present national chairman is Mrs. Emma Guffey Miller, longtime member of the Democratic National Committee from Pennsylvania.

The NWP's drive for equal rights for women has since 1922 been associated with a campaign for an equal rights amendment to the U.S. Constitution.[62] Advocates say that its ratification will mean equal control of children, equal control of property, equal control of earnings, equal rights to make contracts, equal citizenship rights, equal inheritance rights, equal control of national, state, and local government, equal opportunities in schools and universities, equal opportunities in professions and industries, and equal pay for equal work. The amendment would read: "Equality under the law shall not be denied or abridged by the United States or any state on account of sex." Such a goal would appear likely to have the endorsement of most of the women's organizations, but that is not the case. Opponents contend that the amendment would wipe out much hard-won protective legislation for women workers (such as minimum wage and hour laws, laws prohibiting night work and hazardous occupations for women, requiring rest periods, lunchrooms, seats, etc.) and many desirable family and social laws, without offering women any rights they do not already possess.

Proponents reply that true protective legislation ought to cover men as well as women and that existing legislation only serves to keep women out of certain types of work and out of the better-paying jobs.

The Equal Rights Amendment has been supported since 1935 by the National Federation of Business and Professional Women's Clubs and since 1943 by the General Federation of Women's Clubs.[63] Opposed to the amendment have been the trade unions, the Women's Bureau, a number of lawyers and constitutional authorities, including Justices Holmes[64] and Frankfurter, Roscoe Pound, William Draper Lewis, Douglas B. Maggs, Lloyd Garrison, and Dean Acheson,[65] the AAUW, the LWV, the National Board of the YWCA, the National Council of Catholic Women, the National Council of Jewish Women, the National Consumers League, the American Civil Liberties Union, the National Council of Women of the United States, and the National Women's Trade Union League. The President's Commission on the Status of Women said the amendment was not necessary and that the remedy for inequality could be found in the courts.

Evidence of "man's inhumanity to woman" abounded during the Depression, when measures prohibiting the employment of married women were introduced in the legislatures of 26 states, but women's groups were able to defeat the proposals in every state except Louisiana. The Louisiana statute was subsequently declared unconstitutional.

One of the battles fought in the 1930's for equality of status was for the repeal of Section 213 of the National Economy Act of 1933. This provided that U.S. government agencies should not employ someone whose husband or wife held a federal government job. Over three-fourths of the persons dismissed from civil service positions as a result of the act were women. The Women's Joint Congressional Committee, the LWV, the NWTUL, the BPW, and other organizations joined in campaigning against the provision. Chairman Ramspeck of the House Civil Service Committee agreed that "women had taken the rap" when choices had to be made in retiring people, although this had not been spelled out in the language of the economy clause.[66]

The 1940 Republican Platform marked the first time a major political party went on record as supporting a constitutional amendment to provide equal rights for women.[67] Four years later the Democrats joined in backing the proposal.[68] Both parties continued to recommend the amendment until 1960 when the Democrats hedged by stating only: "We support legislation which will guarantee to women equality of rights under the law, including equal pay for equal work." Neither platform in 1964 endorsed the amendment.[69]

So near, yet so far. The rock of Sisyphus keeps getting pushed to the top of the hill, only to fall back down. Practically every one of the possible nominees for president in 1964 had come out for the proposed Equal Rights for Women Amendment;[70] yet neither party would commit itself to it. "Its advocates," explained William Goodman, "appear to have struck a position which politicians can never fully accept nor completely reject."[71]

In recent years the Equal Rights Amendment has gotten to the floor of the Senate four times after approval by the Judiciary Committee. In 1946 the proposal received a majority vote, 38-35, but not the two-thirds required for constitutional amendments. In 1950 the Senate passed the proposal, 63-19, after accepting a rider offered by Senator Hayden. The House did not act on the matter. In 1953 the Senate again passed the proposal, 73-11, after again accepting the Hayden rider.[72] Again the House did not act. The House Judiciary Committee, headed by Representative Emanuel Celler (Democrat-New York), has shown no inclination to conduct hearings on the proposal. In 1960 the Senate again accepted, by a voice vote, the Hayden rider. It then voted by voice vote to recommit the amendment, in effect killing the proposal.[73]

At the moment the "Lucretia Mott Amendment" has little likelihood of joining the "Susan B. Anthony Amendment" in the U.S. Constitution.

The National Council of Women of the United States.[74] Since 1888 the National Council of Women of the United States has worked to improve the status of women. At present, it speaks for 27 autonomous organizations (including the Ladies' Auxiliary to the Veterans of Foreign Wars, the national Woman's Christian Temperance Union, and the National Woman's Party) and individual women. This is a "membership" of five million.

The National Council's role is that of a catalyst, a clearinghouse, and a co-ordinating agency. It brings together its member organizations and opinion leaders for consultation on a subject of concern, for example, Soviet Exchange, Civil Rights, Rightist or Communist infiltration. It also creates programs and makes them available to the members and others. One of its projects was a Register of Women, a national roster of women qualified for appointment at government policy-making levels.

The Council displays the usual sensitivity on the matter of lobbying. The former president, Mrs. Yarnall Jacobs, admitted that the Council made "its position and recommendations known to government agencies" but denied that the organization had ever "lobbied or sought legislative action in the usual sense." [76] Her successor, Mrs. Louis J. Robbins, acknowledged that the Council had "suggested consideration of certain bills to its members." Infrequently, the Council itself takes a position on legislation. Its Executive Committee prepared a list of proposals to be presented to the platform committees of the two political parties in 1964.

Like other women's organizations, the National Council has encountered difficulties because of the character of its membership. Men control the money in the foundations and industrial corporations which are approached for funds for projects. Men must also be enlisted to "sell" an idea; women's sponsorship could kill a serious scheme. While some men regard the National Council as underappreciated, others dismiss it and similar groups as "do-gooders." [78]

American Association of University Women. This organization of over 155,000 members is concerned with opportunities for women in higher education and with community service. One of its purposes is to promote the participation of women in leadership roles in the fields of education, government, politics, business, etc. Like the NWC, it has compiled lists of women qualified for public office. And, like the LWV, it encourages women to participate actively in politics and informs the electorate on candidates and issues. The AAUW, through its study-action programs, passes resolutions on educational, economic and social issues. It opposes practices discriminating against women and encourages their further education through fellowships, continuing education projects, etc.

Periodically, there have been attempts to take the AAUW entirely out of legislative activity on the grounds that such involvement was inappropriate to the purposes of the organization. In 1922 the AAUW convention opposed blanket equal rights amendments. The 1924 convention refused to reiterate this stand. Not until 1938 did the AAUW abandon its neutrality. Then, after the Senate Judiciary Committee reported out the proposed amendment, the AAUW Board of Directors voted to include opposition to the amendment in its legislative program. Delegates to the 1930 convention upheld this position. [79]

Women in Public Office. In 1935 Miss Lillian D. Rock, a lawyer, founded the League for a Woman for President. [80] She predicted a woman president in her lifetime. After a hiatus because of the war, the organization was reactivated as Women in Public Office. The National Advisory Council included Doris Byrne, a New York state legislator and judge, Anna Kross, a New York City judge and corrections commissioner, and Mary Norton, chairman and vice chairman of the New Jersey Democratic Party and congresswoman.

The organization is non-partisan. Its goal is the selection of women for elective and appointive office regardless of party.

The Margaret Chase Smith campaign brought new hope to the committee. Not having many members [81] or a treasury, it looked for a breakthrough to result from the example of an inspiring leader.

Commissions on the Status of Women. All 50 states have organized commissions on women. In addition, the District of Columbia, the Virgin Islands, and the cities of Beaver Dam, Wisconsin, and Cedar Rapids, Iowa, have established these bodies. These groups owe their origin to a presidential commission set up in 1961 to study the status of women. Membership on both the national and state bodies, while not limited to women, tends to reflect female leadership in governmental, academic, and organizational bodies. Perhaps the state commissions have filled the void left by the passing of the state equivalents of the WJCC. In 1965 some

284 state statutes to improve the civic and political status of women were enacted.

Several states also have citizens' councils on the status of women, bringing together representatives of a wide range of women's organizations. These private groups are primarily concerned with lending support to the implementation of commission recommendations.

A critic of the official commissions complained that political considerations by governors, legislators, and commission workers have impaired their effectiveness. Much time, she alleged, is spent trying to justify the commissions' existence and in trying to obtain financial backing. "Women appointed to serve on commissions are usually socially prominent, financially secure, well educated and successful . . . and have little in common with the average woman, who is not so fortunate." [82] Nevertheless, she concluded, the fact that the commissions are state agencies assures some degree of interest and attention to their reports and recommendations.

The National Organization for Women. In 1966 several of the delegates to a Washington conference of state commissions on the status of women decided to form a new national organization to work "to bring women into full participation in the mainstream of American society *now.*" This gadfly group seeks to promote the recommendations of the status of women commissions and to identify other areas in which action is needed. It works to achieve "equality of opportunity in employment and education, and equality of civil and political rights and responsibilities on behalf of women as well as for Negroes and other deprived groups." NOW believes that all the victories of the past four decades can be summed up under one dirty word borrowed from the civil rights movement: tokenism. [83] The organization has expressed its determination to fight the election of "any president, senator, governor or congressman who betrays or ignores women's drive for equality." Its statement of purpose proclaims that it will fight discrimination against women in government, industry, the professions, the arts, the churches, the political parties, the labor unions, in education, science, medicine, law and virtually every other field of importance in American society.

The National Organization for Women argues that Title VII of the Civil Rights Act of 1964 superseded state labor laws applying only to women, and that such laws are contrary to the fourteenth amendment. This view was opposed by the American Nurses Association, the National Consumers League, the National Council of Catholic Women, the National Council of Jewish Women, the National Council of Negro Women, the United Church Women, and the YWCA.

The board chairman of NOW is Dr. Kathryn F. Clarenbach, staff member of the University of Wisconsin, Madison. She is also chairman of the Wisconsin Governor's Commission on the Status of Women. The president is Mrs. Betty Friedan, and among its board of directors are Professor Carl Degler of Vassar; Jane Hart, wife of the senator from Michigan; Marguerite Rawalt, a leader of the National Federation of Business and Professional Women; and Dr. Anna Arnold Hedgemen of the Department of Social Justice of the National Council of Churches. NOW has about 900 members in the United States.

4c. Economic and Professional Groups.

Groups in the economic and professional category include some whose behavior resembles that of women's status groups[84] and others of a broader orientation relating to the teaching profession, to consumers, or to the house of labor. Some have male members, though women are in the majority.

The National Federation of Business and Professional Women's Clubs. The idea for the NFBPWC came about during World War I when the secretary of war was anxious to recruit the help of business and professional women in a concerted war effort. There are now 174,000 members in 3,550 clubs. As part of its purpose of elevating the standards and promoting the interests of business and professional women, the NFBPWC encourages the active participation of women in political activities at the local, state, and national levels.

The organization is non-partisan but not non-political. In 1944 the Federation repealed its rule prohibiting the endorsing of an individual woman for a post of any kind. Since then their Political Alertness project has encouraged local clubs to help place women in policy-making posts, either elective or appointive.

The NFBPWC studies and proposes legislation. Among the measures which it has endorsed are lower tariffs, equal pay legislation, the Equal Rights Amendment, and a uniform retirement age under social security. The NFBPWC had an article in the April 1954 issue of its magazine entitled "How Much Is Your Congressman Worth?" preprinted in leaflet form and circulated to members of Congress. The article advocated raising the salaries of members of congress and the judiciary to make them competitive with those paid in private business.

In 1961 the NFBPWC initiated the movement for the establishment of the President's Commission on the Status of Women. Federation leaders were active in it and in subsequent state commissions.

The National Consumers League for Fair Labor Standards. The National Consumers League was established in 1899 as a vehicle for bringing the power of consumers to bear upon the improvement of working conditions. Its two main areas of activity are consumer protective legislation, for example, truth-in-lending bill, Food and Drug Law,[85] anti-monopoly laws, bills to reduce air and water pollution, anti-usury laws, meat inspection[86] and fair labor standards, such as minimum wage legislation,[87] social security, Medicare, help for migratory labor. The League works closely with federal regulatory agencies and with the Department of Agriculture. It also testifies at congressional hearings and informs its membership of pending legislation, and they, in turn, notify their representatives.

Florence Kelley, daughter of former Congressman William "Pig-Iron" Kelley, was the first general secretary of the League. Jeannette Rankin, the first woman in Congress, became field secretary of the League after her defeat in 1918.

There are active state branches in New York, New Jersey, and Ohio, and individual members in every state. The membership is largely female, though a number of men are listed among the officers. Conventions are held at irregular intervals. Policy statements come from the board of directors, which fills vacancies in its own ranks.

The National Women's Trade Union League. The NWTUL was made up of women unionists and other women sympathetic to trade unionism. Legislative objectives of the NWTUL included better wage and working conditions for women, extension of civil service, equal pay for equal work in the government, child labor laws and the child labor amendment, a department of education in the cabinet, the Cable Act, the Sheppard-Towner Act, workmen's compensation laws, social security, the eight-hour day, elimination of night work, protected machinery, sanitary workshops, separate toilet rooms, seats for women and permission for their use when the work allowed, factory inspection laws, adequate fire protection, control of employment agencies, the initiative, referendum and recall, opposition to the Equal Rights Amendment, and securing appropriations for the Women's Bureau and the Children's Bureau. Leaders of the NWTUL were appointed to various state and federal minimum wage boards.

The NWTUL supported the American Federation of Labor but the AFL, on its side, seems to have had lukewarm feelings toward the League.[88] Some of the AFL leaders wished the NWTUL would disband. The union officials distrusted the NWTUL policy of admitting non-union members. Jane Addams was its first vice president and Lillian Wald, Eleanor Roosevelt, Caroline O'Day and Mrs. Harold Ickes were among its early backers. After 1922, though, the national presidency and most other offices were held by trade union women.

The NWTUL suffered from inadequate financial resources. From 1929 on it had to rely on voluntary help to carry out its legislative program. The 1936 convention was the last to be held until after World War II because of economic difficulties. "In the forties," according to one account of its demise, "other debilitating factors became apparent. The idea of the League had grown old and no longer attracted enough women of imagination and ability to keep it dynamic."[89] The League was dissolved in 1950.

Women hold no important offices in the great nationwide unions and have little or no voice in union policy making, yet one out of five union members is a woman, or 3.4 million women in 1964. Louise M. Young noted: "As soon as the union's principal concern became organizational stability and membership welfare, the women were shunted off to 'educational' jobs."[90] In 1966 the

United Automobile Workers elected the first woman to the executive board.

The AFL-CIO Committee on Political Education has a Women's Activities Department. It solicits financial support, and provides candidates with precinct workers, doorbell ringers, leaflet distributors, baby sitters on election day, and drivers of cars to take voters to the polls.

Teachers' Associations. Although both the National Education Association with 810,000 individual personal memberships and approximately 1,250,000 affiliated through state, territorial, and local groups, and the American Federation of Teachers, with 120,000 members, have majorities of women members, they are male-dominated organizations.

Since 1918, it has been customary for a woman educator to be president of the NEA every other year. The one-year president, however, is very much in the shadow of the permanent executive secretary, a man. [91] Women are more apt to hold NEA presidencies at the local level. In 1949 only 14 of the 52 state education association presidents were women but 36 per cent of the presidents of the 944 affiliated county associations and 50 per cent of the presidents of the 1,753 local affiliated teachers associations were women.

All four of the major officers of the AFT are men but there are six women among the 16 vice presidents. The New York City chapter of the AFT in 1963 had only one woman among its 11 officers. She was the legislative representative. (There was a male associate legislative representative.)

The NEA is the more conservative organization, reflecting the role of administrators among its membership. The AFT uses the concepts and tactics of trade unions. [92] Both lobby at the local, state, and national levels for better pay and working conditions and for expanded programs of aid to education.

4d. Religious Groups

Although the principal concerns of women's groups organized along sectarian lines are religious, welfare, and social, a significant area of their involvement is political. There is sometimes on their part the usual hesitancy of women's groups to acknowledge that they engage in politics. Often they concede only to be working for community betterment or to be operating defensively if the state disturbs the prevailing moral climate.[93]

The Young Women's Christian Association. The YWCA has since its beginning in 1858 had a program of social action, and since 1911 it has had a public affairs program voted by delegates to its national conventions. The National Board of the YWCA has joined with other organizations to support legislation for the abatement of poverty, the abolition of child labor, a living minimum wage, an eight-hour day, protection against continued unemployment, health care for the aged, the United Nations, revision of immigration legislation, federal aid for education, conservation, the abolition of capital punishment, and protection of civil rights.

The YWCA cooperates with organizations like the LWV in campaigns to get out the vote. It sponsors courses in practical politics to help young people to have firsthand knowledge of the political process in their communities. The association has joined with the National Council of Jewish Women in a drive to support the civil rights movement.

The National Woman's Christian Temperance Union. The WCTU was organized in 1874. Its early history is closely connected with the career of Frances Willard. Miss Willard was an advocate not only of abstinence from alcoholic beverages but also of women's suffrage [94] and Christian Socialism. Under her leadership, the WCTU displayed a concern for "social reform of institutions and for aid to the victims of urbanization and industrial development."[95] It came out for a living wage, an eight-hour day, courts of conciliation and arbitration, world peace, civil service reform, and food and drug legislation.

Since the repeal of the eighteenth amendment, however, there has been an underlying tone of political conservatism in the WCTU pronouncements. The organization does include in its program proposals to deal with narcotics, juvenile delinquency, and obscene literature. Among some of its proposals for liquor control are bills to prohibit serving alcoholic beverages on planes, to prohibit liquor advertising in interstate commerce and over the air, and to make uniform chemical tests for drinking drivers the law in all states. A full-time legislative representative is in charge of the WCTU's permanent legislative headquarters in Washington, D.C.

Once the WCTU was on the moral offensive. Now it seems to be on the propaganda defensive. There has been an overall decline in membership. The percentage drop since 1930 has been most conspicuous in New England and the East. [96]

In the 1920's the WCTU had the support of other women's organizations. A Women's National Committee for Law Enforcement was organized. At its meeting Carrie Chapman Catt made a public pledge never to vote for any candidate for office until she knew that candidate to be "dry." [97] The General Federation of Women's Clubs passed resolutions reaffirming its belief in the prohibition law, and the National Congress of Parents and Teachers came out for strict enforcement and against modification.

For the first time in its history, the WCTU openly endorsed a presidential candidate in 1928. Hoover was the golden knight of the "drys," Smith was the champion of the "wets."

It was only a matter of time before the "wets" attempted to steal the arguments and organizational tactics of the "drys." Congresswoman Mary T. Norton, a "wet," observed: "No class of people knows better than women what prohibition has done to the children of this country. We know that morality has decreased. As a woman, I know women want a change." [98]

Mrs. Charles H. Sabin, a Republican national committeewoman with considerable practical political experience (her grandfather had been a secretary of agriculture and her father a secretary of the navy), organized in 1929 the Women's Organization for National Prohibition Reform. By early 1931 it claimed 250,000 members. By 1933 it was claiming to speak for 1,200,000. Leadership was supplied chiefly by society women. The WCTU and the Women's National Committee for Law Enforcement together probably had as many members as Pauline Sabin's organization. [99] The "noble experiment," however, was one of the casualties of the Depression. [100]

Catholic Organizations. The National Council of Catholic Women is a federation of more than 14,000 national, state, diocesan, and local groups with over 10 million women members. It speaks and acts as a unit, with policy statements being declared by its national convention and Board of Directors. Among stands taken by the NCCW are those for equal pay for equal work and liberalization of the immigration law, and against the Equal Rights Amendment, government birth control activities, and the admission of Red China to the United Nations.

The Catholic Daughters of America has 215,000 members in 1,520 local units throughout the country. Its policies are similar to those of the NCCW. The national chairman of social welfare recommends study of a question to the local units. Individuals are urged to write legislators and the organization presents testimony before legislative committees.

Jewish Organizations. The National Council of Jewish Women has a membership of 123,000. Its social action programs are concerned with important state, national and international issues. The usual study-before-action formula is followed. The organization adheres to a liberal orientation. Among the programs it favors are foreign aid, civil rights, liberalized immigration laws, the war on poverty, Medicare, federal aid to public education, and the United Nations. Policy positions on national affairs are determined by the National Committee on Public Affairs which recommends action to the local units.

Hadassah, the Women's Zionist Organization of America, is interested in governmental policies involving civil rights or Israel.

4e. Social Groups

It is rare for strictly social groups like the Order of the Eastern Star, Soroptimists, or Zonta to be active in political affairs. One exception, though, is the General Federation of Women's Clubs, an association of over 800,000 members in 50 autonomous state federations of autonomous clubs of every description.

In 1904 the GFWC organized legislative committees to work for child protection and against child labor, for pure-food laws, for libraries, and for other legislation. More recent campaigns have been for conservation of natural resources, for equal pay for equal work (the GFWC supports the Equal Rights for Women Amendment), for assistance to the American Indian, against roadside billboards, for highway construction, for international trade, for mental health, for more nurses, against drug addiction, against juvenile delinquency, against crime "comic" books, against overcrowded jails, for the United Nations, and against communism.

The State Federation in Wisconsin lobbied successfully against the state's ban on colored oleomargarine. The Wisconsin group was also able to get bills passed to control the use of detergents and to keep state lakes clean. A Community Improvement Program was started in 1955 to encourage the 15,000 clubs in the GFWC to work to better their localities. Prizes and national publicity are given the winning clubs and communities.

One of the periodic projects of the GFWC is the get-out-the-vote drive. Among other organizations with such drives are the DAR[102] and the NFBPWC.[103] The Federation of American Women's Clubs Overseas works for overseas absentee voting.

The GFWC has been criticized for attempting to do too much at one time. There are about 45 different divisions of work. Convention delegates who set the organizations's policies are accused of frequently being uninformed.[104]

How Adequately Do Women's Groups Speak for Women? Women's organizations have tended to attract members from the middle class. Certainly, that is where most of their leadership comes from. These officers, when testifying before Congress of passing resolutions at conventions, claim to speak for millions of women. But are these followers deliverable? According to V. O. Key: "Women, as women, have few common political interests, and hence women's organizations often have difficulty in finding issues in which their numbers have a joint concern, and in avoiding issues that generate schisms. Women's groups with a multi-class membership maintain unity on only the most innocuous matters."[105]

The major women's organizations tend to be liberal in their outlook, with leaders usually in advance of positions held by their membership.[106]

How Concerned Are These Groups with Political Goals? One of the characteristic features of women's groups is their dislike of openly admitting any political programs. Maurice Duverger's UNESCO report observed: "This camouflage of political activities, this attempt to enlist women's support for a particular political view by way of their practical interests, religious convictions or education for citizenship is a most important phenomenon. It probably reflects the present psychological and social attitude of women towards politics, and the doubts many of them still show about political life."[107]

Women's organizations often hesitate to take up questions which are too controversial or partisan for their membership to agree upon.[108] For example, consider the hesitancy with which the LWV committed itself on the League of Nations or the AAUW on the Equal Rights Amendment.

How Effective Are These Organizations in Accomplishing Their Objectives? As might be expected, women's groups have enjoyed their most frequent success in fields which society has defined as woman's domain:[109] welfare, reform, home economics, and education. There has been no victory of the magnitude of the nineteenth amendment, but the LWV can take credit for many a successful local, state, and national campaign. The attention that women's organizations have given to such matters as international organization, conservation, civil rights, and fair labor standards could not but have affected the climate within which these subjects were debated.

Yet women's groups have been handicapped by being outsiders to the political process. They have often displayed formalistic and moralistic views of government. Knowing the truth is only the first step toward becoming free. Passing a resolution, writing a letter, signing a petition may be only ritualistic performances producing catharsis (a feeling of "doing something"). Too many groups become engaged in trivia while the larger problems go untackled. There are token achievements and glorified bookkeeping. Another tendency is an inability to consider power as neutral, rather than as innately bad.

A study of the political role of women's organizations between 1920 and 1941 concluded that the GFWC, the NFBPWC, and the LWV were handicapped by limited funds for legislative work and by their slow machinery for endorsements. These are still limiting factors.

Another deficiency is that of leadership, especially at the local levels. Women's groups lack political "strength in depth," although this is not unique to women's organizations. There are the overactive few and the apathetic many.

A national president of a large women's organization said: "In a volunteer women's organization, you don't have to run; if you're nominated, you're elected." There are uncontested elections and relatively short tenure. Positions are sometimes filled by default—going to whoever has time or the desire for the prestige of office. There are too many titles and too many conferences. Women's societies seem to have more officers and committees than one usually finds in men's groups.

Often there is overlapping membership and leadership. A member of the National Consumers League might also be in the LWV, the NWTUL, and the PTA. In some cases, the same women have risen to leadership positions in several of these groups.

Often women's groups combine forces to achieve a legislative goal. Joint councils exist at all levels. The LWV, the GFWC, and the NFBPWC often send representatives to meetings of boards of education and city councils.

Is Segregation by Sex Necessary for the Representation of Women in the Political Process? What Is Gained and Lost by This Arrangement? Would the influence of women be greater or less if they were in the same interest groups as men instead of in parallel associations? As long as equality has not been achieved in practice, as long as both sexes persist in a mentality of anti-feminism, as long as women's political and civic education is still much less than that of men, women would seem to be better off where they are. Actually, this is a chicken-and-egg problem. Continued segregation may perpetuate women's second-class status rather than be a vehicle for surmounting it.

It can be argued that heterosexual government is less important than better government, that women are really interested in good legislation and administration. Most of their organizations have less concern with representation and recognition than with responsible and responsive government. Their influence can be measured by the way in which legislators listen to their demands.

Women's groups tend to have different interests than men's. Perhaps this reflects the sexual division of labor in our society rather than differences between sexes. Heterosexual organizations may either broaden the female base of concern or neglect those subjects of most interest to women. Male organizations have been indifferent to such issues as the nationality rights of married women, maternity care, censorship of obscenity, international cooperation for peace, conservation, and social legislation. The fight for the child labor amendment showed labor, philanthropic, and feminine groups opposing manufacturing and agricultural groups. Women speak as consumers, men as producers.

Many women have developed talents for leadership and organization in their women's groups that would never have emerged in mixed company. The average female executive in an unpaid public service position is usually married, with a sympathetic husband, with household assistance, and with a family tradition of civic and service responsibilities. Church groups, PTA, Community Chest, Red Cross, and other professional, philanthropic, social and ad hoc political groups are all indebted to these women for their accomplishments. Men lack the time or interest to staff such groups.

It might be useful to speculate as to what extent a "following" developed in voluntary organizations could be transferable to the political arena. A reading of the *Congressional Directory* will impress the reader with the extent to which congressmen think it important to list their membership in veterans' fraternal, and other societies. The difference, though, is that men join such groups to further their political ambitions whereas women are active in such groups in lieu of other political activities.

Women in Government Since 1920

5a. Women in National Government

Before the present century, few women held posts of responsibility in the federal government. Mary K. Goddard was postmaster of Baltimore from 1775 to 1789; Mrs. Sarah De Crow of Hertford, North Carolina—the first woman to serve as a postmaster after the constitution was adopted—was appointed in 1792.[1]

Only on the eve of national suffrage did women begin to get appointments commensurate with their abilities. In 1912 President Taft appointed Julia C. Lathrop head of the newly created Children's Bureau. During the Wilson administration several women were assigned to important posts. In 1913 Mrs. J. Borden Harriman became a member of the U.S. Industrial Commission, and four years later Mrs. Frances Axtell was appointed to the U.S. Employees' Compensation Commission. In 1918 Kathryn Sellers was named judge of the juvenile court of the District of Columbia. A year later Mary Van Kleeck was put in charge of the agency which became the

Women's Bureau; she was succeeded in 1919 by Mary Anderson. Annette Abbott Adams of California became the first woman U.S. attorney in 1918; two years later she was promoted to assistant attorney general. In 1920 Mabel Boardman became a commissioner of the District of Columbia,[2] and Mrs. Helen H. Gardner was appointed to the U.S. Civil Service Commission, Mrs. Estelle V. Collier of Utah was named a collector of customs, and Mrs. Clara Sears Taylor became a member of the Temporary Rent Commission of the District of Columbia.

All of this was before women were able to vote. How much progress has been made in the 45 years since then? Have women been able to compete for any and all offices on the basis of ability, or have they been confined to the sidelines? Who are the women legislators and administrators? What have they done for their country and their sex?

Congresswomen. At the start of each session of Congress, a dozen or so members gather together for a group picture. They are Northerners, Southerners or Westerners, Republicans, Democrats, veterans or freshmen. Some have worked all their lives; for others this is their first position. Some have had political experience, others are strictly amateurs. Some are widowed or single, others are married. About the only thing they have in common is their sex. After all these years, women in politics are still a curiosity, a handful.[3]

A total of 65 women have served in the House of Representatives. Information about some of these women is not readily available.

A. States that have had Congresswomen:

Ala.	0	Hawaii	2	Mass.	2	N. M.	1
Alaska	0	Idaho	1	Mich.	2	N. Y.	7
Ariz.	1	Ill.	7	Minn.	1	N. C.	1
Ark.	3	Ind.	2	Miss.	0	N. D.	0
Calif.	3	Iowa	0	Mo.	1	Ohio	1
Colo.	0*	Kansas	1	Mont.	1**	Okla.	1
Conn.	2	Ky.	1	Neb.	0	Ore.	2
Dela.	0	La.	0	Nev.	0	Pa.	3
Fla.	1	Maine	1	N. H.	0*	R. I.	0
Ga.	3	Md.	1	N. J.	2	S. C.	3***

S. D.	0	Utah	1	Wash.	2	Wyo.	0****
Tenn.	3	Vt.	0*	W. Va.	1		
Texas	1	Va.	0	Wisc.	0		

   * Despite the large number of women in their state legislature.
  ** Jeanette Rankin, the first Congresswoman, was Montana's first and only
      Representative.
 *** All were widows succeeding mates.
**** Despite being first to give women the vote.

B.   **Party**   Democrats—37   Republicans—28

C.   **How Long at Job**

Less than one year—11
Between one and two years—3
One term—10
Two terms—16
Three terms—7
Four terms—6
Five terms—4 (Hansen, Harden, May, Pfost)
Six terms—4 (Church, Dwyer, Kahn, Kee)
Seven terms—2 (Green, Griffiths)
Eight terms—1 (Sullivan)
Nine terms—1 (St. George)
Ten terms—1 (Kelly)
Eleven terms—0
Thirteen terms—1 (Norton)
Fourteen terms—1 (Bolton)
Eighteen terms—1 (Rogers)

D.   **Marital Status**

Single—6
Married—21
Widowed—38

E.   **Husband's Occupation** (Some have more than one career)

Congressman—28
Lawyer—5
Businessman—16
Farmer—2
Educator—1
Entertainment—1
Military—1

F.   Previous Political Experience

None—24
Party—23
Elected governmental Office—15
Appointed governmental Office—13

G.   Occupation (Some have more than one)

None (usually housewife or socialite)—17
Law—9
Government—3   Business—8
Education—13   Agriculture—2
Social Work—11   Entertainment—3

The most publicized women in politics are those in the U.S. Congress. Yet the type of coverage is usually the feature story of the woman's page article. Reporters play up congresswomen, such as Isabella Greenway, Clare Boothe Luce, Helen Gahagan Douglas and Winifred Stanley as "glamour girls," rather than as intelligent legislators. In the twenties, the women were seriously asked by interviewers: "Are we going to have a woman bloc?"[4] Today the stories often dwell on women's taste in clothes and food rather than on their political concerns.[5]

There have been three types of successful congresswomen: (1) a widow of a congressman, (2) a woman with very substantial financial means, or (3) a woman whose husband has a business so flexible that his wife's career does not interfere with home life. Louise Young found that three-fourths of the congresswomen were women of wealth and position and that most had superior education. She concluded: "It appears that a mixture of extraordinary prestige, extraordinary gifts, and extraordinary luck are necessary ingredients for a career in Congress, if one is a woman. It is small wonder the number remains stationary."[6]

Mrs. Harriet Taylor Upton, head of the Women's Division of the Republican Party in the 1920's, admonished women not to reckon on immediate capture of political office. "We can't expect to start from the top in this political game, any more than the men do," she said. "A perusal of the *Congressional Directory* will show that most of the men doing our business on the Hill started as lawyers and district attorneys, and served in the state legislatures previously.[7]

Some women did start at the top, however—the widows of incumbents. Before Clare Boothe Luce was elected to Congress in 1942, almost all the female legislators had been either single or widows. The widow of a deceased officeholder is often endorsed in order to capitalize on the good will generated by her husband, to gain the sympathy vote, or to forestall a general contest of the office.[8] That so large a percentage of the congresswomen were first elected to serve terms of condolence is a reflection of the difficulty of getting female candidates. Often those who serve "through descent" hold office for less than a full term.

Mark Sullivan thought it likely "that historians will say women first entered politics as holders of high office on the basis of sentiment and because of association with male relatives."

A writer observed in 1939: "Both lady senators and the majority of the lady representatives are simple, conventional and on the whole, rather mediocre housewives, who happened in their youth to marry men who later became statesmen and still later died in office."[9]

This comment, no doubt, is unfair to some of the widows. A number acquired skills running the businesses, farms, or ranches left to them and worked hard learning the new role of congresswoman.

In 1922 Mrs. Izetta Jewell Brown ran to succeed her late husband, W. G. Brown, in Congress. She was billed as the "richest woman in politics," having inherited a huge estate in West Virginia. She was also an officer of the National Women's Party. Surprisingly, she was defeated.

All but one of the dozen women running for Congress in 1922, including three for the Senate, were defeated. Among these were three-term state legislator Mrs. Maggie Smith Hathaway, Montana, and two-termer Mrs. Anna L. Saylor, California. The sole victor was Mrs. Winnifred Mason Huck, the first mother to sit in Congress, elected to the remainder of her deceased father's term.

Among the other candidates in the twenties to get a head start on the strength of their relatives' names was Ruth Hanna McCormick, who told an interviewer: "I didn't run for office as a woman. I ran as the daughter of Mark Hanna and the wife of Medill McCormick and therefore equipped for office by heredity and training." [11]

A few legislative widows became more prominent in Congress than their husbands were. Mrs. Edith Nourse Rogers polled a larger proportion of the total vote in the special election than her husband had done the previous fall. She defeated a former governor, went on to serve 18 terms in Congress, and became chairman of the House Veterans Committee in the 80th and 83rd Congresses. [12] Mrs. Frances Bolton, now in her 14th term, is ranking minority member on the Foreign Affairs Committee. Mrs. Margaret Chase Smith is the only widow, and woman, to serve in both the House and Senate.

Sometimes widows are favored by being permitted to assume their husband's committee assignments, whereas other freshman legislators would be given lesser positions.

One tactic which has not worked is to run a woman against a woman incumbent. Clare Boothe Luce was opposed by a woman in 1944. Reva Bosone defeated Ivy Baker Priest in 1950. Katherine St. George won over Marion Sanders and Edith Rogers over Helen M. Fitzgerald-Cullen in 1952. Grace Pfost beat Louise Shadduck and Marguerite Church defeated Helen B. Leys in 1956. Florence Dwyer vanquished Lillian Walsh Egolf in 1962, and Charlotte Reid triumphed over her female opponent in 1964.

A congresswoman's lot is not a happy one, especially if she has a family. A former congresswoman said: "National political life and family life are incompatible." [13] Mrs. Edith Green of Oregon was separated for most of the time by 3,000 miles from her husband who was busy with work in Seattle. Eventually, though, Arthur Green set up shop in the House Office Building and appeared to get a lot more fun out of coping with his wife's constituents than he ever did out of his electrical heating business back home. [14]

Dogs and women are not allowed in the capitol cloakrooms. [15] Female legislators are often treated like outsiders. They are sometimes included in the social programs of legislators' wives. [16] If a congresswoman even seems to confirm the legend of the clacking female, her usefulness is at an end. A male legislator can huff and puff, but a woman must be seen and not heard. [17]

Margaret Chase Smith once noted that she was the least costly member of the Senate. Her male colleagues "have a swimming pool from which I am barred. They have a gym from which I am barred.

They get free haircuts and free care of their hair, and I have to pay for the care of my hair."

A total of sixty-five women representatives in 50 years does not seem like significant representation. However, the situation may be on the verge of marked improvement. At least there are factors pointing toward more professionalism. The trend is toward fewer widows and more wives. The trend is also toward longer tenure. Fewer women retire after finishing a portion of a term. Finally, more "career" congresswomen with state legislative experience are appearing on the scene.[18]

Senators. Only ten women have served as U.S. Senators. Five were elected and seven served less than a year. [19]

The first woman for the Senate was Anne Martin, national chairman of the National Woman's Party, who ran in Nevada as an independent in 1918 and again in 1920, with no success.

In 1922 the Democrats nominated two women in hopeless races. Mrs. Jessie Jack Hooper, an unflagging suffragist and president of her state's LWV, ran against La Follette in Wisconsin. [20] Senator Frank B. Kellogg of Minnesota was opposed for re-election by Mrs. Anna Dickie Olesen in an appeal to the Swedish voter. Mrs. Olesen, the first Democratic national committeewoman from Minnesota, was an officer of the state's Federated Women's Clubs.

The first female senator was appointed in November 1922. She served only two days. Mrs. Rebecca L. Felton achieved this honor at the age of 88. She had been graduated from Madison Female College in 1852. Her husband, William H. Felton, had served as congressman from Georgia from 1875 to 1881. She was his secretary in addition to being a teacher, writer, and lecturer. In her long and busy life, Mrs. Felton had stumped Georgia for prohibition, care for expectant mothers, woman's suffrage, child reform laws, compulsory school laws, and state reformatories for wayward boys and girls. In 1912 she was a delegate to the Progressive Party convention. The death of Senator Thomas E. Watson gave the governor an opportunity for a grand gesture.

Mrs. Felton granted numerous interviews on "how it feels to be a senator" and other topics. In one interview she talked about hats and husbands. "She said that if hats cost less, husbands would last longer, and her proud boast was that she had made her hat with her own hands at a total cost of 50 cents."[21]

The second woman senator served considerably longer. Mrs. Hattie Caraway was the widow of Senator Thaddeus Caraway. She was appointed in 1931 to her late husband's seat and then, thanks to Huey Long,[22] was able to defeat six male opponents in the Democratic primary, including a former governor, a national committeeman, and a former commander of the American Legion, to become the first woman elected to the Senate. She retained as her secretary a man who had served Arkansas congressmen since 1907, and frequently made the statement that she always voted the way "Thad" would have voted. This graduate of Dickson, Tennessee, Normal College, who had been her husband's political and administrative secretary, seldom spoke on the Senate floor, preferring to do crossword puzzles during debate.[23]

According to the journal kept by Allen Drury, a Capitol Hill reporter, "Black-clad Senator Hattie Caraway of Arkansas, adhering to her standard ritual, came in with her big black handbag, fumbled in it for her glasses, put them on, sat for a while, read the paper, voted 'No' on a few amendments and then walked out."[24]

Mrs. Caraway served until 1945, becoming the first woman chairman of a Senate committee, Enrolled Bills—about as minor a post as could be found. In 1938 she defeated Representative John McClellan in the Democratic primary. In 1944, however, she finished a poor fourth in a field of five, losing to Representative J. William Fulbright, whose mother owned an important newspaper in the state. She was consoled by being appointed to a $9,000-a-year position, member of the U.S. Employees' Compensation Commission. In 1946 she was transferred to another sinecure, the Employees' Compensation Appeals Board. "It will always seem too bad," concluded Allen Drury, "that she made so little of her Senatorship . . . It was her misfortune to be a nice little old lady, very unassuming and quiet, thrust by the whim of the electorate into a job far beyond her capacities."[25]

Huey Long was responsible for another woman's reaching the Senate. After his assassination in 1936, his widow, Rose, was appointed to his post. Mrs. Long, whose education had gone no farther than a public school, served for less than a year.

When Hugo Black was appointed to the U.S. Supreme Court in 1937, he left a vacancy in the Senate from Alabama. Governor Bibb Graves could think of no one more deserving of the seat than his wife, Dixie. "She has as good a heart and head as anybody," he boomed. [26] Mrs. Graves was a high school graduate who had served since 1916 as a trustee of the Alabama Boys' Industrial School. She had been in 1915-17 president of the state division of the United Daughters of the Confederacy, and in 1929 had served as vice president of the Alabama Federation of Women's Clubs. She resigned from the Senate after serving four months.

The death of Senator Peter Norbeck of South Dakota in 1938 made possible the election of the first Republican woman senator, Gladys Pyle. Miss Pyle was well qualified for the post [27] but was never sworn in. Congress was not in session between the time of her election (11-8-38) and the expiration of her term (1-3-39).

Mrs. Vera C. Bushfield was appointed by the governor of South Dakota a decade later to succeed her late husband, Harlan J. Bushfield. The widow resigned two months later. [28]

Margaret Chase Smith would seem to be in a class by herself. She is easily the most outstanding of the women to enter the Senate. She would probably be rated among the top ten members presently in that exclusive chamber.

Mrs. Smith is a former teacher, though she only completed high school, newspaperwoman, and businesswoman. At 29 she became president of the Maine Federation of Business and Professional Women's Clubs (1926-27). She married a local newspaper publisher and politician who ran for office 48 times in his life without a defeat. [29]

From 1930 to 1936 Mrs. Smith was a member of the Republican state committee. When her husband went to Congress in 1937, she served as his secretary. When he was dying in 1940, he asked his constituents to elect his wife to fill out his term. Mrs. Smith won and was re-elected four times.

In 1941 she asked for an appointment to her husband's former committee, Labor. House Republican leaders thought her vote would be as undependable as her husband's and turned her down. They thought the Education and Invalid Committee more suitable for a woman. In 1943 she asked for and got an assignment to the Naval

Affairs Committee. She used her position on that committee to see that Maine got "its share of federal industrial contracts."[30]

Mrs. Smith defied traditional proprieties by announcing her candidacy for the Senate in June, 1947, over a year ahead of time. Some Republican leaders suggested that she run instead for the governorship.[31] She had three opponents in the Republican primary including the governor. Her strategy against the two millionaires was to use penny postcards to reach the voters, who "could not help but appreciate that this was all the poor widowed Mrs. Smith could afford in a campaign."[32] Mrs. Smith had strong support from women's groups. She was elected to the Senate by the highest majority and the greatest total vote majority in the history of Maine. She was easily re-elected in 1954 and 1960, the latter time against Democrat Lucia Cormier in the first feminine contest for the Senate, and in 1966.

Mrs. Smith holds the all-time consecutive roll-call voting record with over 2,000 consecutive roll-call votes without a miss.[33] "The Senate is my whole life," she says. "I have no family, no time-consuming hobbies. I have only myself and my job as United States Senator."[34]

Her record is significant in quality as well as in quantity. It is a profile in courage and independence. Mrs. Smith was one of the first senators to attack the excesses of Senator Joseph McCarthy. In June 1950, in her first important speech to the Senate, she delivered a "declaration of conscience." Six Republican senators joined her in the statement. McCarthy attacked the group as "Snow White and the Six Dwarfs."[35]

Mrs. Smith cast a decisive vote that helped Democrats block Eisenhower's appointment of Lewis Strauss to be secretary of commerce in 1959. Although polls showed that most Americans were for it, she voted in 1963 against the test ban treaty. Mrs. Smith also opposed the wheat sale to Russia, once again going counter to public opinion.[36]

She has served as a lieutenant colonel in the Air Force Reserve and is acknowledged champion of reserve legislation in Congress. In 1963 she was rated by a Gallup Poll as one of the four most admired women in the world. Mrs. Smith was elected unanimously in 1967 to be chairman of the Senate Republican conferences.

The death of Senator Dwight P. Griswold of Nebraska in 1954 gave the governor an opportunity to appoint Mrs. Eva Bowring to the Senate for the seven months before the regular elections. Mrs. Bowring was the widow of a cattle rancher, [37] who had served for over 20 years as county commissioner and for about 10 years as state representative and senator. She had held a number of posts in the Republican Party including finance chairman and county chairman, state central committee member, and state vice chairman (the latter from 1946 to 1954). She took particular interest in the highway problems of the state. Mrs. Bowring was not a candidate for election in November, 1954. She served on the Federal Parole Board from 1956 to 1958.

Nebraska briefly gained another woman senator in 1954. Mrs. Hazel H. Abel was elected in November to succeed Mrs. Bowring in the two months remaining in Griswold's term. [38] Mrs. Abel, a former high school mathematics teacher and principal, held posts in her husband's construction and investment companies. She was vice chairman of the state Republican Central Committee in 1954 (succeeding Mrs. Bowring).

In 1958 Senator Symington, Democrat, Missouri, was opposed for re-election by Republican Hazel Palmer, a political novice who was a lawyer and former president of the National Federation of Business and Professional Women's Clubs. He scored an easy victory.

Senator Smith was joined in 1960 by Mrs. Maurine B. Neuberger, the widow of Senator Richard Neuberger. Mrs. Neuberger, like Mrs. Smith, had had ample political experience before entering the Senate. She was married to a writer on politics and conservation who was an Oregon state senator. In 1950 Mrs. Neuberger decided that she would like to run for the lower house. [39] She was elected to three terms. In 1953 Mrs. Neuberger became chairman of the Education Committee even though she was in the minority party in the legislature, the Democrats. She led a fight for the repeal of a ban on oleomargarine. In 1952 she campaigned for her Republican friend, Mayor Dorothy Lee of Portland, for re-election. Her political career came to an apparent end when her husband was elected to the U.S. Senate in 1954. In 1960 she was elected to fill his term for a full term of six years. [40] Mrs. Neuberger has campaigned against cigarettes and the tax-free status of so-called "educational groups" that distribute political propaganda, and has worked for favorable legislation for working mothers and for better consumer education. She announced in 1965 that she would not seek re-election. In 1966 President Johnson appointed her the chairman of the President's Advisory Commission on the Status of Women. She was selected by the President in 1967 to be on the U.N. Arms Control and Disarmament Agency.

According to Mrs. Neuberger, the women senators are treated chivalrously outside the Senate chamber by their fellow senators. For example, they never fail in their courtesy when entering an elevator. On the other hand, sometimes the women are made to feel like intruders in a men's club. There is a barbershop but no beauty parlor. Until recently, there was no rest room provided for lady senators. They either had to make the trip back to the Senate Office Building or "queue up" with visitors to the Senate in front of the public washroom in the floor below the Senate Chamber. [41] Eventually, they were given keys to the Capitol washroom used by the senators' wives. In 1962, Mrs. Smith and Mrs. Neuberger were each given a two-room suite, separated by a powder room, in the front of the capitol. [42]

In 1966 Ruth M. Briggs, a retired Women's Army Corps lieutenant colonel, won the Rhode Island Republican nomination for the Senate but lost to the incumbent, Claiborne Pell.

Miss Katherine Peden, the only woman on the President's National Advisory Commission on Civil Disorders, announced in 1968 that she was a candidate for the Democratic nomination for U.S. senator from Kentucky. Miss Peden, a former state commissioner of commerce, is a past president of the National Federation of Business and Professional Women.

A Woman for President? Way back in 1872 Mrs. Victoria Claffin Woodhull was a pseudo-candidate for president. The glamorous editor-stockbroker-feminist was not taken seriously. In 1884 Mrs. Belva Lockwood, the first woman lawyer admitted to practice before the U.S. Supreme Court, did a little better; she got the entire electoral vote of Indiana. [43]

In 1964, 44 years after the nineteenth amendment, a third woman ran for president. Margaret Chase Smith at 66 became the first woman ever to be an active entrant in a race to win a major party's presidential nomination. Of course, her campaign had the self-imposed handicap of being conducted only when the Senate was not in session voting on legislation. Senator Smith gave talks to small groups, mostly to women and college students. Her effort was not rewarded.

Periodically, the American Institute of Public Opinion asks the poll question: "If your party nominated a generally well-qualified person for president and she happened to be a woman, would you vote for her?" As recently as 1959, 43 per cent of a national sample answered "no." Moreover, only four per cent more women than men were willing to support a female president. [44]

Samuel Lubell, doing interviewing in New Hampshire on the eve of the 1964 primary, found only one voter in fifteen favored the idea. [45] "Why not?" a factory worker said. "A woman couldn't foul things up any more than they are now." A highway engineer thought a woman ought to be put in charge of government spending. A restaurant owner's wife felt a woman would have to do what she thought was right; she would not know how to be a politician. Sometimes an analogy was made to the first Catholic president. [46]

Most of the negative respondents felt that having a woman president would be like going against a law of nature. Women were subservient, emotional, and erratic. How would she be able to give orders to a largely male cabinet and Congress? What would foreign countries think? Could you imagine her as commander-in-chief of the armed forces? What would her husband do?

In the past many of the proponents of women for all offices were unrealistic in considering the process by which a woman might become president. Kathleen Norris, the novelist, argued: "When a woman is made president of the United States, it will not be by either party. She will go in because she believes in some special idea—some new method of handling—well, let's say education or agriculture or public health at home, or world peace abroad, and because the public that is hungering for that special thing believes that it is essential to our safety and progress as a nation that she be given a chance to introduce it." [47]

Much of the naivete has disappeared, but not all of it. There are still women who would like to storm the citadel without going through preparations for a siege. [48] The prospect of attaining the presidency through the vice presidency is still attractive.

Oliver LaFarge wrote in 1947: "A sensible opinion on the matter cannot develop until we have observed, not an occasional oddity like Ma Ferguson, but a large number of woman governors, senators, cabinet members, and so forth. We have never yet had a stateswoman of any significance. Let one arise and real opinions will begin to form." [49]

The following year Clare Booth Luce, a Republican, suggested that the Democrats would do well to nominate their foremost stateswoman, Eleanor Roosevelt, for vice president. Mrs. Roosevelt declined. She felt that the country was not ready for a woman in the post, that it would be wisest to seek this post when the country was ready to accept a woman as president. "In choosing a vice president it should be kept in mind that he may become president during his term of office, so he should be chosen not only because he can fulfill the relatively simple duties of a vice president, but because he could become president, if necessary." [50]

In 1952 Mrs. Luce campaigned for Senator Smith for vice president. [51] Mrs. Smith returned the compliment in 1956, by suggesting that Mrs. Luce, who was then ambassador to Italy, be nominated for vice president. [52]

The male politicians view the matter rather cynically. Thruston Morton, a former Republican national chairman, said of Senator Smith's possible candidacy for vice president in 1964, "We want to win. If she proves in the primaries she can bring us the suffragettes and the old maids, she's in." [53]

Perle Mesta told a story about the India Edwards vice presidential "boom" in 1952. "One naive woman from Florida . . . came up to Sam Rayburn, almost sobbing, to ask, 'Is it true that India is going to withdraw?' Sam gave her one of those glowering looks that only he can give and replied, 'You are damned right she is going to withdraw. If she hadn't agreed to, I wouldn't have let her name come up in the first place.' "[54] Mrs. Edwards herself did not know whether to feel honored or embarrassed.

Eventually, a woman may be nominated for vice president. The other party will then do some political soundings to see whether it should join the trend by nominating its own woman or fight it. [55] Despite the number of vice presidents who have assumed the presidency on the death of the president, most people and most convention delegates do not pay much attention to the qualifications of a vice presidential candidate.

Federal Executives. There are a lot of women who work for the government, but very few who do important work. Only about one out of 75 of the civilian federal executives, GS-14 level or equivalent, are women. [56] Some three-fourths of the men are in grades reached by only one-quarter of the women. The largest group of federal white-collar employees are women at the clerical levels. Women have moved into government but they have been restricted to positions of lower prestige. [57]

In most cases women with comparable education and years of service are at lower grades than men. Not only do fewer women proportionately move above GS-14, but those who do are older than male executives at the same level. More of the women executives have college degrees.   Typically, they are not married, or they have smaller families than men at the same grade. [59] The President's Commission on the Status of Women found that the advancement of single women was noticeably but not strikingly greater than that of married women.

A number of explanations have been offered why women are not represented in greater numbers:

(1) Women are not as career-minded as men. The Civil Service Commission found that women's voluntary quits were between two and a half to three times those of men. The reply is made that women predominate in younger age groups and low-paid occupations where turnover is higher for both men and women. [60] Women who enter the labor market in their forties show very low turnover rates compared with other women.

A study of separation rates among persons appointed in the 1956 class of foreign service officers showed that some 47 per cent of the women had resigned at the end of two and a half years as contrasted with only six per cent of the men. The frequent changes in assignment required by a diplomatic career discourage marriage for women; only 17 out of 307 women career officers are married. No differences were found in the woman's advancement rate as compared with the men in the service. [61]

Women in the upper grades were quite as involved in their

careers as men; they engage more frequently than men in professional activities related to their jobs.

(2) Women lack leadership ability. This is a chicken-and-egg proposition. A large proportion of men at all grade levels believe that women are not as good supervisors or workers as men. Thus they are predisposed to be critical of feminine executives. [62]

(3) Women tend to enter stereotype occupations. A 1954 Department of Labor report concluded that "the best opportunities for women were in social administration services in such programs as social security, child welfare, public assistance, and vocation rehabilitation. Almost half the administrators in these programs were women." [63] The five departments having the highest percentage of female executives are: Health, Education, Welfare, State, Labor, Agriculture, and Commerce. Over one out of three women executives are in HEW and Labor, which have only one out of 20 of the total civilian executives. [64]

Only 3.5 per cent of U.S. lawyers are women, yet women constitute 5.2 per cent of the lawyers in federal agencies as a whole and 6.9 per cent of the attorneys in the U.S. Department of Justice.

Few women are prominent in the private occupations which lead normally to governmental selection and advancement. They lack public visibility in middle and upper levels of private administration. Women are just not thought of when appointments are being made or when honors are being bestowed. "Where are the women?" President Johnson asked when on May 19, 1965, he honored 10 winners of government career service awards. "I just can't believe that the odds are 10 to nothing in favor of men when it comes to making an award based on merit."

Mrs. Anna Rosenberg complained in 1963 that there "certainly are fewer women in important governmental positions today than during the Roosevelt and Truman administrations." [65] In 1947 there were 17 women in federal positions paying $10,000 or more as compared with 1,430 men in the same salary group. In 1955 Philip Young, chairman of the Civil Service Commission, thought that the ratio was still approximately the same. In 1963 it was estimated that women comprised a constant percentage (2.4) of a rising number of upper level federal executive posts. [66] The situation was on the eve of a significant improvement, however.

The new president, Lyndon Johnson, had the disposition and philosophy to single out women for consideration. He launched a talent hunt to bring into governmental service women of ability and to promote to suitable positions those already employed by the government. He told his staff: "Search for qualified women wherever you can find them. Don't overlook a woman for a high post because she is a woman." On another occasion he remarked: "A woman's place is not only in the home, but in the House, the Senate and throughout government service."[67]

President Johnson denied that his purpose was to woo women voters in an election year. A look at his biography will confirm that women have played an unusually prominent role throughout his life.[68] He grew up in a family of three sisters and today is the sole male in a family of four. In addition to the encouragement of his wife,[69] the President is influenced by Mrs. Elizabeth Carpenter, a former Texas newspaperwoman,[70] who was executive assistant to the vice president and serves as Mrs. Johnson's press secretary but is relied on by the President in the matter of women's activities.[71]

The President appointed 73 women to top positions. Another 371 were appointed by executive agencies, and 1,379 others were promoted to positions in the $10,000-and-over class.[72] For a time it seemed that the President and his agency heads were engaged in a numbers game. The problem was that a good woman was hard to find. There are comparatively few women in high corporate jobs who can easily take a leave of absence.[73] Like union leaders or Negro leaders, women executives often lack "job security."

The greatest number of rejections came from women with family obligations. The President offered the post of ambassador to Finland to both Mary Lasker, a philanthropist, and Aline Saarinen, an art critic, but was turned down because of commitments at home.[74]

As a result, the White House compiled two lists: one for women who were available for a permanent full-time job in Washington and the other for those who could come for a week at a time in an advisory capacity.[75]

Inroads have been made on male bastions such as the Interstate Commerce Commission. It remains to be seen whether women will consolidate their gains under Mr. Johnson's successors.

Women at the Top. In the early years women were appointed to positions where they were supposed to have some special insight because of their sex. More recently they have been selected to serve in posts which had been informally defined as "none of their business."

Three men and one woman were proposed in 1912 for chief of the new Children's Bureau. Susan B. Anthony was among those who wrote President Taft urging that a woman be appointed. Taft shocked some by selecting Julia Lathrop as the first woman to head a major bureau in the federal government. The 1912 equivalent of the General Services Administration furnished her office with every item in the list of standard equipment for high federal officials—including a spittoon.

Miss Lathrop, the daughter of a politician, was a Hull House social worker who was appointed in 1893 to the Illinois State Board of Charities. She was succeeded as head of the Children's Bureau by Miss Grace Abbott, another social worker, whose mother had been among the earliest suffragists. Miss Abbott was mentioned for the secretary of labor position in the Hoover cabinet.

From 1934 to 1951 Miss Katharine F. Lenroot, daughter of a Wisconsin congressman and senator, was chief of the Children's Bureau. She had started to work for the bureau in 1915. Her place was taken by Dr. Martha M. Eliot, a physician, who had worked in the bureau since 1924.[78] Dr. Eliot was in turn succeeded by Mrs. Katherine B. Oettinger. Mrs. Oettinger was the first mother to head the bureau. Prior to being appointed in 1957, she was dean of the Boston University School of Social Work, the first woman to head the school. Her husband was a college and community-planning consultant. William V. Shannon described her job as one requiring large talents for discreet lobbying, speechmaking and diplomacy.[79] In 1968 Mrs. Oettinger was sworn in as deputy assistant secretary for population and family planning in the Department of Health, Education, and Welfare.

Another agency which has known only female leadership is the Women's Bureau. It began as a World War I temporary agency, the Women in Industry Service, in the Department of Labor. Its director was Mary Van Kleeck. Her assistant, Mary Anderson, was appointed the first director of the bureau in 1920, when it was renamed and put on a permanent basis. Miss Anderson, a veteran of the women's trade union movement, served until 1944.

Miss Anderson was succeeded by Frieda S. Miller, a former secretary of the Philadelphia Women's Trade Union League who held posts in the New York Department of Labor from 1929 to 1938 when she became New York State industrial commissioner. [80]

In 1953 Mrs. Alice K. Leopold was named director of the Women's Bureau and assistant secretary of labor for women's affairs. Mrs. Leopold had had a long career in politics and public service. For ten years she was a member of the state board of the Connecticut LWV. Encouraged by her mother and husband, a vice president of a New York advertising firm, she had served in Connecticut on over a half dozen civic organizations and projects and was appointed by four governors to boards and commissions on education, housing, labor relations, and minimum wages. She served in the state assembly from 1949 to 1951, being backed by both parties, when she became secretary of state for Connecticut. Mrs. Leopold was secretary and project chairman of the Eisenhower administration's Commission on Intergovernmental Relations.

The Democrats replaced Mrs. Leopold with Mrs. Esther Peterson, who also had a long and impressive record. She entered politics through the trade union movement. [81] Sidney Hillman appointed her Washington representative of the Amalgamated Clothing Workers. Later she became the legislative representative of the AFL–CIO Industrial Union Department. [82] In 1964 President Johnson appointed her adviser to him on consumer problems. Mrs. Peterson, who retained her post as assistant secretary of labor, was succeeded as consumer affairs' adviser in 1967 by Miss Betty Furness, a television personality. There was some surprise by consumer groups and congressmen at the choice of a person without experience in this area. However, her familiarity to housewives was seen by some observers as an asset.

When Mrs. Peterson assumed her new responsibilities, her position as director of the Women's Bureau was taken by Mrs. Mary D. Keyserling. Mrs. Keyserling is an economist who has held a number of government posts including that of director of the International Economic Analysis Division of the Department of

Commerce. She has also been general secretary of the National Consumers League and president of the Woman's National Democratic Club. Her husband, Leon, was a member of President Truman's Council of Economic Advisers.

Since a large number of women worked for the government, albeit at the lower levels, it was considered proper for Woodrow Wilson to appoint women to the Civil Service Commission and the U.S. Employees' Compensation Commission.

Wilson's choice to be the first woman appointed to the Civil Service Commission was Mrs. Helen Gardener. At the age of 19 she had been made head of the Ohio State Normal School. She was the liaison officer between the National American Woman's Suffrage Association and three successive administrations in Washington.

At her death in 1926, Coolidge appointed Mrs. Jessie Dell, a member of the Woman's Party, who had been in the government service for 25 years, mostly in the War Department. She was succeeded in 1927 by Mrs. Anna C. Tillinghast, a collector of customs.

From 1933 to 1946 the woman on the three-member commission was Mrs. Lucile McMillan, a national committeewoman from Tennessee and the widow of an elderly politician who had became successively congressman, governor, and ambassador. In 1946 Frances Perkins was named to the Commission.

Eisenhower selected Mrs. Barbara Bates Gunderson, a national committeewoman from South Dakota. She initiated the first government-wide program to spotlight top-calibre career women in the federal service, honoring them in public ceremonies. The present woman commissioner and deputy director is Miss Evelyn Harrison, an engineer.

Mrs. Frances C. Axtell was appointed by Wilson to be one of three commissioners on the U.S. Employees' Compensation Commission. For two years she was its chairman. Her successor as chairman in 1921 was Mrs. Bessie P. Brueggeman, a St. Louis social leader and daughter of an unsuccessful Republican candidate for mayor of St. Louis, who, in turn, was succeeded by Roosevelt-appointee Mrs. Jewell W. Swofford, secretary of the Missouri Democratic State Committee. Succeeding Mrs. Swofford was Mrs. Hattie Caraway, a former U.S. senator. In 1950 Mrs. Caraway's place on what was now the Compensation Appeals Board was taken by Miss Grace McGerr.

In 1924 another bureau was created which from the start has had a woman chairman, the Bureau of Home Economics. Its first chief, who served under both Republican and Democratic Administrations, was Dr. Louise Stanley.

In 1936 Jane M. Hoey organized and became director of the Bureau of Public Assistance of the Social Security Administration. She had previously served with a number of public and private health and social agencies. [83] In 1940-41 she was president of the National Conference of Social Work. Miss Hoey remained head of the bureau until 1953. [84]

Another New Deal agency to start with a woman member was the Social Security Board. Mary W. Dewson, head of women's activities for the Democratic National Committee, served as the first woman member (1937-38).

Miss Dewson was succeeded by Mrs. Ellen S. Woodward. Mrs. Woodward, the daughter of the late Senator William V. Sullivan and the widow of a judge, had served in the Mississippi state legislature from 1926 to 1928 and had been the state's director of community development from 1930 to 1933, as well as Mississippi Democratic national committeewoman from 1932 to 1934. She went to Washington as head of women's and professional projects of the Civil Works Administration, the Federal Emergency Relief Administration, and the Works Progress Administration. Mrs. Woodward served on the Social Security Board from 1938 to 1946 when she became director of Inter-Agency and International Relations for the Federal Security Administration.

Another agency which has built up a precedent for female leadership is the Passport Office. This is a singular breakthrough because neither the work of the agency nor its personnel would require "a woman's touch." In 1928 Mrs. Ruth Shipley became the first woman to achieve the rank of division chief in the State Department. She was a Patent Office clerk from 1903 to 1909. Mrs. Shipley left for Panama with her husband who was in the employ of the Panama Canal Administration. She returned to Washington in 1914 with a husband who had fallen ill and took a job as State Department clerk to support him and their small son. He died in

1919. Her brother, Bruce Bielaski, was director of what is now the FBI. Her rise in the department was steady: special assistant (1920), drafting officer (1921), member of the Board of Review (1922-27), assistant chief of the Division of Coordination and Review (1924-28), chief, Passport Division (1928).

Upon Mrs. Shipley's retirement in 1955, Frances G. Knight became director. Miss Knight,[85] a public relations expert, was a U.S. government employee for all but two years since 1934. In World War II she was public counsel division chief in the Office of Civilian Defense. She joined the State Department in 1949 as a radio information specialist for the Voice of America. In 1953 she became assistant deputy administrator in the Bureau of Security and Consular Affairs, which administered the Passport Office.

Women have held a number of positions in the Treasury Department beginning with Wilson's appointment of Mrs. Estelle V. Collier to be a collector of customs. From 1923 to 1929 Mrs. Mabel G. Reinecke, who had been secretary of the Women's National Republican Committee, was collector of internal revenue for Chicago. She had been the first woman appointed to the Cook County Board of Assessors. In 1922 Mrs. Reinecke was promoted to assistant to the controller. At the controller's death, she was appointed to his place. Thereafter, she became a member of Cook County Board of Election Commissioners.

Former Wyoming Governor Nellie Tayloe Ross was appointed director of the mint in 1933. This set the pattern for a number of women to hold offices in the mint. Nellie Ross ran the mint efficiently, installing mechanical and electronic devices which made it possible to operate with 1,000 workers instead of the previous 4,000. She also was well liked by the coin collectors.

When Mrs. Ross retired in 1953, Eisenhower appointed Mrs. Alma K. Schneider to be superintendent of the Denver mint[86] and Mrs. Rae V. Biester to be superintendent of the Philadelphia mint.[87] Mrs. Schneider, a national committeewoman from Colorado, had become assistant director of the women's division of the Republican national committee in 1945 and was chosen one of the two female vice chairmen of the national committee in 1952. Since 1945 she was a real estate salesman. Mrs. Biester, the first woman head of the Philadelphia mint, had been active for 30 years in public affairs. In

1947 she was elected treasurer of Delaware County, Pa. In 1953, she was president of the American Legion Auxiliary. The Kennedy administration had Miss Eva B. Adams as director of the mint and Mrs. Fern Miller as superintendent of the Philadelphia mint. Miss Adams was a teacher and lawyer who had been administrative assistant for three senators from Nevada from 1940 to 1961, Senators McCarran, Brown, and Bible.

President Truman appointed the first woman controller of customs, Mrs. Margaret Daly Campbell, who served from August 1952, to August 1953.

The highest rank that a woman has held in the Treasury Department is that of assistant secretary. Miss Josephine Roche of Colorado served in the post from 1934 to 1937. She had inherited coal mines from her father and was president of the Rocky Mountain Fuel Company. She was also a director of the United Mine Workers' Welfare and Retirement Fund. As assistant secretary, she was in charge of the U.S. Public Health Service.

Mrs. Marion Banister, a writer, and the sister of Senator Carter Glass, became the first woman assistant treasurer of the United States in 1933. She served until 1951 when she was succeeded by Mrs. Mabelle Kennedy, Democratic national committeewoman from Oklahoma. By that time President Truman had appointed Georgia Neese Clark treasurer of the U.S. Mrs. Clark had been active in the Kansas Democratic Party since 1932. Both her parents were active Democrats. Since 1936 she was Democratic national committeewoman. She inherited from her father a bank, general store, grain elevator, and farm land, and had familiarity with financial affairs.

Mrs. Clark was succeeded in 1953 by Mrs. Ivy Baker Priest of Utah, assistant to the Republican national chairman.[88] In 1966 Mrs. Priest was elected treasurer of California. The Kennedy administration appointed Mrs. Elizabeth R. Smith, Democratic national committeewoman from California, who was succeeded in 1962 by former Congresswoman Kathryn Granahan. During Mrs. Granahan's illness in 1967, William Howell served as acting treasurer. His appointment that year to be treasurer of the United States ended a tradition that the job would go to a woman. Eisenhower selected Mrs. Pearl Carter Pace to be on the Foreign Claims Settlement Commission. Johnson named Mrs. Elizabeth S. May to the board of directors of the Export-Import Bank. Mrs. May had been professor of economics and dean at Wheaton College. She had also served as an economic analyst for the Treasury Department and Budget Bureau.

The highest rank which women have held in the Justice Department is that of assistant attorney general. Mrs. Annette Adams was appointed in 1920 to this post; she was the first woman to hold a sub-cabinet office. Prior to this she had been the first woman district attorney of the United States, serving in northern California from July 1918, to June 1920. Mrs. Adams was appointed presiding judge of the third district California court of appeals in 1942. She was later elected to the appellate court.

Mrs. Adams was succeeded in 1921[89] by Mabel Walker Willebrandt.[90] Mrs. Willebrandt had been a teacher and principal of a girls' school. She was a lawyer who became public defender of women in Los Angeles. She was also president of the Professional Women's Club of Los Angeles. As assistant attorney general, Mrs. Willebrandt was in charge of the division handling cases under the prohibition and tax laws. She also helped to attain a model federal prison for women.[91]

Mrs. Willebrandt was passed over for a federal judgeship in part because President Coolidge was apprehensive of a senate row over the confirmation of the first woman judge.[92] In part, though, Mrs. Willebrandt had a talent for stirring up strong feelings pro and con. It was said of her, "It is rarely that a man turns up in politics with Mrs. Willebrandt's characteristics, and if he does, he can't get away with it"[93]

She had the political savvy to come out early for Hoover in 1928 and was rewarded with the chairmanship of the Credentials Committee of the GOP convention. Mrs. Willebrandt was the most popular Republican speaker in 1928, especially in the Middle West.[94]

Frequently, though, her tactless speaking and letter writing resulted in bad publicity. In 1926 a judge quashed an indictment in a liquor case because she had written an indiscreet letter to the jury foreman telling him how badly she wanted him to find an indictment in the case. In 1924 she had written another "personal" letter to the president of the Law Enforcement League of Philadelphia, complaining about another assistant attorney general, nine or 10 U.S. attorneys, and the two Pennsylvania senators. A few months later the letter leaked out to the press. In 1928 she went around the country urging that Methodists and Presbyterians rise up and defeat Tammany "wet" Governor Al Smith.

On another occasion, at the time of a big New Jersey bootleg case, she informed the U.S. attorney there, with plenty of publicity, that she wanted Assistant U.S. Attorney Van Riper to keep his hands off the prosecution. Both the federal attorneys were proteges of Senator Edge, a wet Republican. New Jersey dries took up the issue and Attorney General Stone promised a full investigation. A few weeks later, Van Riper was out of his job.[95] It was suspected that she had a file of political dynamite about eminent Republican wets. Some leaders hesitated to tangle with her because of a suspicion that if pushed to it, she would open her files.[96]

President Truman appointed Dr. Kathryn McHale to the newly created Subversive Activities Control Board in 1950. Dr. McHale, a college professor, had been executive director of the AAUW from 1929 to 1950. She served until 1956. Eisenhower named Dorothy Lee to be chairman of the board. Another Eisenhower appointment of a police-work nature was that of former Senator Eva Bowring to the Federal Parole Board.

The highest position awarded to a woman in the Defense Department was that of assistant secretary in charge of manpower. Mrs. Anna M. Rosenberg served in that post from 1950 to 1953.[97] Mrs. Rosenberg was a specialist in labor relations.[98] In 1943 she served actively on 14 boards and commissions. President Roosevelt and Truman sent her to Europe to interview GI's about conditions, morale, demobilization, weapons, ammunition, clothing, food, etc. As top woman in the Pentagon, Mrs. Rosenberg was a challenge to the stereotype of a woman. "Leaders in both industry and labor believe that one of the qualities which make her successful is her ability to be objective after the facts are in. She takes sides, not blindly, but intelligently."[99]

Former Congresswoman Mrs. Cecil Harden was the first woman to hold a high office in the post office department when she was appointed in 1959 special assistant to Postmaster General Arthur Summerfield. She had been on the House Post Office Committee and her job made her the principal adviser to the postmaster general regarding the 55,000 women in the postal service.

Mrs. Dorothy Jacobson held the highest rank of any woman in the Department of Agriculture. She was named by Johnson to be assistant secretary of agriculture. Previously, she served with the Minnesota state department of education. The department of agriculture was headed by another Minnesotan, Orville Freeman.

The first woman to serve on an independent regulatory commission was Frieda B. Hennock, who was named to the Federal Communications Commission in 1948.[100] Miss Hennock was the youngest practicing lawyer in New York City when admitted to the bar in 1926.[101]

Not until Lyndon Johnson became president was another woman appointed to a regulatory commission. He named Mary Gardiner Jones to the Federal Trade Commission, Dr. Mary Bunting to the Atomic Energy Commission, and Mrs. Virginia Mae Brown to the Interstate Commerce Commission. Mrs. Bunting, a microbiologist and biochemist, was president of Radcliffe College. Mrs. Brown, a lawyer, was former assistant attorney general of Maryland and a member of the state's Public Service Commission. She was the first woman in the United States to be appointed a state insurance commissioner.

Only two women have ever served in the Cabinet. The first was Frances Perkins who served from 1933 to 1945 as secretary of labor. The other was Mrs. Oveta Culp Hobby who was secretary of health, education, and welfare from 1953 to 1955.[102]

The Republicans had promised in 1920 to have a woman in Harding's cabinet; however, the male heads of the bureaus and agencies which would have been placed in the proposed Department of Welfare objected to serving under a woman secretary. Some women were apprehensive that Congress would slight a department headed by a woman, when making appropriations.

Miss Perkins, who was Mrs. Paul Caldwell Wilson in private life, had had a distinguished career before being named by President Roosevelt to the Cabinet. From 1910 to 1912 she was executive secretary of the Consumers' League of New York. She was an investigator for the Factory Investigation Commission after the 1911 Triangle Shirtwaist fire. From 1912 to 1918 she was secretary of the Committee on Safety of New York City. Al Smith named her to the State Industrial Commission in 1919. Miss Perkins was appointed to the Industrial Board in 1923 and became its chairman in 1926. Governor Roosevelt promoted her to his cabinet as industrial commissioner in 1929. It seemed only logical that he should take her along to Washington in a similar capacity.

The AFL had wanted Dan Tobin of the Teamsters, chairman of the Democratic Labor Campaign Committee, to be secretary of labor. Said AFL President William Green, "Labor will never be reconciled to her appointment." Miss Perkins had a stormy dozen years as secretary. She tried to avoid the limelight and was inept at press relations. The press retaliated by intermittently rumoring her resignation. [103]

One of her subordinates, Mary Anderson of the Woman's Bureau, wrote: "All through the time she was secretary of labor, I think Miss Perkins rather minimized the importance of women's problems because she knew that a good many of the representatives of organized labor did not like her very well, partly because she was a woman and partly because they thought of her as a social worker and not a real labor person. So every time there was a chance to single out women, she leaned over backward not to do it." [104] Wendell Willkie, the 1940 Republican presidential candidate, pledged that if elected, he would appoint a secretary of labor "who wasn't a woman." [105]

Yet on her retirement as secretary, the United Mine Workers called her the best of the Labor Department heads since creation of that agency. From 1945 to 1953 Miss Perkins served on the Civil Service Commission.

It is not widely known that President Eisenhower did not appoint Oveta Culp Hobby directly to the Cabinet. She was named in 1953 to be head of the Federal Security Administration, which later became part of the new Department of Health, Education, and Welfare. [106] Mrs. Hobby was the daughter of a former Texas state legislator and the wife of a former governor and publisher of the Houston *Post*. She was 26 when she married the 53-year-old widower. She became parliamentarian of the Texas House at age 20 and wrote a book on parliamentary law. [107] During World War II she held the rank of colonel, the highest rank in the Women's Army Corps. Mrs. Hobby succeeded her husband as editor and publisher of the *Post*. She was also president of the Texas League of Women

Voters. In 1952 she headed Democrats for Eisenhower. Mrs. Hobby announced in 1953 that she preferred to be referred to as "Mrs. Secretary" and not as "Madam Secretary." A major event in her management of the Health, Education and Welfare Department was the mishandling of the distribution of the new Salk polio serum in 1955. Like Frances Perkins, she had poor relations with the press. Mrs. Hobby retired in 1955, giving as the reason her husband's ill health. Under President Kennedy she served as a member of the National Advisory Council for the Peace Corps and was on the President's Committee on the Employment of the Physically Handicapped.

Women in Foreign Affairs. Only 10 women have ever served as a U.S. minister or ambassador to a country. At the present time, we have over 100 such envoys.

Former Congresswoman Ruth Bryan Owen served from 1933 to 1936 as U.S. minister to Denmark. After her marriage to a Danish subject, she intended to continue as minister. However, Danish law gave the wife of a Dane his nationality. Therefore, she felt compelled to resign from the Foreign Service. [108]

In 1937 Roosevelt appointed Mrs. Florence J. Harriman, widow of the railroader, J. Borden Harriman, to be minister to Norway. Mrs. Harriman was a veteran of the suffrage struggle. Woodrow Wilson had appointed her to the Federal Industrial Relations Commission. She was founder of the Women's National Democratic Club and was national committeewoman for the District of Columbia. She served until 1940 when the country was overrun by Germany.

Our first woman ambassador was Mrs. Eugenie Anderson of Minnesota, who was appointed by President Truman to be ambassador to Denmark (1949-53). [109]She was the first woman envoy with a family. Her husband, an artist, was son and heir of the man who invented puffed wheat and puffed rice. He and their two children went with her to Denmark. Mrs. Anderson had been a member of her local school board, state vice chairman of the Democratic Party, and Democratic national committeewoman. From 1955 to 1960 she served as chairman of the Minnesota Commission for Fair Employment Practices.

In 1962 President Kennedy appointed her minister to Bulgaria, the most difficult post in east Europe for American diplomats because of the suspicion and coolness with which the Bulgarian Communist government viewed the United States.[110] When she retired in 1964, it was agreed by diplomats that she had done much to better U.S.–Bulgarian relations.

Mrs. Perle Mesta served as minister to Luxembourg[111] from 1949 to 1953.[112] She was the widow of the owner of the Mesta Machine Works and knew about the steel-producing business, having sat on the company's board. Mrs. Mesta was also a generous contributor to Truman's 1948 campaign. She was a renowned partygiver and her service in Luxembourg became the subject of an Irving Berlin musical, "Call Me Madam."

Eisenhower appointed former Congresswoman Clare Booth Luce to be ambassador to Italy. She served from 1953 to 1956. To facilitate protocolary seating at diplomatic functions, her husband, publisher Henry Luce, was given the simulated rank of minister. He spent half the year in Italy, "cultivated industrialists and political leaders, and gave her the benefit of his observations."[113] At official dinners Mrs. Luce was seated as a lady, rather than as an ambassador, ahead of her diplomatic senior colleagues.

The first woman to reach the top of the career foreign service ladder was Frances E. Willis. A Stanford Ph.D. who had studied at the University of Brussels, Miss Willis had taught history at Goucher College and political science at Vassar. She entered the foreign service in 1927 as a means of adding to her experience. Eisenhower appointed her minister to Switzerland (1953-57). From there she moved to posts in Norway (1957-61) and Ceylon (1961-64). In 1960 she was a member of the U.S. delegation to the U.N. General Assembly.

President Johnson's first woman ambassador was Mrs. Katherine E. White who was sent in 1964 to Denmark. Her father, Abram I. Elkus, was Woodrow Wilson's ambassador to Turkey. In 1928 she accompanied her mother, an alternate, to the Democratic convention. She is married to a vice president of a management-consultant firm. Mrs. White was New Jersey Democratic vice chairman from 1954-1964. She was a three-term mayor of the community of Red Bank, chief of the state's Garden State Parkway, and a national treasurer of the American Association of University Women. In 1960 she was defeated for Congress.

The second Johnson appointment, Miss Marguerite Tibbets, ambassador to Norway, entered the foreign service in 1946.

Mrs. Patricia R. Harris was named in 1965 to be ambassador to Luxembourg, the first Negro woman to have ambassador rank. Prior to her appointment, she was an assistant professor of law at Howard University. Her husband is a lawyer. In 1966 Mrs. Harris was named to the U.S. delegation to the United Nations.

Miss Carol C. Laise, a career foreign service officer, became ambassador to Nepal in 1966. Previously, she served as director of the State Department's Office of South Asian Affairs. In 1967 she married Ellsworth Bunker, a widower who had been ambassador to Argentina, Italy and India. The 72-year-old roving ambassador is now U.S. ambassador to South Vietnam. They are the only husband-and-wife ambassador team in U.S. history.

Women have also been named to delegations from the U.S. to the United Nations. The women's organizations, which are among the foremost supporters in our country of international organization, have since the 1920's urged the appointment of women to conferences on world peace and disarmament.

In 1932 the State Department, under pressure from women's organizations, announced that if they could all get together and agree on one woman to attend the Geneva Disarmament Convention, the administration would take the matter "under consideration." The officers of 30 national women's groups met and agreed on submitting the name of Judge Florence Allen of Ohio. The administration turned this name down because Judge Allen was a Democrat. The women's organizations then proposed the name of Dr. Mary Wooley, president of Mount Holyoke College and a good Republican. After some hesitation, she was included in the delegation. A convincing argument was that women, half of the eligible voters, wanted their vote heard in the cause of peace. [114]

In 1944 a group of women complained about the exclusion of women from the Dumbarton Oaks Conference. They drew up a list of names they believed qualified to participate in the formation of the United Nations. Once again, a woman from the academic community was selected. Dr. Virginia C. Gildersleeve, dean of Barnard College, was the only woman U.S. delegate to the 1945 San Francisco Conference. Miss Gildersleeve had worked with the League of Nations Association and was a founder and two-time president of the International Federation of University Women. She was also chairman of the Advisory Committee of the WAVES.

The first woman named U.S. representative to the U.N. General Assembly was Mrs. Eleanor Roosevelt in 1946. From 1947 to 1952 she served as U.S. representative to the U.N. Human Rights Commission and the Economic and Social Council.

Mrs. Roosevelt's alternate from 1950 to 1952 was Mrs. Edith S. Sampson. In Chicago, Mrs. Sampson had moved from social worker to probation officer to trial lawyer and had served as chairman of the Executive Committee of the National Council of Negro Women.

Other women to serve as alternates in the Truman years were Ruth Bryan Owen Rohde, Congresswoman Helen Gahagen Douglas, and Anna Lord Strauss, president of the LWV.

President Eisenhower appointed Mrs. Mary Pillsbury Lord to be U.S. representative to the U.N. Commission on Human Rights and alternate to the General Assembly. She served from 1953 to 1961. Mrs. Lord had grown up in a political family, which included a three-time governor, a state senator with 10 years' service, a school board member, an alderman, and a mayor of Minneapolis. She was a social worker who was elected in 1948 chairman of the U.S. Committee for the United Nations International Children's Emergency Fund. In 1952 she was elected president of the National Health Council. Mrs. Lord also served in 1952 as co-chairman of Citizens for Eisenhower.

Congresswoman Frances Bolton was a U.N. alternate delegate under Eisenhower, as were actress Irene Dunne and singer Marian Anderson.

The Kennedy-Johnson female U.N. representative was Mrs. Marietta Tree. In 1964 she was given the rank of ambassador and was U.S. representative to the Trusteeship Council and to the Human Rights Commission of the Economic and Social Council. She is known as a giver of interesting parties. "You just never know what you'll find when you get to Marietta Tree's," one guest said. "It could be Henry Luce or a Democratic precinct worker—or both."[115] She was once a *Life* researcher, and is a tireless Democratic party worker. In 1954 and 1958 she co-managed a losing congressional campaign for Anthony B. Akers in New York. In 1956 she headed the Volunteers for Stevenson committee in New York and in 1960 was deputy chairman of the Citizens Committee for Kennedy. Her brother, Endicott Peabody, became governor of Massachusetts. Mrs. Tree has long been active in civil rights activities and has served as director of the National Urban League and as a member of the New York City Commission on Intergroup Relations and the National Committee Against Discrimination in Housing. Her successor in 1965 as U.S. representative to the U.N. Trusteeship Council was Mrs. Eugenie Anderson.

Dr. Zelma W. George served as a U.N. alternate under Eisenhower and Kennedy, 1960-62. She has been a social case worker, probation officer, college teacher, educational administrator, community center director, singer, and newspaper columnist. Her husband, a lawyer, was president of the Civil Service Commission of Cleveland. Mrs. Edison Dick, a board member of many social welfare, mental health and foreign relations organizations, was U.S. representative to the Social Commission of the Economic and Social Council. Mrs. Carmel Carrington Marr, a Negro lawyer, was an adviser to the U.S. Mission to the U.N. In 1966 Mrs. Patricia Roberts Harris, who served two years as ambassador to Luxembourg, was named to represent the U.S. on both the Social and Legal Committees.

One position on the U.S. delegation which has been reserved to women from the start in 1947 is that of representative to the U.N. Commission on the Status of Women. The post was held from 1947 to 1949 by Dr. Dorothy Kenyon. Miss Kenyon, a doctor of jurisprudence, was first deputy license commissioner of New York City from 1936 to 1938, when she was appointed municipal judge. She served until 1940. She had been active in the League of Nations Committee on the Status of Women and was a proponent of the draft of women. Miss Kenyon was also legal adviser to the Cooperative League of the U.S.A. and a director and former president of the Consumers League of New York.

She was succeeded in 1950 by Mrs. Olive Remington Goldman, a teacher at the University of Illinois and an unsuccessful candidate for Congress in 1946 and 1948. Mrs. Goldman had held a number of short-term governmental posts. She was married to a professor of English.

President Eisenhower's delegate to the Status of Women

Commission was Mrs. Lorena Hahn, a former teacher, who had served in 1936-37 as head of the American Legion Auxiliary. She was married to a Nebraska banker. In 1948 she was chief of Women's Affairs for the U.S. zone of occupation in Germany.

President Kennedy appointed Mrs. Gladys Tillett as his representative to the Status of Women Commission. Mrs. Tillett had served in the 1940's as head of women's activities for the Democratic Party.

Women in the Judiciary. Women are few on the federal bench. In 1964 there were only three women federal judges out of 425. Out of more than 100 judges named by President Johnson, only one has been a woman.

President Wilson appointed Kathryn Sellers to be judge of the Juvenile Court of the District of Columbia. She served from 1918 to 1934.

President Coolidge named Genevieve R. Cline of Ohio in 1928 to be judge of the U.S. Customs Court in New York. She had been appraiser of merchandise at the Port of Cleveland. Miss Cline had read law in her brother's office. For six years she was chairman of legislation of the Ohio Federation of Women's Clubs. Judge Cline retired in 1954.

In 1930 Annabel Matthews became the first woman member of the U.S. Board of Tax Appeals. For 15 years she had been an income tax expert and lawyer with the Bureau of Internal Revenue. She served on the Tax Appeals Board until 1936.

The highest position in the judiciary ever held by a woman was judge of the Circuit Court of Appeals. Florence E. Allen of Ohio was appointed to this tribunal in 1934 by Franklin Roosevelt.[116] She served until 1959. Miss Allen, the daughter of a former congressman from Utah, had practiced law in Ohio from 1904 to 1919. She was attorney for the suffragists at the time she was appointed assistant county prosecutor for Cuyahoga County, Cleveland. In 1920 she was elected judge of the Common Pleas Court of the county. In 1922 Miss Allen won a six-year term on the state Supreme Court and was re-elected in 1928. She was unsuccessful in 1926 in a campaign for the Democratic nomination for U.S. senator. She was defeated by Atlee Pomerene, an anti-suffragist. Miss Allen eventually became chief judge of the U.S. Sixth Circuit.[117]

President Roosevelt's other appointment of a woman judge was that of Miss Carrick M. Buck to be judge of the Circuit Court of Hawaii. She served from 1934 to 1958.

President Truman appointed Burnita S. Matthews in 1950 to be the first woman ever to serve as U.S. District Court Judge. Mrs. Matthews was a lawyer in Washington, D.C., for over 20 years. Her father had been the clerk of a county chancery court and later a tax collector. After teaching music in the public schools and working in the suffrage movement, Mrs. Matthews became a lawyer. She headed a corps of young women lawyers in the National Woman's Party doing research on legal discrimination against women. She is credited with being the author of many federal and state laws on this subject. Mrs. Matthews taught at the Washington College of Law and was president of the National Association of Women Lawyers and of the Women's Bar Association of the District of Columbia. She is still on the court. Her husband is an attorney.

Dr. Marion Harron was appointed by Roosevelt in 1936 to what was then the U.S. Board of Tax Appeals. When it was transformed into the Tax Court of the U.S. in 1946, Miss Harron received an appointment from President Truman.

In 1946 President Truman appointed Mrs. Nadine Lane Gallagher to be the first woman judge of the Municipal Court of the District of Columbia. She served until 1957. Mildred Reeves, Ellen K. Raedy, Lucy S. Howorth, Mary C. Barlow, and Catherine B. Kelly were later judges of the Municipal Court.

In 1951 Miss Frieda Hennock of the Federal Communications Commission was named a U.S. District Court Judge by President Truman.

President Eisenhower appointed Miss Mary H. Donlon to the U.S. Customs Court in 1955. Her mother had been a worker for woman's suffrage. Miss Donlon was editor-in-chief of the *Cornell Law Quarterly.* For 10 years she held the office of chairman under Governor Dewey of the New York State Workmen's Compensation Board. Miss Donlon retired from the bench in 1966.

Another Eisenhower appointee was Mrs. Irene Scott, who became a member of the Tax Court in 1960. She served as an attorney with the Internal Revenue Service from 1937 until her appointment to the court, holding such posts as member of the

Excess Profits Tax Council and as staff assistant to the chief counsel.

President Kennedy named Mrs. Sarah T. Hughes a U.S. District Court judge. Mrs. Hughes had served for 26 years as a judge in the Texas District Court, at first appointed and then four times elected. She was an unsuccessful candidate for Congress in 1946. In 1952 Judge Hughes was president of the National Federation of Business and Professional Women's Clubs.[118] Her husband was assistant chief attorney for the Dallas region of the Veterans Administration.

In 1966 President Johnson selected Constance Baker Motley, civil rights attorney and borough president of Manhattan, to be a U.S. District Court judge.

Supreme Court Justice Tom Clark said in 1962, "Out of the 93 persons who have sat on the Supreme Court, not one yet has been a woman. Too bad, for they always have the last word, except here, where the last word really counts."[119]

Summary. Women have held comparatively few positions of importance in the federal government. Although they comprise over 50 per cent of the nation's population, they have held only two per cent of the legislative posts and even less than that in the executive and judicial departments.

Some presidents such as Roosevelt and Johnson have gone out of their way to reward capable women. Most, however, have been stingy in doling out appointments to deserving women.

A few offices have been reserved or captured by women. Many more have never had a woman officeholder. Still other positions have had occasional representation by women. Despite their frequently distinguished service, there has been no breakthrough for women in the federal government.

5b. America's Congresswomen: 1917 to 1967

Miss Jeannette Rankin (Republican, Montana, 3/4/17–3/4/19; 1/3/41–1/3/43). Graduate of the University of Montana. A social worker. Before going to the Capitol as the first congresswoman, Miss Rankin was president of the Montana branch of the National American Woman Suffrage Association. She worked for the suffrage in Washington State in 1910, in California in 1911, and in Montana from 1912 to 1914. Montana voted for suffrage in 1914, and she was elected congresswoman-at-large in 1916, as a Republican, though the state went Democratic. She voted against the declaration of war in 1917 [1] and again in 1941. Miss Rankin ran twice unsuccessfully for the Senate, the second time as an independent, but was elected to the House in 1940 as a pacifist. She was defeated for re-election in 1942. In 1968, at the age of 87, she was still active in pacifist causes.

Miss Alice M. Robertson (Republican, Oklahoma, 3/4/21–3/4/23). Studied at Elmira College, New York. After working in the Indian Office in Washington from 1873 to 1879, she taught at an Oklahoma Indian Territory girls' school, which later became the University of Tulsa. Theodore Roosevelt appointed Miss Robertson a postmaster. She served from 1905 to 1913, and was then replaced by a Democrat. She was an anti-suffragist. Before becoming a congresswoman at the age of 66, she operated a cafeteria. Miss Robertson did not mind being placed on the low-prestige Indian Affairs Committee of the House; her immediate ancestors were missionaries to the Cherokees and Creeks. Her defeat in 1922 resulted from her vote against the soldiers' bonus of 1921. Miss Robertson then retired from politics, which she denounced as too unclean for women.

Mrs. Winifred Sprague Mason Huck (Republican, Illinois, 11/7/22–3/4/23). Elected to the seat of her late father, William E. Mason. Her previous occupation was journalism and lecturing. She failed to secure the primary nomination for a full term in 1922. Since Congress was in recess at the time of her election, she never assumed her seat. Mrs. Huck campaigned unsuccessfully in early 1923 for the seat of another late representative.

Mrs. Mae Ella Nolan (Republican, California, 1/23/23–3/4/25). Educated at St. Vincent's Convent, San Francisco. Mrs. Nolan succeeded her late husband, John I. Nolan, and was re-elected. She campaigned as a "wet" and on a pro-labor ticket. Mrs. Nolan was not a candidate for renomination in 1924.

Mrs. Florence Prag Kahn (Republican, California, 2/17/25–1/3/37). Educated at the University of California, Berkeley. Mrs. Kahn was a high school teacher whose mother had been a teacher and a member of the San Francisco School Board. She was a partner in her husband's political and other interests and received twice as many votes in 1928 as her husband and predecessor had ever received. She possessed parliamentary skill and frequently presided over House debate. Florence Kahn objected to being placed on the Indian Affairs Committee and was put on Education; she continued to fight until she persuaded the House leaders of her party to put her on the Military Affairs Committee, a major committee of which her husband had been chairman. Mrs. Kahn was an unsuccessful candidate in 1936.

Mrs. Edith Nourse Rogers (Republican, Massachusetts, 6/3/25–9/10/60). Attended Rogers Hall School and Madame Julien's School, Paris. Mrs. Rogers served with the American Red Cross during World War I, and was appointed by both Harding and Coolidge as presidential adviser on the care of disabled soldiers. She succeeded her husband, John Jacob Rogers, and was re-elected. Mrs. Rogers was the first woman member of Congress whose name was attached to a piece of major legislation. She was interested in veterans' aid and hospitals, and was one of the sponsors of the GI Bill of Rights. Mrs. Rogers was an articulate champion of high tariffs. Her district was a textile producer. Like many businesswomen, Edith Rogers preferred suits to dresses for work. "A suit blends in," she said. "It doesn't stand out like a sore thumb." She also promoted aviation, the Women's Army Corps, and the Foreign Service. Mrs. Rogers died in office.

Mrs. Mary Norton (Democrat, New Jersey, 2/4/25–1/3/51). Mrs. Norton attended Packard Business College and became a secretary. After marrying a businessman, she engaged in welfare work. During World War I she ran a Red Cross workroom and was president of a child care center. Mrs. Norton was asked by Mayor Frank Hague of Jersey City in 1920 to be Hudson County's woman representative on the State Democratic Committee. He assured her that she would have no work to do and informed her that a meeting of Jersey City women was being called for the following week. In the following year she was promoted to state vice chairman and in 1932 she became chairman.[2] In 1923 she was elected to the County Board of Freeholders, the first woman in New Jersey to hold this post. In 1924 she became the first Democratic woman to be elected to Congress. Mrs. Norton was a foe of prohibition. In 1932 she declined to permit her name to be posted for vice president.[3] Mrs. Norton was at different times chairman of the House District of Columbia, Administration, Labor and Education Committees. In 1943 she complained that much important legislation had been "stolen" from the Labor Committee because the committee was headed by woman. Mrs. Norton helped get the 1938 Wage and Hour Bill through the House, and fought unsuccessfully for a permanent FEPC. She retired in 1950.

Mrs. Katherine Langley (Republican, Kentucky, 12/5/26–3/4/31). Attended the Woman's College of Richmond, Virginia, and Emerson College of Oratory in Boston. She taught expression at the Virginia Institute in Bristol, Tennessee. During World War I she was chairman of a county Red Cross society. Her father, James Madison Cudger, Jr., had been a congressman from North Carolina. For 14 of her husband's 19 years in Congress, she was his secretary, besides serving six years as clerk for the Committee on Public Buildings and Grounds. In 1920, Mrs. Langley became the first woman vice chairman of the Kentucky Republican State Central Committee. In 1927 her husband was convicted of violation of the prohibition law. She was elected to fill his vacated seat. Her daughter served as her secretary.[4] She was defeated for re-election in 1930.

Mrs. Pearl P. Oldfield (Democrat, Arkansas, 1/9/29–3/4/31). Went to Arkansas College. She succeeded her husband, William P. Oldfield, the Democratic whip. Mrs. Oldfield was not a candidate for renomination in 1930. She gave as the reason for her retirement that woman's place is in the home.

Mrs. Ruth Hanna McCormick (Illinois, Republican, 3/4/29–3/4/31). Attended Miss Porter's School in Connecticut. She was an active member of the "Bull Moose" Party and was chairman of the congressional committee of the National American Woman's Suffrage Association. Mrs. McCormick led a faction in the Suffrage Association which sought to dissolve the organization in 1919, and thus force the organized feminists into the political parties. The daughter of Senator Mark Hanna and the wife of Senator Medill McCormick, she served as chairman of the first woman's executive committee of the Republican National Committee and was national committeewoman for over a third of a century. After her husband's death, she owned and operated a dairy breeding farm and was a newspaper publisher. She ran for representative-at-large for the state of Illinois[5] and defeated a former governor. In Congress she campaigned against the World Court. Mrs. McCormick defeated the Senate incumbent in the 1930 Republican primary, but lost in the general election.[6] In 1932 she married Albert Gallatin Simms, who was also a member of the 71st Congress.

Mrs. Ruth Baker Pratt (Republican, New York, 3/4/29–3/4/33). A graduate of Wellesley College. Mrs. Pratt was the widow of a prominent Republican and Standard Oil executive. She was a suffrage leader, was active for years in civic affairs, and became the first woman member of the New York City Board of Aldermen (1925-29). Mrs. Pratt was also a member of the Republican National Committee (1929-43) and was a delegate to the national conventions of 1924, 1932, 1936, and 1940, and an alternate in 1944. Mrs. Pratt was an unsuccessful candidate for re-election to Congress in 1932. From 1943 to 1946 she was president of the Women's National Republican Club.

Mrs. Ruth Bryan Owen (Democrat, Florida, 3/4/29–3/4/33). Attended the University of Nebraska. She was the daughter and secretary of William Jennings Bryan. From 1918 to 1928, she was a popular Chautauqua performer like her father.[7] After the death of her British army officer husband, she taught speech at the University of Miami and was vice-president of its Board of Regents. Mrs Owen lost her first primary contest for Congress in 1926 by 770 votes. In 1928 she defeated the seven-term veteran for the nomination.[8] Unlike her father, she supported protective tariffs. She also spoke out for women's causes, such as mother's pensions and the creation of a Department of Home and Child. In 1932 Mrs. Owen, a "dry", was defeated for renomination in a campaign involving repeal of prohibition. In 1933 she was appointed U.S. minister to Denmark. Mrs. Owen had been on the House Foreign Affairs Committee. She resigned from the diplomatic service in 1936, after marriage to a captain of the Danish Royal Guard.[9]

Mrs. Effegene Wingo (Democrat, Arkansas, 11/4/30–3/4/33). This great-great-granddaughter of Representative Matthew Loche attended Union Female College, Mississippi, and Maddox Seminary, Arkansas, and then went into educational and research work. She was not a candidate for renomination in 1932.

Mrs. Willa B. Eslick (Democrat, Tennessee, 8/4/32–3/4/33). Attended Dick White College, Milton College, Winthrop Mode School, Peabody College, and Metropolitan College of Music. During World War I, she was chairman of her county's Council of National Defense. Mrs. Eslick was a member of the Tennessee Democratic State Committee. She was elected to her late husband's seat. She was not eligible for re-election, not having qualified for nomination as required by the state Law.

Mrs. Kathryn O'Loughlin McCarthy (Democrat, Kansas, 3/4/33–1/3/35). Attended Kansas State Teachers College and the University of Chicago Law School. A lawyer who had served a term in the state legislature, Miss O'Loughlin defeated eight male opponents in the 1932 primary.[10] In February, 1933, she married one of her opponents, state Senator Daniel McCarthy. She was defeated for re-election in 1934. Mrs. McCarthy was a delegate to Democratic state conventions in 1930, 1931, 1932, 1934, and 1936, and to the Democratic national conventions in 1940 and 1944.

Mrs. Virginia Ellis Jenckes (Democrat, Indiana, 3/4/33–1/3/39). Mrs. Jenckes had a high school education. She was a farmer since 1912, and inherited a farm from her husband. Mrs. Jenckes was secretary of the Wabash Maumee Valley Improvement Association from 1926 to 1932 and fought for flood control legislation. She was elected to Congress as a "wet," defeating two former members of Congress. Mrs. Jenckes was an unsuccessful candidate for re-election in 1938.

Mrs. Isabella Greenway (Democrat, Arizona, 10/3/33–1/3/37). A graduate of Miss Chapin's School of New York. Mrs. Greenway was the was the widow of a "Rough Rider" colonel and magnate. In 1918 she was chairman of the Women's Land Army of New Mexico. In 1929 she became the owner and operator of a cattle ranch, an inn, and an airlines. She was also Democratic national committeewoman from Arizona. "She was for some time," noted Louise Young, "the acknowledged leader of the Democratic organization of her state and thus takes her place among the small group of women in American politics whose political power was inherent—in this case upon property holdings—and not contingent upon their relationship to a politically powerful husband or family." Mrs. Greenway was elected representative-at-large to fill the vacancy left by the resignation of Lewis W. Douglas. She was not a candidate for renomination in 1936.

Mrs. Marian Williams Clarke (Republican, New York, 12/18/33–1/3/35). A graduate of Colorado College. She was elected to her late husband's seat. Mrs. Clarke was a candidate for renomination in 1934, but withdrew her name before the primary election. She was an alternate to the 1936 Republican convention.

Mrs. Caroline Goodwin O'Day (Democrat, New York, 1/3/35–1/3/43). Studied at the Lucy Cobb Institute in Georgia and in France, Germany, and Holland. She was a social worker and was the widow of a Standard Oil executive. Mrs. O'Day was commissioner of the New York state Board of Social Welfare from 1923 to 1934, president of the Rye, N.Y., school board, and a vice president of the Consumers' League and the League of Women Voters. She held a number of offices in the Democratic Party, including vice chairman of the New York state Democratic committee (1916–20), associate chairman (1923–42), and national committeewoman for the Virgin Islands. Mrs. O'Day was elected from the at-large seat from New York. Her Republican opponent in 1934 was Natalie Couch, a lawyer and secretary to a New York state appellate division judge. Mrs. O'Day was not a candidate for renomination in 1942 and died the day after her term expired.

Mrs. Nan Wood Honeyman (Democrat, Oregon, 1/3/37–1/3/39). Attended the Finch School (N.Y.C.). She was president of the Oregon LWV before entering Democratic Party politics and becoming state vice chairman. Mrs. Honeyman served in the state House of Representatives from 1935 to 1937, when she was elected to Congress. She was an unsuccessful candidate for re-election in 1938 and 1940. In 1941 Mrs. Honeyman was named senior representative of the Pacific Coast Office of Price Administration. That same year she was appointed by the Multnomah County commissioners to fill a vacancy in the state senate. In 1942 she became a U.S. collector of customs. Mrs. Honeyman's daughter later became Democratic national committeewoman for Oregon.

Mrs. Bessie Williams Gasque (Democrat, South Carolina, 9/13/38–1/3/39). Studied at the Greenville, S.C., Woman's College. Mrs. Gasque was active in dramatics and was an author and lecturer.

She was elected to complete the term of her late husband, Allard H. Gasque. Mrs. Gasque was never sworn in and seated, since Congress did not meet between the date of her election and the expiration of her term.

Miss Jessie Sumner (Republican, Illinois, 1/3/39–1/3/47). Attended Smith College, the University of Chicago, Columbia University, and Oxford University. Miss Sumner was a lawyer. She was unsuccessful in a 1932 primary contest for Illinois state attorney, but in 1937 was elected county judge to fill out the term of her late uncle. She held this post at the time she was elected to Congress. Miss Sumner was considered "one of the best rough-and-tumble arguers in the House." [11] She was an isolationist. Miss Sumner was not a candidate for renomination in 1946. She returned to her farming and banking interests.

Mrs. Clara G. McMillan (Democrat, South Carolina, 11/7/39–1/3/41). Studied at Confederate Home College, S. C., and Flora MacDonald College, N. C. Mrs. McMillan succeeded her late husband, Thomas S. McMillan, She was not a candidate in 1940. In 1946 she was appointed an information liaison officer for the Department of State.

Mrs. Frances Payne Bolton (Republican, Ohio, 2/27/40–present). [12] Mrs. Bolton had a public school education, but holds honorary degrees from about 14 colleges and universities. She is the great-granddaughter of a judge, the granddaughter of a Cleveland city council member, and the granddaughter of U.S. Senator Henry B. Payne. Mrs. Bolton was active in public health, nursing education, social service, and education. She founded the U.S. Cadet Nurse Corps. In 1940 she was elected to fill the unexpired term of her deceased husband. Mrs. Bolton was a delegate to the eighth session of the U.N. General Assembly in 1953. She is an internationalist, and is ranking Republican on the House Foreign Affairs Committee. Her son, Oliver, was a Representative with her in the 84th and 88th Congresses. They frequently opposed each other in voting.

Mrs. Florence R. Gibbs (Democrat, Georgia, 10/1/40–1/3/41). Attended Brenau College in Georgia. She succeeded her late husband, Willis B. Gibbs.

Mrs. Margaret Chase Smith (see details of her career in the section on Senators.) She occupied the seat of her late husband, Clyde Smith, in 1940. In 1948 she advanced to the U.S. Senate.

Mrs. Katherine Edgar Byron (Democrat, Maryland, 5/27/41–1/3/43). Mrs. Byron was president of the PTA of Williamsport, MD., in 1935. From 1938 to 1941 she was town commissioner. She had been encouraged by her husband to run for the Town Council. She was elected to her late husband's term in Congress. Mrs. Byron was not a candidate for renomination in 1942.

Mrs. Veronica Boland (Democrat, Pennsylvania, 11/19/42–1/3/43). Attended Scranton Technical High School. Mrs. Boland succeeded her late husband, Patrick, in the 77th Congress. She was not a candidate for re-election.

Miss Winifred Stanley (Republican, New York, 1/2/43–1/3/45). A graduate of the University of Buffalo and the University of Buffalo Law School. As a lawyer, Miss Stanley crusaded for the right of New York's women to serve on juries. At the age of 29 she was selected assistant district attorney of Erie County. She was elected from a field of eight to be representative-at-large from New York and at 34 was the youngest woman ever to be sent to Congress. Miss Stanley was voted one of the nation's ten best-dressed women. That honor did not help her retain her seat, which was reapportioned out of existence. In 1945 she was appointed counsel to the New York state employees retirement system.

Mrs. Clare Booth Luce (Republican, Connecticut, 1/3/43–1/3/47). Educated at boarding school. Mrs. Luce was the stepdaughter of Congressman Albert E. Austin, and wife of the founder of the *Time-Life* establishment. She was secretary to Mrs. Belmont's Woman's Party, managing editor of *Vanity Fair,* playwright, actress and war correspondent.[13] Mrs. Luce won the 1942 nomination for Congress by defeating six opponents, including Miss Vivien Kellems, the industrialist. She defeated the incumbent, who had himself gained the seat from her stepfather. She was not a candidate for renomination in 1946. In 1952 she was unsuccessful in an attempt to secure the Republican nomination for senator from Connecticut. In 1964 Mrs. Luce was mentioned as a Conservative Party candidate for senator from New York. From 1953 to 1956 she was ambassador to Italy. In 1959 she was nominated to be ambassador to Brazil, an assignment she never undertook.

Mrs. Willa L. Fulmer (Democrat, South Carolina, 11/7/44—1/3/45). A graduate of Greenville, S.C., Female College. Mrs. Fulmer was elected to fill the vacancy caused by the death of her husband, Hampton P. Fulmer. She was not a candidate for re-election.

Mrs. Chase G. Woodhouse (Democrat, Connecticut, 1/3/45—1/3/47; 1/3/49—1/3/51). Attended McGill University, Montreal, the University of Berlin, and the University of Chicago. Mrs. Woodhouse was a professor of economics and senior economist of the Federal Bureau of Home Economics. She was president of the Connecticut LWV, three times president of the Connecticut Federation of Democratic Women's Clubs, and executive director of the Women's Division of the Democratic National Committee. In 1941-42 she was secretary of state for Connecticut. Mrs. Woodhouse was elected to Congress in 1944 but defeated in 1946, elected in 1948 but defeated again in 1950. She was defeated by the incumbent in 1944 and 1948. Mrs. Woodhouse is chairman of the Connecticut Commission on the Status of Women.

Mrs. Emily Taft Douglas (Democrat, Illinois, 1/3/45—1/3/47). Attended the University of Chicago. This actress-daughter of sculptor Lorado Taft is the wife of Senator Paul Douglas. She was an organizer for the Illinois LWV, and became chairman of the Illinois league's Department of Government and Foreign Policy. She was elected at-large representative in 1944, defeating the incumbent, but failed in her attempt at re-election in 1946.

Mrs. Helen Gahagan Douglas (Democrat, California, 1/3/45—1/3/51). Attended Barnard College of Columbia University. She was an opera singer and actress. Her husband is actor Melvin Douglas. In 1940 she became Democratic national committeewoman for California and vice chairman of the Democratic state central committee. Mrs. Douglas rented an office and hired a secretary at her own expense. She had a liberal record in Congress and ran for the Senate in 1950 against Richard Nixon. An internal split among the Democrats cost her the election.

Mrs. Helen Douglas Mankin (Democrat, Georgia, 2/12/46—1/3/47). Studied at Rockford, Illinois College and Atlanta Law School. Mrs. Mankin was a lawyer whose parents were both lawyers and teachers. Her husband was an engineer. She served five successive terms in the state legislature, (1937-46) and worked for better salaries for teachers, modern health legislation, segregation of youthful offenders, a state department of labor, and a truly secret ballot. Mrs. Mankin was elected to Congress to fill the vacancy caused by the resignation of Robert Ramspeck, defeating 17 male opponents in the special February 1946 Democratic primary, but was an unsuccessful candidate for renomination in 1946. She won the popular majority in the primary, but carried only one of the three counties in the congressional district. Under the Georgia County unit system, a weighted vote favoring rural areas meant defeat. Mrs. Mankin tried again, without success, in 1948.

Miss Eliza Jane Pratt (Democrat, North Carolina, 5/25/46—1/3/47). Attended Queens College, N. C. Miss Pratt was a newspaper editor at Troy, N.C., in 1923-24, and was secretary to the members of Congress from the Eighth Congressional District of North Carolina from 1924 to 1946. She succeeded her employer, the late Representative William O. Burgin, but was not a candidate for renomination in 1946.

Mrs. Georgia Lusk (Democrat, New Mexico, 1/3/47—1/3/49). Graduate of State Teacher's Colleges in New Mexico and Colorado. Mrs. Lusk was the widow of a cattle rancher who died a few years after their marriage, leaving her the ranch and three small sons. She became a teacher and rose to county superintendent of schools and state superintendent of public instruction. Mrs. Lusk was elected to Congress at-large in 1946, but was an unsuccessful candidate for renomination in 1948. She was a delegate to the Democratic national convention in 1924 and 1948. From 1949 to 1953 she was the first and only woman member of the War Claims Commission.

Mrs. Katharine St. George (Republican, New York, 1/2/47—1/3/65). Educated in private schools and abroad. Mrs. St. George was married to a former chairman of the board of the First National Bank of New York, and president of the St. George Coal Corporation. She was an officer of the Red Cross since 1918, a member of her town board since 1931, and president of its board of education since 1936. Mrs. St. George was one of the few women in the nation to be county chairman of a political party. In Congress she sponsored an Equal Rights Amendment and became the first woman to serve on the House Rules Committee.[15] She was defeated for re-election in 1964.

Mrs. Cecil Murry Harden (Republican, Indiana, 1/2/49–1/3/59). Attended Indiana University. Mrs. Harden was a schoolteacher who became active in the Republican Party in 1932, after her husband had been appointed a postmaster. In 1944 she became a national committeewoman, an office she held until 1959. Mrs. Harden lost her bid for a sixth term in Congress in 1958.

Mrs. Reva Beck Bosone (Democrat, Utah, 1/3/49–1/3/53). Studied at Westminster Junior College, the University of California, and the University of Utah College of Law. Mrs. Bosone taught high school in Utah from 1920 to 1927, and then studied law. Her husband was a lawyer. She served in the state House of Representatives from 1933 to 1936, and was the author of the state's minimum wage and maximum hour law for women and children, an unemployment insurance law, and a water control law. She was elected municipal judge of Salt Lake City in 1936. Judge Bosone achieved a reputation for reducing the traffic death toll by a system of stiff fines. She was elected to Congress in 1948 and 1950, but was unsuccessful in 1952 and 1954. Under Kennedy she was judicial officer for the Post Office.

Mrs. Edna F. Kelly (Democrat, New York, 11/8/49–present). Attended Hunter College, New York. Her father-in-law had been postmaster of Brooklyn, and was one of the first Democrats ever elected in what was then a largely Republican borough. Her husband became a New York City court justice. His death in an accident left her a widow at 35.[16] Mrs. Kelly became the disciple and ally of Irwin Steingut, then minority leader of the state assembly. She was appointed in 1943 associate research director of the Democratic Party in the legislature. In 1944 she became chief research director. She was also Democratic woman leader of her election district. Mrs. Kelly was elected to Congress in a special election after the death of the incumbent. She is a high-ranking member of the House Foreign Affairs Committee and was named a delegate to the 18th session of the U.N. General Assembly. Since 1956 Mrs. Kelly has been Democratic national committeewoman from New York.

Mrs. Vera D. Buchanan (Democrat, Pennsylvania, 7/24/51–11/26/55). Attended public and parochial schools. Mrs.

Buchanan was elected to fill the vacancy caused by the death of her husband, Frank Buchanan, and was twice re-elected. She died in office.

Mrs. Marguerite Stitt Church (Republican, Illinois, 1/3/51–1/3/63). Graduate of Wellesley College and Columbia University. She taught psychology at Wellesley in 1915 and was a psychologist for the State Charities Aid Association in New York City during World War I. She succeeded her late husband, Ralph Edwin Church, in Congress. Mrs. Church was an internationalist. She authored a bill banning transportation of fireworks into a state where its use is illegal.

Miss Ruth Thompson (Republican, Michigan, 1/3/51–1/3/57). A graduate of Muskegon Business College, she also studied law. After working as registrar of the county probate court of Muskegon, Michigan, she served three terms as probate judge, 1925-37. From 1939 to 1941, Miss Thompson was in the state legislature. Thereafter, she had governmental experience in the legal section of the Social Security Board, the Labor Department, the Adjutant General's office and with the army of occupation in Europe. She was elected to Congress in 1950, and was twice re-elected, but was an unsuccessful candidate for renomination in 1956.

Mrs. Elizabeth Kee (Democrat, West Virginia, 7/17/51–1/3/63). Attended Roanoke Business College. Mrs. Kee was active in Democratic politics since 1922. She was secretary to her husband, a Congressman who became chairman of the Committee on Foreign Affairs. Her son, a former foreign service officer, became her administrative assistant when she entered Congress. During this time she wrote a weekly newspaper column and sponsored a library for handicapped children. Mrs. Kee was re-elected in 1951 to fill the unexpired term of her late husband and was re-elected.

Mrs. Gracie Bowers Pfost (Democrat, Idaho, 1/3/53–1/3/63). Graduated from Link's Business University, Idaho. Mrs. Pfost was chemist for a milk products company for two years. From 1929 to 1939 she was deputy county clerk, auditor, and recorder of Clayton County. From 1941 to 1951 she was Canyon County treasurer. Mrs. Pfost was an unsuccessful candidate for Congress in 1950, losing by 783 votes, but won in 1952, defeating Representative John T. Wood by almost the same margin by which he had beaten her two years before. She waged a colorful campaign, including riding in rodeos. Mrs. Pfost once challenged an opponent to a log-birling contest on Lumberjack Day, "remarking as she arose dripping wet, having hit the water at the same instant as her adversary, 'Orofino's pure water sure tastes good.'"[17] She favored government hydroelectric projects. Her support of a Hell's Canyon dam earned her the nickname of Hell's Belle. In 1962 Mrs. Pfost ran unsuccessfully for senator against the interim Republican Senator Len Jordan.

Mrs. Leonor K. Sullivan (Democrat, Missouri, 1/3/53–present). Attended Washington University in St. Louis. Prior to marriage she was director of a business training school. She served as her husband's congressional administrative assistant from 1942 to 1950,[18] and was his campaign manager. A Republican won the special election after his death, but Mrs. Sullivan, after serving as administrative assistant to another congressman, defeated him in the regular election of 1952. She won a hard primary battle against six opponents, five of whom were men. She has shown an interest in consumer legislation, including federal inspection of poultry, processing plants and truth-in-lending bills. Mrs. Sullivan is secretary of the House Democratic caucus and is the only woman on the Democratic Steering Committee of the House.

Mrs. Elizabeth Farrington (Republican, Hawaii, 7/31/54–1/3/57). Studied at the University of Wisconsin. Mrs. Farrington was president of the National Federation of Republican Women and of the League of Republican Women of Washington, D.C. She succeeded her late husband as territorial delegate to Congress from Hawaii[19] and was re-elected. Mrs. Farrington lost her bid for a second full term in 1956.

Mrs. Coya G. Knutson (Democrat, Minnesota, 1/3/55–1/3/59). Studied at Concordia College, Minnesota, Minnesota State Teachers College and the Juilliard School of Music. Mrs. Knutson taught high school, was a farmer and a 4-H leader, and had experience in the restaurant business. She was a member of her county welfare board from 1948 to 1956. From 1951 to 1954 she served in the state legislature. She became Minnesota's first congresswoman in 1955, after defeating a 12-year veteran in a campaign against the Eisenhower farm program, and became the first woman placed on the House Agriculture Committee. Mrs. Knutson was the only Democratic member of Congress to lose to a Republican challenger in 1958 after her political enemies published a "Coya, come home" letter from her husband. Her comeback attempt in 1960 was unsuccessful.

Mrs. Martha W. Griffiths (Democrat, Michigan, 1/3/55—present). Attended the University of Missouri and the University of Michigan Law School. During World War II, she was a government contract negotiator. She and her husband are members of G. Mennen Williams' law firm. In 1949 her husband was Democratic state chairman. Mrs. Griffiths served two terms in the state legislafure, 1949-52,[20] but was unsuccessful as a candidate for Congress in 1952. In 1953 she became the first woman ever appointed recorder and judge of the Recorder's Court.[21] Her husband was a probate judge. She was elected to Congress in 1954, campaigning from a 40-foot house trailer. Mrs. Griffiths, a supporter of the Equal Rights Amendment, made the speech which put the prohibition of discrimination for reason of sex in the 1964 Civil Rights Act. She has received aid in her campaigns from the Business and Professional Women's Clubs.

Mrs. Edith Green (Democrat, Oregon, 1/3/55—present). Attended Willamette University, the University of Oregon, and Stanford University. Her father was active in politics. For 14 years, Mrs. Green was a teacher. She was also a leader of the Oregon Education Association and the PTA. In addition, she did commercial radio work. Her first campaign for Congress was against a well-known radio personality. Mrs. Green has been supported by the Business and Professional Women; they have even urged that she be named secretary of Health, Education and Welfare. She is an advocate of equal rights legislation and author of the Equal Pay Bill, but has always opposed the Equal Rights Amendment. Her efforts resulted in women's being included in the Job Corps.

Mrs. Iris F. Blitch (Democrat, Georgia, 1/3/55—1/3/63). Studied at the University of Georgia and South Georgia College. Mrs. Blitch was associated with her husband in the drug business, in farming, and in naval stores operations. She was an unsuccessful candidate for the state House of Representatives in 1940, but was elected to the state Senate in 1946. She served in the state House from 1949 to 1950, but was defeated in 1950. In 1952 she was again elected to the Georgia Senate. Mrs. Blitch was the prime mover of a bill giving women the right to serve on Georgia juries. From 1948 to 1956, she was Democratic national committeewoman. She was elected to Congress in 1954.

Mrs. Kathryn Granahan (Democrat, Pennsylvania, 11/6/56–1/3/63). Attended Mount St. Joseph College, Philadelphia. From 1940 to 1943 Mrs. Granahan was a supervisor of public assistance in the state auditor general's department. After the death of her husband, William Granahan, she was elected to fill his vacancy.[22] Mrs. Granahan crusaded in Congress against the sale and distribution of salacious and pornographic material, especially against the mailing of obscene literature. President Kennedy named her treasurer of the United States.

Mrs. Florence P. Dwyer (Republican, New Jersey, 1/3/57–present). Mrs. Dwyer is the wife of an industrial relations man. She became interested in politics through the PTA. She was state legislative chairman of the New Jersey Business and Professional Women. This familiarity with the legislative process led to her being chosen secretary to the assistant majority leader and speaker, and parliamentarian of the Assembly. From 1949 to 1957, Mrs. Dwyer served as an assemblywoman. She worked for equal pay for women, for the improvement of teachers' salaries and for state school aid. She was chairman of the Educational Committee. After her election to the Assembly she attended Rutgers Law School. In 1956 Mrs. Dwyer was elected to Congress, defeating the incumbent.[23] She has been mentioned for the Senate but turned down an invitation to run in 1964.

Mrs. Catherine May (Republican, Washington 1/3/59–present). Studied at Yakima Valley Junior College, the University of Washington, and the University of Southern California. Mrs. May was a high school English teacher, a women's editor, and a radio newscaster. She and her husband, a real estate and insurance broker, joined the Young Republican Club in 1951. He persuaded her to run for the state legislature in 1952, and she served for six years. In 1958 she was elected to Congress. Mrs. May represents a 100 percent rural district and is on the Agriculture Committee. She has served on the Joint Committee on Republican Principles.

Mrs. Jessica M. Weis (Republican, New York, 1/3/59–5/1/63). Attended private schools and Bryn Mawr. Mrs. Weis held many positions in the New York Republican Party. From 1937 to 1952 she was vice chairman of the Monroe County Republican Committee. In

1940 and 1941 she was president of the National Federation of Republican Women. In 1944 Mrs. Weis became a member of the Republican National Committee. She was elected to Congress in 1958[24] and died in office in 1963.

Mrs. **Edna Oaks Simpson** (Republican, Illinois, 1/3/59–1/3/61). Mrs. Simpson was elected to the seat previously held by her husband, Sidney. She did not seek renomination in 1960.

Mrs. **Julia B. Hansen** (Democrat, Washington, 11/8/60–present). Graduated from the University of Washington. Mrs. Hansen, married to a retired logger, was manager of a title insurance and casualty insurance business. She served eight years on the Cathlamet City Council. From 1939 to 1960 she was a member of the state legislature. Mrs. Hansen was Democratic leader and became Speaker pro tempore in 1955. In 1960 she was elected to fill the vacancy caused by the death of the incumbent and was re-elected for the full term.

Mrs. **Catherine D. Norrell** (Democrat, Arkansas, 4/25/61–1/3/63). Studied at Ouachita Baptist College and the University of Arkansas. Mrs. Norrell was a public schoolteacher and director of the music department at Arkansas Agricultural and Mining College. She succeeded her husband, William F. Norrell, after his death in 1962. In 1963 she was named deputy assistant secretary of state for Educational and Cultural Affairs.

Mrs. **Louise G. Reece** (Republican, Tennessee, 5/24/61–1/3/63). Graduated from Miss Spence School, New York, Mrs. Reece was the granddaughter of Senator Nathan Goff and daughter of Senator Guy Goff of West Virginia. She was manager of Goff Properties and was chairman of the board of directors of two banks. Her husband, Representative Carroll Reece, was a former Republican national chairman. She filled the vacancy caused by his death in 1962.

Mrs. **Charlotte T. Reid** (Republican, Illinois, 1/3/63–present). Attended Illinois College, Jacksonville. She left college to become a professional singer. As Annette King, she was for three years on the Don McNeill radio show. In 1962, her lawyer husband died while campaigning for Congress.[25] She did not seek the office, but was put forward by the party. Mrs. Reid won and two years later was re-elected.

Mrs. Irene B. Baker (Republican, Tennessee, 3/1/64–1/3/65). Mrs. Baker was the widow of Representative Howard H. Baker. She was elected to fill the vacancy caused by his death.[26] Later that year her son, Howard H. Baker, Jr., ran unsuccessfully for the U.S. Senate. She did not seek renomination.

Mrs. Patsy T. Mink (Democrat, Hawaii, 1/3/65–present). Studied at the University of Hawaii and the University of Chicago Law School. Mrs. Mink is a lawyer who was active in the Hawaii Young Democrats. She served in the territorial House of Representatives and Senate and in the state Senate before being elected to Congress.[27] Mrs. Mink holds an at-large seat. Her husband, a geologist, was her campaign manager.

Mrs. Lera M. Thomas (Democrat, Texas, 3/30/66–1/3/67). Mrs. Thomas, the widow of long-time Congressman Albert Thomas, was elected to fill the vacancy caused by his death. She was urged to run by both Houston daily newspapers. As a tribute to her late husband, two Democrats and a Republican who had filed for the next two-year term stepped aside so that she would be unopposed. Mrs. Thomas did not seek re-election.

Mrs. Margaret M. Heckler (Republican, Massachusetts, 1/3/67–present). Studied at Albertus Magnus College and Boston College Law School. Mrs. Heckler, a housewife and lawyer, upset Joseph W. Martin in the Republican primary, ending the former Speaker's 42-year House career. She is married to an industrial investment broker. From 1963 to 1966 she was the only Republican elected to the Massachusetts Governor's Executive Council.

Women in State Government

On the eve of national woman suffrage, a circular appeared signed by the Men's Patriotic Association of Pittsburgh. "If women are given further suffrage, they might hold any office, judge, senator, or by political accident, president of the U.S. Their advancement could be extended rapidly by the ruthless male office holder who would not care if a woman was second so long as he was first . . . . It is not the right order of affairs to expect men to take orders or directions from women officials, or to encourage women to exert that authority." [1]

At about the same time, the Republican speaker of the New York Assembly, Thadius Sweet, denounced a number of women's groups that lobbied for social legislation as "criminal agitators." A portent of what might happen nationally was the reaction of the newly enfranchised women of New York. They got a young woman who was a Republican to run against Sweet on the Democratic ticket. She came close to defeating him.[2]

It seemed to the men as though the militant feminists were "muscling in" on a male preserve. Toward the end of the 1920 campaign, a seasoned old-timer asked Alice Moyer-Wing, a suffragist turned Republican,[3] what she wanted in the way of patronage if their party won. She did not understand what he was talking about. He laughed and said: "Ain't that like a darn fool woman?" Nevertheless, despite the horror of the idea to many old-timers, the new governor appointed her to head the Missouri Industrial Inspection Department.

By 1924 she aspired to run for Congress but met with hostility and scorn from the male leaders. One remarked: "Taking yourself mighty serious, ain't you? Funny about women that way. Plumb serious. But let me tell you something: You won't get 500 votes in this entire district of 11 counties." She came in third with 32,000 votes, and the new governor reappointed her department chairman.

Another woman office seeker met with a rebuff from the men of Arkansas in 1920. She had to withdraw her candidacy after a decision that, despite woman's suffrage, she was disqualified from contesting for the office on the ground of sex. A similar law existed in Georgia.[4] Iowa amended its consitition in 1926 to allow a woman to hold state office.

As late as 1942 women were barred by the Oklahoma constitution from holding such offices as governor, lieutenant governor, and attorney general.[5] In referenda in 1923, 1930 and 1935, the voters of Oklahoma, male and female, voted down the rights of women to hold major state offices.[6]

To what extent have women been able to overcome this initial discrimination? With what frequency have women been elected or appointed to state legislative, executive, and judicial positions?

Legislators. Women hold only four per cent of the nation's

7,700 state legislative seats.[7] A much smaller percentage is in the upper houses. Between 1896, when Wyoming became the first state to grant women the vote, and 1920, a total of 60 women served in state legislatures.[8] A number of women served as state representatives in Colorado in the 1890's.[9]

Gains have usually been made by women in presidential election years, when political interest is high and the vote is large. Women tend to appeal to independent voters. They also profit from the coattail effect, running in marginal districts and being swept in with the rest of the ticket.[10] The Depression saw a dip in the number of women elected; the seats became more attractive to men.[11] On the other hand, the relative absence of men during World War II gave women an opportunity to increase their number of seats. When the men returned, there was a reduction in the female representation.

In 1961 there were 194 women in the lower houses of 43 states,[12] but 144 of these came from just three states, Connecticut, New Hampshire, and Vermont.[13] These three New England states have disproportionately large legislatures, all in need of redistricting. Each of Vermont's 246 cities and towns have one seat in the House, regardless of population. Thus Stratton, Vermont, with 36 residents, has one seat, as does Burlington, with over 36,000 residents.[14] Connecticut had 294 members of its House, elected on a town-by-town basis, which has been declared unconstitutional. Each member received a salary of $2,000 and expenses of $500.[15] Yet the 59 women who served in 1963, including only three women in the 24-member senate, still had to campaign for their positions.[16]

Two other states with legislative houses of over 200, Georgia and Massachusetts, have fewer than five women each, and Pennsylvania, another state with a large legislature, has less than 10.

In the 1966 election Maryland chose four women to be state senators and 11 as members of the house of delegates, seven per cent of the legislature, as against the national average of three to four percent.

Three women were elected to the Wisconsin legislature in 1924, but in the 40 years since there were never more than that number in any one session. There were only two in 1964-66 and three in 1967. There has never been a woman in the state senate. New York, which paid a salary of $10,000, had only four women in the 1965 legislature. In the first 20 regular sessions of the North Carolina General Assembly since women got the vote, only 15 women held seats, for a total of 24 terms.

Women enter politics and seek public office for the same variety of reasons as do men.[17] There are differences in the backgrounds of male and female legislators, however. Fewer women are lawyers or business executives,[18] more are widows[19] and teachers.[20] Legislative posts are part-time and relatively poorly paid jobs. In most cases, they require two to three months' absence from home every other year. This is ideal for many women and for self-employed business-men.[21]

Women legislators have come a long way since the early 1920's. At that time Mrs. Lottie Holman O'Neill, the first woman elected to the Illinois legislature, introduced 10 bills, most involving protection of women and children. The only one to pass was a bill to save wild flowers. She was able to keep plugging away, though, and was still in the legislature in the 1960's after serving nine terms in the house and three in the senate. Mrs. Cora Woodbridge, a California legislator, exclaimed dolorously: "Vote for a boxing bill and you are all right."[22]

Women, like men, seek committee posts in fields which are of interest to them. Men are concerned about hunting and fishing regulations, a tax on cigars, employment preference for Korean War veterans, penalties for fixing athletic contests, and the payment of policemen and firemen. Women pay special attention to matters of health, equal pay, public welfare, education, consumer protection, and wayward children.[23] There is no reason, however, to restrict women to "women's subjects." Female legislators have served with distinction on such committees as appropriations, finance, judiciary, and ways-and-means.

Although outnumbered 194 to 52, the Vermont lady legislators managed in 1952 to elect one of their own, Mrs. Consuelo Northrop Bailey, speaker of the House. Their technique was simple but effective: While male legislators split their votes among five veteran candidates for the job, the women voted as a solid bloc, thereby exploding the male notion that a group of women could never agree or work together on anything. Of the women's performance, one male veteran opined: "They ain't any worse than men."[24]

Because so many women have had service in state legislatures, it would be impossible to look at more than a few of them. Mrs. Nellie Nugent Sommerville of Mississippi, a state legislator in the 1920's was a power in the state Democratic Party. Her daughter, Lucy Sommerville Howorth, followed her into the state legislature in 1932.[25] Miss Mildred Barber was one of the first three women elected to the Wisconsin legislature in 1924.[26] She was only 23. Her father had been in the state senate and her mother was a postmistress. As an only child, she was heavily exposed to politics. Miss Barber retired from politics at the end of her first two-year term. She ran for re-election but was defeated. After teaching for a year, she settled down to the life of a housewife. "When I married, my husband was not inclined toward politics," she said, "so I didn't stay active, but every time I got to a picnic I was in there pitching for the current candidates. I couldn't resist."

Miss Barber's story illustrates some factors which have recurred in a number of cases. There have been several very young and ambitious women who have won legislative seats. These victories have been played up by newspaper and magazine feature story writers, more so than if politically precocious males had been elected. These and other women need the encouragement of their families to embark on and continue their political careers. Some, like Mrs. Sommerville, may, in turn, be setting an example for their children.

Anna Brancato was first elected to the Pennsylvania legislature in 1932 when in her twenties. She campaigned in Italian, Hebrew, and English and was valuable to her party as a vote-getter among Italians and women. Her platform advocated modification of the Sunday blue laws, repeal of prohibition, and improvement of social conditions. Miss Brancato served a term as vice president of the State Young Democrats. Her husband was a deputy attorney general of Pennsylvania.

Miss Nancy Brown ran for the Maryland legislature at 21 in 1962, while a senior at the University of Maryland. She was elected, becoming the youngest woman legislator in the country.[27] Miss Brown attended law school at night so as not to interfere with her legislative duties. Now Mrs. Burkheimer, she was re-elected in 1966.

In 1948 Mary Shadow, a Tennessee Democrat, became at 23 the

youngest woman legislator when she was successful in a district that was largely Republican. She had taught political science at Tennessee Wesleyan College and defeated the Republican assemblyman who had served almost continuously since 1908. Miss Shadow was the only woman in the legislature. After a pet bill of hers was tabled on the last day of the legislature, she burst into tears and was led from the assembly.[28] Her parents were not impressed by her political position. "They think I ought to get married and forget politics," she said. Despite the frustrations of political life, Miss Shadow sought and won re-election in 1950.

Miss Betty Jane Long was elected to the Mississippi state legislature in 1955 after defeating four male opponents in the primary. A pretty 27-year-old lawyer, she was the only woman among the hundred law students at the University of Mississippi.

Twenty-four-year-old Jane Noble, an Indiana legislator in 1949, attended De Pauw University over weekends and maintained an A average. She was the daughter of a newspaper editor and had served with Army Intelligence as a WAC. When she ran in 1948, she received more votes than Truman in her district. Her boyfriend, a De Pauw junior, whom she saw weekly, did not approve. "It's one thing for a girl to serve a term in the legislature," he said, "but another for her to enter politics permanently."[29]

In 1958 Gloria Schaffer became at 27 a Connecticut state senator, the only woman at the time. She was nominated because the party leaders thought no Democrat could win in her overwhelmingly Republican district, "so it would be all right to nominate a woman." She had run unsuccessfully for the lower house in 1956. Miss Schaffer won re-election in 1960 and 1962 and was chairman of the Welfare Committee. She was known for her sponsorship of penal reforms.[30]

In 1966 80-year-old Eleanor Dougherty, a professor of history and political science, was elected to the Montana legislature.

Mrs. Charolotte Giesen of Radford, Virginia, married into a political family. Her husband and father both had served as mayor of their city. She was elected to the city council in 1954 and to the House of Delegates of the Virginia General Assembly in 1957. Mrs. Giesen was re-elected in 1959 but defeated in 1961. In 1962 she was again elected to the city council.[31]

Mrs. Bernice MacKenzie, an Ohio state representative, is the daughter of a one-time city councilman and board of education member. She got into politics while practicing law and served two terms as councilman-at-large in Canton. Mrs. MacKenzie is now serving her fifth term in the state legislature.[32]

Mrs. Florence J. Beckers, South Dakota representative in 1951, was the daughter, granddaughter and niece of men active in state political affairs. She had engaged in teaching, photography, and the retail drug business and was president of the state Business and Professional Women's Clubs.

Mrs. Janet Hill Gordon, a Republican state senator in New York, learned to campaign when her father, James P. Hill, ran for judge. She became a lawyer and was in partnership with her husband. After six terms in the Assembly, she was elected to the Senate.

Richard and Maurine Neuberger of Oregon were not the only husband-and-wife team to serve together in a state legislature. Orene and John Farese of Mississippi were the second such combination. Mrs. Farese, a teacher and state senator, had a father who was active in politics. Her lawyer-husband had been elected county attorney and state senator prior to moving to the House of Representatives.

Dorothy Jackson Miller was admitted to the Maryland bar at 22. She and her art-school director husband became Democratic precinct leaders and she entered the legislature in 1951.

Mrs. Lucille H. McCollough moved to the Michigan statehouse after four years on the Dearborn City Council. She got started in politics in 1947 when she and her husband helped form a homeowners' group. Mrs. McCollough was the group's spokesman before the city council.

Senator Kathleen A. Foote was the third woman to be elected to the unicameral Nebraska legislature. She was victorious at 28, being helped by newspaper stories that, if successful, she would be the first woman to be elected, as well as the youngest member in the coming session.[33] Her husband, a farmer, worked for the State Game Commission. Their children grew up among the legislators. Debate on a tax bill was once interrupted so that everybody could attend a birthday party for her two-year-old. Mrs. Foote took time out in the spring of 1956 to have her third baby and resumed her duties after missing only eight and a half legislative days.

Mrs. Wanda Sankary of California did not let a pregnancy stand in the way of her legislative campaign. Her son was born the day after her election.[34] She was the first Democrat elected from her district in nearly 20 years and was also the first woman lawyer in the California Assembly. Mrs. Sankary was in law partnership with her husband.

Mrs. Blanche Cowperthwaite also carried a child during her campaign for the Colorado House of Representatives. Her fourth baby was born a month after the 1954 race. She was president of the Denver chapter of the American Association of University Women and was active in the real estate business.

Another woman who refused to let a little thing like having a baby disturb her legislative routine was Senator Florence Murray of Rhode Island. The day before she gave birth she was at the statehouse, lawmaking as usual. A week after her baby was born, she returned to duty. Both she and her husband are now judges.

Mrs. Margery Graves of the New Hampshire legislature had assistance from her two college-aged children in the clerical work of her campaign. At the time that Mrs. Graves served in 1951 there were 29 married women, 12 widows, and five unmarried members of the New Hampshire legislature. Some women, as in Congress, got their opportunity for office after the death of their mates. Mrs. Caroline Blanchard of Wisconsin succeeded her husband, the late assembly speaker, in 1964. She was re-elected. Mrs. Augusta T. Larson of Arizona was, with her husband, a teacher and champion of the rights of the Navajos. She was appointed to complete her husband's legislative term and was subsequently re-elected.

Some women are married to politically active men who are themselves unavailable for candidacies. Mrs. Ruth Doyle, a Wisconsin assemblywoman, the wife of a member of the old LaFollette law firm, was also a leader of Americans for Democratic Action. Harold Ickes' wife, Anna, served three terms in the Illinois Senate.

Mrs. Kathryn Stone, who has served in the Virginia House of Delegates since 1954, is the wife of a department of the army management specialist. They co-authored two books on city management. Mrs. Stone moved from leadership in the state LWV to the state legislature. She was the only legislator to oppose the "massive resistance" approach to the desegregation of schools. The barrage of insults from male legislators reduced her to tears, but she refused to retreat. Mrs. Stone was vindicated through being twice re-elected and is now chairman of the Governor's Committee for Youth.

The husband of Mabeth Hurd Paige was a professor of law at the University of Minnesota. She, too, was a lawyer. He encouraged her service as president of the Minneapolis Woman's Christian Association, national board member of the LWV, and state legislator. She was in the Minnesota legislature from 1923 to 1944 and became the chairman of its Welfare Committee.

Senator Suzanne Loizeaux of New Hampshire, a veteran of 15 years of newspaper publishing and editing, was called the "unofficial majority floor leader."[35] Another writer-senator was Mrs. Eudochia Bell Smith of Colorado, who, after 12 years in the state legislature,[36] was appointed by President Truman district land register of the Department of the Interior. She began her career as a newspaper-woman and was married to a newsman. Once after answering a number of phone calls for his wife, her husband said with affected resignation, "Yes, yes, this is the senator's stooge."

A Colorado legislator who served on and off for 22 years was Mrs. Betty Pellet. She was first elected in 1940. Before that time, no woman had ever been elected from a rural section of the state. She went on to become minority floor leader. Mrs. Pellet was encouraged in her political career by her semi-invalid husband, a mine owner. She was a successful candidate for her local school board in the 1920's. For 18 years she was vice chairman of her county Democratic Party and boasted that in 45 years she had never missed a local party caucus. At one time in her county, women held all the legislative, executive, and judicial offices except that of sheriff. Mrs. Pellet had her share of political setbacks. She supported Josephine Roche's unsuccessful attempt to become governor of Colorado and was herself defeated in a contest for a congressional seat.

Mrs. Doris M. Barnes, a widow and businesswoman in Wrangell, Alaska, was on the city council from 1944 when she became mayor. From 1949 to 1953 she served in the territorial House of Representatives and was in the Senate from 1943 to 1957. In 1960 she began another term as mayor.

Mrs. Harriet R. Stone of Vermont served in many capacities at the local level before being elected to the legislature. She was justice of the peace 12 years, auditor eight years, selectman three years, overseer of the poor seven years, cemetery commissioner nine years, town clerk 14 years and town treasurer nine years. She has been a member of the House since 1959.

Another veteran was Mrs. Hilda Brungot of New Hampshire. Mrs. Brungot began her political career at the 1930 state constitutional convention, being elected to replace her recently deceased father, a veteran legislator. She was a delegate to state constitutional conventions in 1930, 1938, 1948, 1956, and 1959, and served in the legislature from 1931 to 1937 and from 1941 to 1960. She had a "Margaret Smith" attendance record—never missing a roll-call vote and being absent from her legislative seat only two days in 15 terms.

Dr. Rachel D. Davis, a physician from a family of doctors, argued her case before her North Carolina Assembly colleagues in behalf of special legislation permitting her to adopt a daughter although she was unmarried.

Mrs. Eleanor F. Slater, a Rhode Island representative, became active in politics through an interest in the condition of the schools her two boys were attending. She helped form a citizens' committee and ran successfully for the school board. She was elected to the legislature in 1958 and is now serving her fourth term. Mrs. Slater has also become vice chairman of the Democratic State Committee.[37]

Mrs. Dorothy Bell Lawrence was rated by the Citizens Union of New York as the most independent member of the state legislature. She was brought up in a home where it was always in order for a woman to do things. Her father died when she was a child and her mother taught school in Georgia. Mrs. Lawrence has worked all her life.[38] She came to New York to teach and soon got involved in Girl Scouts and political affairs. From 1941 to 1943 she was secretary to Congressman William Pheiffer. In 1943 she became the only woman leader of a political party in New York City. In 1945 she was appointed assistant secretary of the State Workmen's Compensation Board and in 1954 became its secretary. Mrs. Lawrence was elected to the Assembly in 1958 and served until 1964. In 1961 she was an unsuccessful Republican candidate for Manhattan borough president, the first woman nominated for a borough presidency by either major party. She left the legislature to become a commissioner on the Unemployment Insurance Appeal Board.

Mrs. Lawrence did not find her sex much of a handicap in her career. [39] Her husband and his father, both engineers, had a horror of politicans, a reversal of the usual male attitude. She invited her husband to visit her political club, and he left impressed. Dorothy Lawrence found that one way to be known as a legislator was to introduce bills in fields that men did not monopolize. Among her bills were those to halt child beating by parents, to test babies for P.K.U., and to regulate the use of X-ray machines. Her stand against teacher spanking was acclaimed by the Civil Liberties Union but opposed by five women legislators. When Mrs. Lawrence was in the New York Assembly, there were as many as seven women in the legislature; now there are four. There have never been many women lawmakers in the Empire State. [40]

For about a year in 1964-65, Mrs. Constance Baker Motley was the only woman in the New York Senate. As assistant counsel of the NAACP Legal Defense and Educational fund since 1949, she has worked on virtually all the major rights cases and by early 1964 had won seven cases before the U.S. Supreme Court. She was appointed by Governors Harriman and Rockefeller to the nine-member State Advisory Council on Employment and Unemployment Insurance. In February 1964, Mrs. Motley was offered the Senate nomination after another candidate had been ruled off the ballot on an election law technicality. She was re-elected in November 1964. [41] In February 1965, she was selected by the Manhattan members of the New York Council to fill a vacancy as borough president. She won election to that office in November 1965. In 1966 she was appointed to a federal judgeship.

Mrs. Aileen B. Ryan served four terms in the New York Assembly. Prior to her entry into politics, Mrs. Ryan was a teacher, civic leader, and radio commentator. She also attended New York Law School. The local party leaders had been looking around in 1958 for someone with a community record. When they decided on her, they first asked her lawyer-husband. [42] He told her and she was delighted. Mrs. Ryan has been commended for her legislative efforts in behalf of consumer protection, curbing juvenile delinquency, medical treatment of drug addicts, school bus inspection, subway safety, and day-care centers for children. She is vice president of her local political club. In 1965 she was elected to the New York City

Council. She was unsuccessful in a bid for a congressional seat in 1966.

Another woman presently in the New York Assembly is Mrs. Constance Cook. Had she been a man, it seems likely that, with her background, she would have risen higher. Mrs. Cook received a law degree from Cornell and did graduate work at Columbia, the University of Oslo, and the Hague Academy of International Law. She became confidential law assistant to Governor Thomas E. Dewey and then served as counsel to a number of state commissions. Her husband is the president of Finger Lakes Flying Services.

In 1967 California's 10 million women were represented by three members of their sex in the State Assembly. Mrs. Pauline Davis had served since 1952 and was active in the field of natural resources. Mrs. March Fong and Mrs. Yvonne Brathwaite were in their first term. Mrs. Fong holds a Ph.D. in education from Stanford. Mrs. Brathwaite is an attorney.[43]

Where do women legislators hope to go? Some aspire to Congress or a judgeship or to be selected secretary of state. Most, though, look no farther than re-election.

Legislative Officers. A few women have been honored by being named by their legislative colleagues, male and female, to be floor leaders or presiding officers.[44]

Mrs. Maggie Smith Hathaway, a Montana state legislator since 1916, was elected Democratic floor leader in 1921. She was an unsuccessful candidate for Congress the next year. In 1925 she was appointed chief of the Bureau of Child Protection.

The second woman to be a floor leader was Miss May M. Carty, minority leader of the New Jersey Assembly in 1930. Miss Carty, a Democrat, was serving her seventh term. She gained the post by virtue of her seniority.

Mrs. Reva Beck Bosone became Democratic floor leader in the Utah House of Representatives in 1935. Nellie H. Jack of Utah was floor leader in the 1947 session. After 14 years in the House of Representatives, she advanced to the state Senate.

Miss Lucia M. Cormier was Democratic minority leader of the Maine House in 1960. Miss Cormier was a former chairman of a high school modern language department and proprietor of a stationery and bookshop. She had a strong interest in educational problems, plugging tax loopholes, and aid for the aging. She was an unsuccessful candidate for Congress in 1950 and opposed Margaret Chase Smith for the Senate in 1960,[45] Miss Cormier was president of the Maine Federation of Democratic Women's Clubs and national committeewoman from 1948 to 1956.

Mrs. Marion W. Higgins was Republican majority leader of the New Jersey Assembly in 1964. In 1965 she achieved the post of speaker. Miss Margaret A. Mahoney became Democratic majority leader of the Ohio Senate in 1949. In 1949 and 1950 she was also president pro tem of the senate. Miss Mahoney, a lawyer, served as a representative from 1938 to 1942 and as a state senator from 1943 to 1950. From 1951 to 1953 she was chief of the Division of Securities of Ohio. She served in 1953-56 and 1959-62 as director of the state Department of Industrial Relations.

The first woman speaker of a statehouse was Mrs. Minnie D. Craig of North Dakota who was elected to this post in 1933. Mrs. Craig, the wife of a banker, had served as a Republican national committeewoman and was the only woman in the legislature.

The second woman in the country so honored was Mrs. Consuelo Northrop Bailey of Vermont, who was chosen in 1953. In 1955, after being the first woman in the country to be elected lieutenant governor, she became the only woman in the country's history to have presided over both chambers of the state legislature. The Northrop family had been active in Vermont politics even before the American Revolution. She was the fourth member of her family to occupy the same House seat, which was first held by her father in 1902. Mrs. Bailey attended the University of Vermont and Boston University Law School. She was appointed in 1925 city prosecutor of Burlington by the City Council and was elected states attorney of Chittenden County in 1926. In 1930 she was elected state senator and was the only woman lawyer and the youngest woman, at 31, ever to sit in the Vermont Senate. From 1931 to 1937 she served as secretary to U.S. Senator E. W. Gibson. Since 1936 she has been a member of the Republican National Committee. She also served for a time as state vice chairman. In 1940 she married a Burlington attorney. Mrs. Bailey returned to the Vermont legislature in 1951 as representative. In 1952-53 she served as vice chairman of the Republican National Committee, and later became GOP secretary.

Mrs. Vera G. Davis, a Republican, served in the Delaware Senate from 1947 to 1949, the state's first woman senator, and became president pro tem in 1949. Her election was the result of a move by the eight-member Democratic minority in the 17-member Senate; their eight votes plus her own gave her a majority. She was elected to the House in 1953 and became state treasurer in 1956.

In 1965 Maryland had a female president pro tem of the Senate, Mary L. Nock, and Wyoming had a female speaker pro tem of the House, Mrs. Edness K. Wilkins. After six terms in the House, Mrs. Wilkins, a Democrat, was elected to the state Senate.

State Executives.[46] Few positions of importance were held by women in state government prior to the suffrage. Even today the percentage of women in key posts is quite small.[47] Florence Kelley was appointed in 1893 by Governor Altgeld of Illinois as the chief inspector of the new State Factory Inspection Department. Her father, William, had been for almost 30 years a member of Congress from Pennsylvania and earlier had been a judge in Philadelphia. Miss Kelley attacked child labor, sweatshops, inadequate safety precautions, and callous judges.

The position which Miss Kelley held is representative of the offices given to women in the decade after they received the vote. Frances Perkins served as industrial commissioner of New York from 1919 to 1921 and from 1923 to 1933 and was chairman of the State Industrial Board from 1926. Mrs. Alice Moyer-Wing was designated industrial commissioner of Missouri in 1921. Mrs. Kate Burr of North Carolina became commissioner of Public Welfare in 1921 after two years as director of Child Welfare. In 1923 Dr. Ellen C. Potter was named commissioner of Public Welfare of Pennsylvania. Mrs. Mabel Bassett was elected Oklahoma commissioner of Charities and Corrections in 1922. These women were usually succeeded by other women, thereby establishing some sort of female claim to these offices.[48]

Mrs. Charles Bennett Smith, the wife and secretary to a Buffalo publisher who became a congressman, served as president of the New York State Civil Service Commission from 1924 to 1931.[49] In 1927 Mrs. Esther M. Andrews was elected to the Massachusetts Governor's Council after having been appointed to fill an unexpired term. Mrs. R. L. Eaton of Florida was elected in 1928 to be the state railroad commissioner. The first woman to be a state budget commissioner was Jean W. Wittich of Minnesota. She served from March 1931 to May 1933.

In 1928 Miss Gladys Pyle was re-elected secretary of state of South Dakota by the greatest number of votes ever cast there for a constitutional officer. The Depression, however, set back the movement for female executive advancement. The League of Women Voters reported in 1939 a shrinkage in the number of women officeholders since 1929.

At present, there are still obstacles to the representation of women in the administrative system. The Democratic state vice chairman of Michigan has indicated that former Governor Williams sought, like President Johnson, to find women for top elective and appointive positions but found it difficult to persuade qualified women to accept apppointment.[50] If they were married, family responsibilities made it hard for them to accept. If single, they hesitated to leave their present positions because the competition within their profession was so great.

The New York Committee on the Education and Employment of Women discovered that there was discrimination against the promotion of women even in the Civil Service.[51] They analyzed 12 open competitive Civil Service examinations and found that the number of women appointed did not compare favorably with the percentage of the women who passed the test. These examinations were in fields where women are qualified and accepted, such as accounting, banking, guidance counseling, and for positions as senior attorney, business consultant, senior statistician and laboratory technician. In six of the exams where 20 per cent of the candidates were women, and half of the group, including half the women, passed the examination, the Committee found that 30 per cent received promotions but only six per cent were women.

Few women have attained state-wide elective posts. In 1953 only 31 women held such posts in 21 states. These included secretary of state, state treasurer, state auditor, superintendent of public instruction, register of state lands, state tax collector, and state librarian. Three women were members of state boards of education, four were regents of state universities,[52] and one was a member of a state board of agriculture.[53]

Superintendent of Public Instruction. There are certain positions where women are easily accepted as qualified candidates. Among these are the posts of chief librarian and superintendent of public instruction. These are fields where women workers outnumber the men and where women have had opportunities to acquire administrative experience. Even so, most of the state superintendents are male.

A few superintendents of public instruction have had political experience. One of these was Mrs. Pearl A. Wanamaker of Washington who was elected to the state House of Representatives in 1928 and served in the House until her election in 1936 to the state Senate. She became superintendent in 1941.

Estelle Reel, who was elected Wyoming state superintendent of public instruction in 1894, serving until 1898, was the first woman in the United States to be elected to a state office. Women have held the office of state superintendent in Colorado almost continuously since they received the suffrage in the 1890's. [54]

Montana's only general election for state-level office in 1964 was for superintendent of public instruction. Miss Harriet Miller, the incumbent, was elected to her post in 1956 and 1960 as a Republican. Early in 1964 she quit the Republican Party and filed as a Democrat. Miss Miller was re-elected by a bigger majority than ever before.

A predecessor of Miss Miller, Mary Condon, was dean of students at Eastern Montana College. She filed for superintendent of public instruction at the urging of some of her students. Miss Condon became president of the Council of Chief State School Officers.

Secretary of State. The responsibilities and the title of this office vary from state to state. Sometimes the position is elective, at other times appointive. One common element, though, is its remoteness from political power. It is a safe place to put a woman if a party wants to balance its ticket. [55]

Since 1922 the office of secretary of state in New Mexico has been held by a woman. [56] It was, therefore, quite natural that both parties in 1964 nominated a woman for the post. A similar tendency has taken place in South Dakota, Alabama, and Connecticut.

Since 1944 when Miss Sibyl Pool was appointed secretary of state of Alabama after serving two terms in the legislature, [57] four women have taken turns being elected secretary of state,[58] treasurer, and auditor.[59] Mrs. Agnes Baggett served in all three posts and is once again secretary of state. She served in the secretary of state's office from 1927 to 1946, and from 1946 to 1950 was assistant clerk of the Supreme Court. Mrs. Baggett was also state legislative chairman of the American Legion Auxiliary. She served as secretary of state from 1951 to 1955. Her successor as secretary of state, Mrs. Mary Texas Hurt Garner, was admitted to the Alabama bar in 1952 and was a member of the state attorney general's staff from 1953 to 1954 when she was elected secretary of state.

In 1966 men opposed women for Alabama auditor and secretary of state, arguing that if Mrs. Wallace could seek the governorship, men could seek "women's offices," but the male candidates went down to defeat.

The female monopoly of the secretaryship of state in Connecticut began in 1938 when Mrs. Sara B. Crawford was elected. At the same time her daughter, Mrs. Sara Crawford Maschol, was elected to the state legislature. Mrs. Chase Woodhouse was elected in 1940 with the highest majority of any state official. By the time Mrs. Alice Leopold ran in 1950, against three other women, the post was safely in distaff hands.

The present Connecticut secretary of state, Mrs. Ella T. Grasso, served two terms in the legislature, becoming assistant House leader in 1955. She is regarded as one of the closest advisers to John M. Bailey, the Democratic state and national chairman. In 1965 she became the Democratic floor leader at the state constitutional convention. She polled more votes than any of the other candidates on the Connecticut Democratic ticket when she won re-election in 1966.

One secretary who did not have female successors was Mrs. Belle Reeves of Washington. She was elected to the state legislature in 1922. On the death of the secretary of state in 1938 she was appointed by the governor to the post. In 1940 Mrs. Reeves was elected to the office and was re-elected in 1944, receiving the largest vote ever cast for a candidate for public office in the state up to that time. She died in 1948.

The cause of women in public office was given a setback in New York in 1928 when Mrs. Florence M. S. Knapp, first and only woman ever elected to a statewide office in the Empire State, was convicted of grand larceny and sentenced to a 30-day jail term for misappropriating funds. Mrs. Knapp, a widow, was elected secretary of state in 1924 after a distinguished career as an educator. She had been elected district superintendent of schools of Onondaga County and had later been in charge of forming Cornell University extension farm bureaus and home bureaus. Mrs. Knapp was the first woman Republican vice chairman of her county.[60]

There had been some objection made when 5,700 of the 7,600 census takers Secretary Knapp appointed in 1925 were women, but it was not for that reason that the office of secretary of state was made appointive rather than elective. Only after her term had expired and she became Dean of the College of Home Economics at Syracuse University was she accused of more than the customary charge of using the census for party patronage. Mrs. Knapp was arrested for payroll padding, diverting for her own use unearned pay alleged to have been acquired for work done on the census.

Thirty years later New York had its second woman secretary of state,[61] Mrs. Caroline K. Simon. Hers was the first appointment made by Governor Rockefeller, a sign that his administration was to be "above politics." Her predecessor had been Carmine Di Sapio, alleged "boss" of the state Democratic Party. Mrs. Simon[62] grew up in a political home.[63] Her mother, a cousin of French Socialist leader Leon Blum, was active in a political party and her father in a local improvement association. After graduating from law school, she became a volunteer for the American Civil Liberties Union, the LWV, the Women's City Club, and the Legal Aid Society. She was horrified by the "circus" atmosphere of the Women's Court. There were no women on juries because the law said only male citizens were eligible. Mrs. Simon helped to organize a state group during the thirties to change the law to omit the word "male." From 1944 to 1945 she was a member of the State Workmen's Compensation Board. In 1945 she began a 10-year membership on the State Commission Against Discrimination. From 1956 to 1959 she served as a member of the State Youth Commission.

Mrs. Simon was the first woman nominated for a citywide office by a major party when she became in 1957 Republican candidate for president of the New York City Council. She had the editorial support of the *New York Times, Herald Tribune, World-Telegram, Daily News, El Diario, Post* and *Town and Village* and was designated "highly qualified" by the non-partisan Citizens Union. In losing, she polled more votes than any citywide candidate ever had on the Republican line and ran 100,000 votes ahead of the ticket, including the candidate for mayor.

In 1958 Mrs. Simon was designated legal adviser to the U.S. Delegation to the U.N. Human Rights Commission. In 1963 she was appointed judge of the state Court of Claims. Mrs. Simon once said that a woman in politics "has to know how to look like a girl, act like a lady, think like a man and work like a dog." She never takes a day off, being aware that people will say that she is like all women, taking time off for family life. She did take a "sabbatical" from law when her two children were born, but used the time for self-improvement. Mrs. Simon declined to run for Congress because she did not want to divide her life between Washington and New York.

Mrs. Helen Holt, secretary of state of West Virginia in 1958-59, was the widow of U.S. Senator Rush Holt. She had been a college biology teacher and a member of the state House of Delegates.

Wyoming's secretary of state, Thyra Thomson, is the widow of Keith Thomson, former congressman who was elected to the U.S. Senate in 1960 just prior to his death.

Mrs. Elwill Shanahan, a registered nurse, was appointed in 1966 to fill the unexpired term of her husband as Kansas secretary of state. She won election in November to a full term.

Mrs. Mary H. Carr was appointed secretary of state of Tennessee in 1944, succeeding her husband who was inducted into the army. She was elected to a full term in 1944 by the state legislature.

Mrs. John Wise, the wife of an electrical engineer associated with the State Industrial Commission, was appointed secretary of state, after the death of Fred R. Zimmerman in 1955. She had labored valiantly for the Republicans, becoming vice chairman of the State Republican Voluntary Organization, president of the Wisconsin Federation of Republican Women, and secretary of the National Federation of Republican Women. She was also president of the Madison LWV and state legislative chairman of the AAUW. Mrs. Wise won endorsement of the 1956 state convention to run for secretary of state but was defeated in the primary.

Miss Genevieve Blatt, secretary of state of Pennsylvania, waged two lively uphill campaigns for the U.S. Senate in 1964. She was victor in the primary by 491 votes out of 921,731 cast, but lost to the incumbent, Senator Hugh Scott. Miss Blatt attracted a sizable bloc of independent support as well as a loyal feminine following. In 1962 she was the only Democrat to survive a Republican landslide. Miss Blatt is a lawyer with considerable experience in local and state political and governmental positions. From 1942 to 1950 she was president of the Young Democratic Clubs of Pennsylvania and from 1948 to the present she has been secretary of the Democratic state committee. From 1945 to 1949 she was deputy state treasurer. Miss Blatt was elected secretary of state in 1954 and was twice re-elected.

Another secretary of state to meet defeat in an attempt to enter the U.S. Congress was Goldie Wells of South Dakota. Miss Wells had also served as vice chairman of the Democratic state central committee.

Treasurer, Auditor, and Other Financial Offices. Despite all the jokes about women's not being able to handle a checkbook, they are coming into their own in state and local government in financial offices. They have two qualities which are highly praised: compared to men, women are honest and non-partisan. Not being policy-making jobs, treasurer and auditor are "safe" places to put women on the ticket.

Often the women who run for these posts have had long careers of public service. Mrs. Myrtle P. Enkling held public office in Idaho from 1915 to the early 1940's. She was at one time the only woman state treasurer in the country and was elected in 1940 to her fifth consecutive term. Miss Evelyn Gandy, Mississippi state treasurer from 1960 to 1963, defeated two male opponents by an overwhelming majority in 1959. She started in politics in 1939, at the age of 16, by campaigning for the late Governor Paul Johnson, Sr. At the University of Mississippi Law School she was student president and the first woman editor of the *Journal*. Miss Gandy spent three years as legal assistant to Senator Bilbo and then was elected to the legislature. From 1952 to 1959 she was attorney for the state department of public welfare. After winning the 1959 primary she was named assistant attorney general and served until she was sworn in as treasurer. In 1968 she started another term as state treasurer.

Dorothy Gardner, state auditor of Indiana, served 24 years as an elected or appointed official. For eight years she was a county clerk. She was in the state Senate for 12 years. For two years she was superintendent of the women's prison. From 1961 to 1964 she was state auditor.

Arizona has known only two auditors, both women, since 1927. Mrs. Ana Frohmiller served from 1927 to 1950 when she ran unsuccessfully for governor. Succeeding her was Mrs. Jewel W. Jordan. Mrs. Jordan had been appointed in 1943 as sheriff of Maricopa County, succeeding her late husband.

A number of women have moved from treasurer to auditor. The first to do so was Mrs. Berta E. Baker of North Dakota who held both offices in the 1950's. In 1953 she again served as auditor. Pennsylvania state law prevented Mrs. Grace M. Sloan, the state's first woman treasurer, from seeking re-election in 1964. Instead she ran for auditor general.[64]

Mrs. Minnie A. Mitchell was appointed in 1952 to fill the term of her late husband as Wyoming state treasurer. She won election to a full term. Since 1955 she has been state auditor. Mrs. Mitchell was vice president and president of the National Association of State Auditors, Comptrollers, and Treasurers. Similarly, Mrs. Alta E. Fisher was appointed state treasurer of Montana in 1949, replacing her late husband. Mrs. Grace Urbahns was named Indiana's treasurer in 1926 after the death of her husband.

Another treasurer who owed her initial appointment to sympathy for a widow was Mrs. Dena Smith of Wisconsin. For 32 years she was manager of music departments in Milwaukee stores. She served as her husband's secretary during the nine years he was state treasurer and was appointed in 1957 for the balance of his term. She was an unsuccessful candidate in the 1958 election. After the 1960 Republican convention chose someone else as their candidate, she defeated him in the primary and went on to win four elections. Mrs. Smith was the first woman elected in Wisconsin to a statewide constitutional office.

In 1967 Mrs. Ivy Baker Priest Stevens, former treasurer of the United States, became treasurer of California. She is married to a Beverly Hills realtor.

Attorney General. A number of women have been appointed assistant attorney general but only one, Miss Anne X. Alpern,[65] was ever named attorney general. Miss Alpern's career shows the rewards of persistence. It also illustrates the value of having a male sponsor. She became assistant city solicitor of Pittsburgh in 1934. She took only two extended leaves from this job—for a honeymoon in 1937 and for two months' maternity leave. In 1942 Mayor David Lawrence made her Pittsburgh's first woman solicitor. Eleven years later she was elected after bipartisan endorsement to be a judge on Allegheny County's Common Pleas Court. When Lawrence became governor of Pennsylvania, he named his former city solicitor to be state attorney general. Miss Alpern was the first woman to practice before the Federal Power Commission and the first woman to be elected president of the National Institute of Municipal Law Offices, an organization of the legal officers of 750 cities throughout the U.S. and Canada. Governor Lawrence, her patron of long standing, elevated her to the Pennsylvania Supreme Court.

Governor. In 1920 the Democrats of Rhode Island nominated Elizabeth Upham Yates for governor, the first time such an honor has ever gone to a woman. She ran ahead of her ticket but lost. Mrs. Alice Lorraine Daly was nominated for governor of South Dakota in 1921 by the state's Nonpartisan League Party, the second largest party in the state. She was active in the LWV.

In the 46 years since then, only three women have ever succeeded in being elected governor, each time thanks to husbands who preceded them in that post. Mrs. Nellie Tayloe Ross became governor of Wyoming, the first territory in the U.S. to give women the vote,[66] after the death of her husband in 1925. Being in mourning, Mrs. Ross did no active campaigning. Her campaign manager was Joseph O'Mahoney, who later became a U.S. senator. She had had no previous political experience. Subsequently, however, she served as vice chairman of the Democratic National Committee, 1928-32, and as director of the U.S. mint, 1933-53. In 1928 her name was placed in nomination for vice president.

Miriam A. ("Ma") Ferguson of Texas had the assistance of her husband, an impeached and thereby disqualified former governor. Their slogan was "Two governors for the price of one." Another slogan, reflecting their opposition to the Ku Klux Klan, was "A

Bonnet or a Hood." Mrs. Ferguson, whose husband had disapproved of the women's rights movement, [67] was elected in 1924 but defeated in 1926 [68] and 1930. She won again in 1932 but came in fourth in the Democratic primary in 1940. About the only thing for which her administration is remembered is the release of 3,600 convicts on full pardons, conditional pardons, and furloughs. The previous governor had freed only 400 in four years.

Not too many women since Mrs. Ferguson have won their party's nomination for governor. Republican Gladys Pyle was defeated for governor of South Dakota in 1930. Democrat Josephine Roche ran for Colorado governor in 1934; she carried the cities but lost the country districts. [69] Democrat Ana Frohmiller lost her race for governor of Arizona in 1950 to Republican Howard Pyle by some 3,000 votes, despite the fact that Arizona is primarily a Democratic state. [70]

When Governor George Wallace of Alabama [71] was thwarted in 1966 in his attempt to have the state constitution changed to permit his re-election, he put up his wife as the nominal candidate. Lurleen Wallace, a former dime store clerk whose only political experience had been visiting the 67 counties of the state in her husband's 1962 campaign, admitted that she would only serve as caretaker, a vote for her would be a vote for him. Their slogan was "Let George do it." The Wallace candidacy swept the Democratic primary and easily won the general election. [72]

Mrs. Consuelo N. Bailey, lieutenant governor of Vermont in 1955-56, is the only woman to be elected to that understudy post.[73] By Vermont tradition, a lieutenant governor campaigned for the governorship. Mrs. Bailey ignored the precedent and chose not to run for the office. Matilda R. Wilson was appointed lieutenant governor of Michigan November 19, 1940, to fill an expiring term. Maude Frazier, a Nevada state legislator, was appointed in July 1962, to serve out the unexpired term of the late lieutenant governor.

Women in the Judiciary. Of the nations's 8,748 judges, only 300 are women. [74] Most of these serve at the local level, often being restricted to family and juvenile courts. Florence E. Allen of Ohio became the first woman to be elected to state Supreme Court when she won in 1922. [75] She was re-elected in 1928 and in 1934 became a U.S. Circuit Court judge.

Sarah T. Hughes' appointment in 1935 to complete an unexpired term as judge of the Texas District Court created a furor. One state senator announced that he would vote and work against her confirmation by the legislature because "she ought to be at home washing dishes." Mrs. Hughes, a member of the legislature, responded: "If his wife had stayed at home washing dishes, he would not have been elected to the senate." The senator's wife had been an unceasing worker in her husband's campaign. And just to prove that Judge Hughes could wash dishes, one newspaper carried a front-page picture of her before a steaming pan of dishes in her kitchen. Her previous experience in police work, law, and politics including three terms in the legislature, and support by business and professional women, led to her confirmation by a large majority. [76] Mrs. Hughes was known for advocating jury service for women. After 26 years as Texas district court judge, she was nominated in 1961 to be a U.S. district court judge. She came into the news prominently in 1963 when she administered the presidential oath of office to Lyndon B. Johnson.

Annie Lola Price was appointed to the Alabama court of appeals in 1951 and was subsequently elected. She had been a court reporter for 12 years and from 1947 to 1950 was legal adviser to Governor James Folsom. Miss Price is now the presiding judge.

Judge Florence K. Murray was the first woman ever named to the Rhode Island Superior Court. She was one of eight women lawyers in the state and had been lieutenant colonel of the Women's Army Corps and state senator. Her husband, Paul F. Murray, was judge of the Newport Probate Court.

Mrs. Jennie Loitman Barron is on the Massachusetts Superior Court, a lifetime post. In 1926 she was the first woman to be elected to the Boston school committee, receiving more votes than the mayor! Mrs. Barron formerly served as judge on the Boston Municipal Court. She was known for her interest in rehabilitating young offenders and in reconciling hundreds of families. Mrs. Barron was once named American Mother of the Year. Her husband, Samuel Barron, is a lawyer.

Governor Rockefeller appointed two women to the New York Court of Claims, Mrs. Dorothea E. Donaldson and Mrs. Caroline K. Simon.

Only three women now sit in state supreme courts—North Carolina's Justice Susie M. Sharp, [77] Hawaii's Justice Rhoda V. Lewis, and Arizona's Lorna Lockwood. Anne X. Alpern of Pennsylvania served in 1961. [78] Miss Lockwood, who became in 1960 the second woman in the U.S. to be elected to a state's highest court, was elected by her colleagues in 1965 to be chief justice. She had previously been assistant state attorney general, state representative for three terms, superior court judge for 10 years, and public affairs chairman of the National Federation of Business and Professional Women's Clubs. Her father, Alfred C. Lockwood, was chief justice three times during his 18 years on the Supreme Court. She was re-elected to the court in 1966.

One of her colleagues said of Justice Lockwood: "Her most enduring quality is patience, patience and patience. She will listen to both sides of every question. Furthermore, she has overcome the emotional reaction common to many women. She has all the qualities that make a great judge." [79]

Women have little part in the government of most states other than through their right to vote. Men are the movers; women are the ornaments. They have been accorded token recognition. Their apointments have usually clustered around certain activities regarded as "women's areas"—those dealing with juveniles, school affairs, health, welfare, and libraries. Men have to be reminded to appoint women; ordinarily, males do not think of females for governmental positions. Some men, however, have given women opportunities to hold important offices.

Just as we have traced the relative absence of women at the national level in part to their secondary role at the state level, normally a training ground, so we turn to the local level for part of the answer to the limited role of women at the state level.

5d. Important State Executive Offices Held by Women

Alaska, Florida, Georgia, Hawaii, Illinois, Maine, Massachusetts, Missouri, New Hampshire, North Carolina, Ohio, Oregon, Rhode Island, South Carolina, and Utah have elected no women to important state executive offices. Given the fragmentary nature of the reporting, this roster can claim to be no more than 90 per cent complete:

ALABAMA

GOVERNOR

Mrs. Lurleen Wallace	Democrat	1967-

SECRETARY OF STATE

Miss Sibyl Pool	Democrat	1944-50
Mrs. Agnes Baggett	Democrat	1951-54
Mrs. Mary Texas Hurt Garner	Democrat	1955-58
Mrs. Bettye Frink	Democrat	1959-62
Mrs. Agnes Baggett	Democrat	1963-66
Mrs. Mabel Amos	Democrat	1967-

TREASURER

Miss Sibyl Pool	Democrat	1951-54
Mrs. Agnes Baggett	Democrat	1959-62
Mrs. Mary Texas Hurt Garner	Democrat	1963-64
Mrs. Agnes Baggett	Democrat	1967-

AUDITOR

Mrs. Agnes Baggett	Democrat	1955-58
Mrs. Mary Texas Hurt Garner	Democrat	1959-62
Mrs. Bettye Frink	Democrat	1963-66
Mrs. Melba Till Allen	Democrat	1967-

ARIZONA

AUDITOR

Mrs. Ana Frohmiller	Democrat	1927-50
Mrs. Jewel W. Jordan	Democrat	1951-

SUPERINTENDENT OF PUBLIC INSTRUCTION

Mrs. Sarah Folsom	Republican	1965-

ARKANSAS

TREASURER

Mrs. Nancy J. Hall	Democrat	1962-

CALIFORNIA

TREASURER

Mrs. Ivy Baker Priest Stevens	Republican	1967-

COLORADO

TREASURER

Mrs. Virginia Blue	Republican	1967-

SUPERINTENDENT OF PUBLIC INSTRUCTION

Mrs. Mary C. C. Bradford		1915-24
Katherine L. Craig	Republican	1927-30
Mrs. Inez J. Lewis	Democrat	1931-46
Mrs. Nettie S. Freed	Republican	1946-51

CONNECTICUT

SECRETARY OF STATE

Mrs. Sara B. Crawford		1939-40
Mrs. Chase Going Woodhouse	Democrat	1941-42
Mrs. Frances Burke Bedick		1943-44, 1947-48
Winifred McDonald	Democrat	1949-50
Mrs. Alice K. Leopold	Republican	1951-53
Mildred P. Allen	Republican	1955-58
Mrs. Ella T. Grasso	Democrat	1959-

DELAWARE

SECRETARY OF STATE

Miss Fannie Harrington		1925-

TREASURER

Mrs. Vera G. Davis	Republican	1957-58
Mrs. Belle Everett	Democrat	1959-

IDAHO

TREASURER

Myrtle P. Enking	Democrat	1933-44
Mrs. Ruth G. Moon	Democrat	1945-46
Mrs. Lela D. Painter	Republican	1947-52
Margaret Gilbert	Republican	1952-54
Mrs. Ruth G. Moon	Democrat	1955-59
Miss Marjorie Ruth Moon	Democrat	1955-

SUPERINTENDENT OF PUBLIC INSTRUCTION

Mae L. Scott	Republican	1903-06
S. Belle Chamberlain	Republican	1907-10
Grace M. Shephard	Republican	1911-14

Bernice McCoy	Republican	1915-16
Miss Ethel E. Redfield	Republican	1917-22
Elizabeth Russum	Republican	1923-26
Mabelle M. Lyman	Republican	1927-28
Myrtle R. Davis	Republican	1929-32

INDIANA

TREASURER

Mrs. Grace B. Urbahns	Republican	1926-30
F. Shirley Wilcox		1949-50

AUDITOR

Dorothy Gardner	Republican	1961-64

IOWA

SECRETARY OF STATE

Mrs. Ola Miller	Democrat	1933-37

SUPERINTENDENT OF PUBLIC INSTRUCTION

Miss May E. Francis	Republican	1923-26
Agnes Samuelson	Republican	1927-38
Jessie M. Parker	Republican	1939-54

KANSAS

SECRETARY OF STATE

Mrs. Elwill Shanahan	Republican	1966-

SUPERINTENDENT OF PUBLIC INSTRUCTION

Miss Elizabeth Wooster		1921-22

STATE PRINTER (an elected office)

Lily M. Washabough	Democrat	1957-61

KENTUCKY

SECRETARY OF STATE

Mrs. Emma Guy Cromwell	Democrat	1925-28
Miss Ella Lewis	Democrat	1929-32
Miss Sara W. Mahon	Democrat	1933-36
Mrs. Thelma L. Stovall	Democrat	1957-60; 1965-

TREASURER

Mrs. Emma Guy Cromwell	Democrat	1929-32
Miss Pearl Frances Runyon	Democrat	1951-56

AUDITOR

Miss Mary Louise Foust	Democrat	1957-60

LOUISIANA

SECRETARY OF STATE

Miss Alice Lee Grosjean	Democrat	1930

REGISTER OF STATE LANDS

Mrs. Lucille May Grace	Democrat	1931-52
Mrs. Ellen Bryan Moore	Democrat	1952-56
Mrs. Lucille May Grace	Democrat	1956-57
Mrs. Ellen Bryan Moore	Democrat	1960-

MARYLAND

SECRETARY OF STATE

Miss Vivian V. Simpson	Democrat	1949-50

MICHIGAN

LIEUTENANT GOVERNOR

Matilda R. Wilson		1940

SUPERINTENDENT OF PUBLIC INSTRUCTION

Clair L. Taylor	Republican	1957-58

MINNESOTA

SECRETARY OF STATE

Mrs. Virginia Holm	Republican	1953-54

MISSISSIPPI

TREASURER

Miss Evelyn Gandy	Democrat	1960-63; 1968-

MONTANA

TREASURER

Mrs. Alta E. Fisher		1949
Mrs. Edna J. Hinman	Republican	1954-57; 1961-64

SUPERINTENDENT OF PUBLIC INSTRUCTION

Miss May Trumper		1921-22
Miss Ruth Reardon		1937-40
Miss Elizabeth Ireland		1941-48
Miss Mary M. Condon	Democrat	1949-56
Miss Harriet Miller	Republican	1957-
	Democrat (since 1964)	

NEBRASKA

TREASURER

Bertha I. Hill	Republican	1958-59

NEVADA

LIEUTENANT GOVERNOR

Maude Frazier	Democrat	1962

SUPERINTENDENT OF INSTRUCTION

Mildred Bray	Democrat	1937-50

NEW JERSEY

TREASURER (Acting)

Mrs. Katharine E. White	Democrat	1962

NEW MEXICO

SECRETARY OF STATE

Mrs. Soledad C. Chacon	Democrat	1923-26
Mrs. Jennie Fortune	Democrat	1927-28
Mrs. E. A. Perrault	Democrat	1929-30
Mrs. Marguerite P. Baca	Democrat	1931-34
Mrs. Elizabeth F. Gonzales	Democrat	1935-38
Mrs. Jessie M. Gonzales	Democrat	1939-42
Mrs. Cecilia T. Cleveland	Democrat	1943-46
Mrs. Alicia Romero	Democrat	1947-50
Mrs. Beatrice B. Roach	Democrat	1951-54
Mrs. Natalie S. Buck	Democrat	1955-58
Mrs. Betty Fiorina	Democrat	1959-62
Mrs. Alberta Miller	Democrat	1963-66
Mrs. Ernestine D. Evans	Democrat	1967-

SUPERINTENDENT OF PUBLIC INSTRUCTION

Miss Isabel Eckles		1923-26
Mrs. Georgia L. Lusk	Democrat	1931-34; 1943-46
Mrs. Grace J. Corrigan		1939-42

NEW YORK

SECRETARY OF STATE

Mrs. Florence M. S. Knapp	Republican	1925-26
Mrs. Caroline K. Simon	Republican	1959-63

NORTH DAKOTA

TREASURER

Mrs. Berta E. Baker	Republican	1929-32

AUDITOR

Mrs. Berta E. Baker	Republican	1955-56

SUPERINTENDENT OF PUBLIC INSTRUCTION

Laura J. Eisenhuth		1893-94
Emma B. Bates		1895-96
Miss Minnie J. Nielson	Republican	1919-26
Bertha R. Palmer	Republican	1927-32

OKLAHOMA

AUDITOR

Imogene E. Holmes	Democrat	1962-63

PENNSYLVANIA

SECRETARY OF STATE

Sophia M. R. O'Hara	Republican	1939-42

SECRETARY OF INTERNAL AFFAIRS

Miss Genevieve Blatt	Democrat	1959-

TREASURER

Mrs. Grace M. Sloan	Democrat	1961-64

AUDITOR

Mrs. Grace M. Sloan	Democrat	1965-

ATTORNEY GENERAL

Anne X. Alpern	Democrat	1959-60

SOUTH DAKOTA

SECRETARY OF STATE

Miss Gladys Pyle	Republican	1927-30
Mrs. Elizabeth Goyne		1931-34
Myrtle Morrison		1935-36
Miss Goldie Wells	Democrat	1937-38
Olive Ringsrud		1939-40
Annamae Riiff	Republican	1948-50
Geraldine Ostroot	Republican	1951-56
Clara Halls	Republican	1957-58
Selma Sandness	Democrat	1959-60
Mrs. Essie Wiedenman	Republican	1961-64
Miss Alma Larson	Republican	1965-

AUDITOR

Fay Albee	Republican	1957-58
Mrs. Harriet Horning	Democrat	1959-60
Mrs. Betty Lou Larson	Republican	1961

STATE TREASURER

Hazel Dean		1945-46

TENNESSEE

COMPTROLLER

Mrs. Jeanne S. Bodfish	Democrat	1954

SECRETARY OF STATE

Mrs. Mary H. Carr		1944-46

TEXAS

GOVERNOR

Mrs. Miriam A. Ferguson	Democrat	1925-26; 1933-34

SECRETARY OF STATE

Mrs. Emma Grigsby Meharg	Democrat	1925-26
Mrs. Jane Y. McCallum	Democrat	1927-33

VERMONT

LIEUTENANT GOVERNOR

Mrs. Consuelo N. Bailey	Republican	1955-56

AUDITOR

Anne Powers	Republican	1941-43

VIRGINIA

SECRETARY OF THE COMMONWEALTH

Mrs. Thelma Y. Gordon	Democrat	1947-52
Miss Martha Bell Conway	Democrat	1953-

WASHINGTON

SECRETARY OF STATE

Mrs. Belle C. Reeves	Democrat	1938-48

SUPERINTENDENT OF PUBLIC INSTRUCTION

Mrs. Josephine C. Preston	Republican	1913-29
Mrs. Pearl A. Wanamaker	Democrat	1941-57

WEST VIRGINIA

SECRETARY OF STATE

Mrs. Helen Holt	Republican	1958-59

WISCONSIN

SECRETARY OF STATE

Mrs. Glenn M. Wise	Republican	1955-56

TREASURER

Mrs. Dena A. Smith	Republican	1957-58; 1961

WYOMING

GOVERNOR

Mrs. Nellie Tayloe Ross	Democrat	1925-26

SECRETARY OF STATE

Mrs. Thyra Thomson	Republican	1963-

AUDITOR

Mrs. Minnie A. Mitchell	Republican	1955-

TREASURER

Mrs. Minnie A. Mitchell	Republican	1952-54

SUPERINTENDENT OF PUBLIC INSTRUCTION

Estelle Reel	Republican	1895-98
Rose A. Bird Maley	Democrat	1911-15
Edith K. O. Clark	Republican	1915-18
Mrs. Katharine A. Morton	Republican	1919-35
Esther Andersen	Republican	1939-46
Miss Edna B. Stolt	Republican	1947-54
Miss Velma Linford	Democrat	1955-63

5e. Women in Local Government

Women seem to have made their greatest gains in local government where competition is not great. Local political positions are often concerned with matters that are of special interest to women, are frequently part time, and are poorly paid. Said one woman mayor: "I might say that our election was due to the fact that in small towns men best fitted for public office often refuse to serve on the ground that they would 'hurt their business.' We had no business to hurt." [1]

In 1952 there were 235 women in state legislatures, only 28 in other state elective offices, but about 10,000 women were serving as county officials in the 3,072 counties of the United States. [2] Most of them were county clerks, tax collectors and assessors, treasurers, recorders, auditors, registers of deeds, clerks of court, and superintendents of schools. A few were judges of probate or orphans' court, public administrators, and controllers. Occasionally, a woman was elected county commissioner.

By 1959 it was reported that over 20,000 women were serving in county positions and another 10,000 in city posts. [3] The New York State Governor's Committee on the Education and Employment of Women reported in 1964 that the number of women officials and administrators increased by 37 per cent in the preceding decade. Here, if anywhere, was a breakthrough.

"Petticoat politics" has always been the stuff of feature stories. There is usually a set formula. The town is decaying, everyone knows something is basically wrong, but no one will do anything. Finally,

the women come together, since the men have abdicated responsibility. A reform slate of females is agreed on. To the shock of
everyone, the amateurs are elected. They confound prophecy by
doing a superb job and then, a la Cincinnatus, retire from politics.

This morality play unfolded in Jackson, Wyoming, in 1920[4]
when five women defeated an all-male ticket, including two husbands
of women candidates, for the city government.[5] The women were
re-elected. Similarly, in Yoncalla, Oregon, five females triumphed
over male incumbents who were too shocked to make any public
statement.[6]

An all-woman government was chosen in Des Lacs, New York,
in 1922 although most of the women refused to vote.[7] Columbus
City, Iowa, got a five-woman town government in 1924 from what
started as a male joke. A larger vote was cast than ever before. One
woman defeated her husband for a seat on the council. Three of the
five victors were schoolteachers. The mayor and council were
interviewed and photographed dozens of times for newspaper and
magazine feature stories.[8] If they did nothing else, they at least put
their town on the map.

There were two main lines of accomplishment: a physical
city-cleaning and a moral clean-up. Dr. Amy Kaukonen, mayor of
Fairport, Ohio, at 25 also took on the positions of chief of police,
board of health director, and chemist. She cracked down on
bootleggers.[9] At the other end of the age scale was Mrs. Mary
McFadden, 80-year-old mayor of Magnetic Springs, Ohio.

The women's government of Grover, Colorado, did such a
popular job after its election in 1928 that it was still in power in
1934. Mayor Ella Jacobsen of Waterloo, Nebraska, won as a write-in
candidate against her husband. Winslow, Arkansas, had distaff
government from 1925 to 1929, and Denning, Arkansas, had it from
1937 to 1941. When the female chief of police slapped the female
mayor of Friendly, West Virginia, it made news.

Stephenson, Michigan, a village of 700, elected a slate of women
to all its offices in 1929. They were pledged to a community
improvement program. Despite the Depression, they created a park
in the center of town, installed a new fire siren, acquired a village
dump, inaugurated an annual clean-up campaign, improved the
streets, installed additional water mains, and repaired the city hall.

And they also balanced the budget. In 1936 the "City Mothers" announced their retirement from office. Mrs. Grace Sanders, six times elected village president, stated that they had entered politics to further community projects, not merely to be office holders.[10]

In Cotter, Iowa, a slate of women won in a write-in campaign, defeating a slate composed of their husbands, but then decided they did not want the offices. The tables were turned in Altomont, Missouri, and Hughes, Arkansas, when all-male tickets triumphed in 1930 over all-female tickets. Four years later an all-male slate in Bradgate, Iowa, bested the all-female ticket which had been victorious in 1930.

In recent years such communities as Washington, Virginia; Walsenburg, Colorado; Ellisville, Illinois; and Seal Beach, California, have gotten publicity for turning over local affairs to their women. The women of Walsenburg, a town of 5,000, had a violent disagreement in 1959 with the male officials. Women of both parties united to support an all-woman slate which won every office. Once in power, the female administration pulled the town out of the red.

Legislative Board Members. In the first decade of suffrage women served as councillors and aldermen in Macon, Georgia; Gloucester and Cambridge, Massachusetts; Des Moines, Iowa; Cleveland, Ohio; and New York City, New York.

Mrs. E. W. Bemis was elected in 1922 the first woman commissioner of Cook County, Illinois (Chicago). She was the only one of six female candidates to triumph. Earlier in 1922 she had been appointed to fill a vacancy. Mrs. Bemis was for many years a director of the Chicago Woman's City Club.

When Ruth McCormick was nominated for Congress by the Republicans, Democratic leaders in Chicago countered by nominating four women for the Cook County Board of Commissioners. They were elected in part because of an "All-Parties Committee of Women." One of the county commissioners was Mrs. Elizabeth Conkey. Mrs. Conkey, whose brother was a state senator and whose husband was captain of a Great Lakes steamboat, had been long active in Democratic politics. She was president of the Democratic Women's Club of Chicago, now the Federation of Illinois Women's Democratic Clubs, and Democratic national committeewoman, 1928-60. In 1930 she became the first woman jury commissioner in

Cook County and in 1931 became commissioner of public welfare.

From the thirties until the fifties not many women succeeded in getting elected to city councils. When Miss Rosalind Wiener[11] won a seat on the Los Angeles City Council in 1953, she became the first woman on that panel in 36 years. At 22 she was America's youngest legislator. She had been active in the Los Angeles Young Democrats and left law school to run for the council. Mrs. Wyman is still on the council.

Mrs. Alice B. Wainwright, a Democrat, became Miami's first woman city commissioner. In 1957 Mrs. Constance H. Dallas was elected the first woman to serve on the Philadelphia City Council.

Mrs. Myrna Harms, a politically inexperienced 54-year-old homemaker, became the first woman ever elected to the Peoria, Illinois, City Council in 1953. She had taught high school and was a public relations officer in the WAVES. Her husband ran a flower shop. Mrs. Harms ran as a nonpartisan.

In 1960 Miss Mary Kanane became the first woman elected as a freeholder (commissioner) of Union County, New Jersey. There were eight men on the board. Her father had been a postmaster appointed by Theodore Roosevelt. She was a secretary in the surrogate judge's office. As a candidate, she met commuters' trains in different cities, attended picnics, and wrote items for the papers. She was re-elected in 1962. In 1963 Miss Kanane was elected surrogate judge. There was only one other woman surrogate in the state, appointed to complete her husband's term. [12]

Mrs. Elsa Johnson, a Republican who had been active in women's organizations and in education and neighborhood programs, was elected Minneapolis alderman in 1961. She was the first woman to serve on the city council in the city's 110-year history. Mrs. Johnson won re-election in 1963.

Mrs. Vel Phillips became the first woman alderman in the 110-year history of the Milwaukee Common Council when she was elected in 1958. From 1958 to 1964 Mrs. Phillips was Democratic national committeewoman from Wisconsin.

Among the 183 cities in Wisconsin none have women mayors, but there are 27 women on city councils.[13] On the county level, 13 of the 72 counties in the state had one or more women as county board members in 1964, for a total of 22 women.[14]

Mrs. Ray Andrews Brown was elected to the Madison Common Council in 1951, the first woman ever elected. She had had a long career as a high school teacher before her election. In 1962 Mrs. Brown was elected by her aldermanic colleagues to be president of the common council.

In 1949 Miss Mary B. Beck became the first woman elected to the Detroit Common Council. She was a lawyer who was fluent in six languages other than English, and made each one count in her campaigns. Miss Beck was accustomed to making speeches four nights a week. In 1952 she became president pro tem of the common council, after polling the greatest number of votes of all candidates running for the council. She is now in her fourth term on the council.

Mrs. Melanie Kreuzer, a Republican councilman-at-large in Syracuse, New York, since 1950, was elected president of the common council in 1953. She was married to a manufacturer and had been a civic worker of 25 years' standing, being active in the Community Chest, Red Cross, Girl Scouts, and other groups.

Mrs. Mary A. Hepburn is president pro tem of the Montgomery County Council in Maryland.[15] Her father held a non-elective position in the U.S. Capitol and her interest in politics was sparked at a very early age. She is a lawyer and has served on the County Board of Appeals. Miss Hepburn is active in the Republican Party and was president of the State Federation of Republican Women.

In 1955 in New York State an unprecedented total of 445 women ran as Democratic candidates for local office. Most were fated to lose since they were usually not given hopeful districts.[16]

One councilwoman felt that the women of her ward were solidly behind her and her efforts. She thought that women found it easier to talk over their problems with another woman and that this was a good argument for putting a woman on a civil service commission.[17] She acknowledged that "women can't hold to feminine advantages in practical politics. You have to be a politician first and a woman second." Some men resented her presence as the only woman on the council. Since she had a husband to support her, they did not feel that she should be there. At first they thought she was just a wealthy woman indulging a whim. When it turned out that she was a hard worker, had more education than most of her colleagues, and was not submissive in temperament, thinskinned males were annoyed all the more.[18]

Another councilwoman felt that neither men nor women react well to women in politics. "There is no chivalry as women have removed themselves from a feminine category and have placed themselves in a competitive position." She thought that women often support their sex prior to an election but that after a woman is elected, she becomes more of a target than a male officer. Some women politicians are too aggressive. She encountered pettiness, gossip, envy and rivalry.[19]

In 1925 Mrs. Ruth Pratt became the first woman on the New York Board of Aldermen.[20] She was associate leader of her "silk stocking" district and was designated candidate for alderman by the male leader. It took a while for her 64 colleagues to get over the novelty of having a woman among them. "At committee meetings, where informality rules," Mrs. Pratt wrote in 1927, "the members have paid me the compliment of smoking, and the greater one of swearing in a restrained and gentlemanly manner, if the necessity for profanity arises."[21]

Few women have served on either the New York City Board of Aldermen or its successor, the City Council. In 1949 Genevieve Earle was the only woman member, having served for over a decade. At the present time, two women are on the 37-member council.

Mayors. The first woman mayor was Susanna M. Salter of Argonia, Kansas, who was elected in May 1887, and served for a year for a dollar. Most of the women mayors have served in small communities. It is rare to have a female mayor in a city of over 30,000. In 1952 there were only ten women mayors in the country.[22] In 1964 there were 112.[23]

The first major city to have a woman mayor was Seattle. Mrs. Bertha K. Landes[24] was president of the Seattle City Council in 1924.[25] She became acting mayor while the incumbent was attending the Democratic National Convention. Mrs. Landes took advantage of her office to promote a police captain to acting chief and embark on a crusade against bootlegging and other crimes. The bootleggers called their nemesis "Big Bertha." The mayor returned and reinstated the old police chief. Two years later Mrs. Landes, a Republican running in a non-partisan election, defeated the old mayor for the job. Her campaign was handled by clubwomen. She was defeated for a second term.[26]

In 1948 Portland, Oregon, elected a veteran female official and crusader against vice. Mrs. Dorothy M. Lee, a lawyer and daughter of an admiral, was chairman of the Oregon Crime Commission from 1931 to 1935 while in the state legislature. She served two terms in the Oregon house and five in the senate. She was a supporter of civil rights and an opponent of racetrack and slot machine gamblers. For several years, she served as a member of the Portland Traffic Safety Commission. In her last term in the senate, Mrs. Lee came within one vote of being elected president of the senate, equivalent to lieutenant governor in other states. In 1940 she became a municipal judge. The City Council of Portland appointed her commissioner of Public Utilities in 1943. That year she was also appointed to a vacancy on the city council, resigning from the senate. She was elected in 1944 to the remainder of the term and elected to a full four-year term in 1946. Mrs. Lee, aided by a bipartisan campaign committee, was elected mayor in 1948, defeating the former mayor, a Republican like herself. Her husband, a chemical engineer, tried to arrange his schedule to coincide with hers, and attempted to join her on out-of-town trips. She was defeated for re-election by a candidate with the slogan "a man for a man's job."[27] President Eisenhower appointed Mrs. Lee to the Federal Parole Board.

A third West Coast city to have a woman mayor was Sacramento, California. Bell Cooledge, a former schoolteacher and vice president of Sacramento Junior College, was elected to the city council in 1948 by a larger plurality than any of her fellow councilmen. They promptly elected her mayor.

Two other Pacific mayors in the sixties were Mrs. Ruth Benell of Pico Rivers, California, and Miss Joanna Boatman of Kalama, Washington. Both had served on their city councils prior to their elevation. Mrs. Benell was a schoolteacher and Miss Boatman was a nurse.

Fewer women have become mayors in other sections of the country. Mrs. Edith P. Welty became mayor of Yonkers, New York, in 1949, to fill out the unexpired term of the mayor who resigned. The office of mayor went to the candidate for the council who received the largest number of proportional representation votes. She had been a member of the council since 1939, having been elected to five two-year terms. Ironically, the previous week Mrs. Welty had been defeated in the Republican primary as a candidate for another term.

In 1957 Mrs. Katherine Elkus White became the first Democrat in 20 years to be elected mayor of Red Bank, New Jersey, a community of 12,700. While still mayor she became commissioner of the New Jersey Highway Authority. Mrs. White was appointed by President Johnson to be ambassador to Denmark.

Mrs. Eleanor P. Sheppard became mayor of Richard, Virginia, in 1962. She was chosen by the city council on the 25th ballot. In 1954 she became the first woman elected to the city council, and in 1960 she was named the city's vice mayor. She could have had the mayor's job in 1960 but turned it down. Mrs. Sheppard's husband was a candy salesman. He was delighted at her selection.

Mrs. Norma B. Handloff, former state president of the Delaware LWV, is mayor of Newark, Delaware. Mrs. Patricia Sheehan has received praise for her performance as mayor of New Brunswick, New Jersey. In 1967 Mrs. Fern Buckler took office as mayor of Laurel, Mississippi.

The year 1967 was an auspicious one for women at the mayoralty level. Mrs. Louise Day Hicks, a lawyer, ran first in a non-partisan primary ballot for mayor of Boston. Since about 55 per cent of the city's registered voters are women and since polls showed that most of Hicks' supporters were women, her election seemed quite likely. Her father, the late William J. Day, was a Boston municipal judge. A younger brother who is a lawyer was her campaign manager. Mrs. Hicks' husband, a design engineer, took charge of her headquarters when she was out campaigning. Her slogan, "Boston for Bostonians," reflected the stand she had taken as a city school board president. It was this position that gave her notoriety as well as backing. Mrs. Hicks' election was opposed by both Democratic Senator Edward Kennedy and Republican Governor Volpe. She went down to defeat.

Victorious in 1967 were Republican Ann Uccello of Hartford, Connecticut, and Democrat Eileen Foley of Portsmouth, New Hampshire. Miss Uccello won a narrow victory in a Democratic stronghold. Her four years on the city council and an appeal to

Italian voters were factors in her election. She had had a long career in various positions with a local department store.

Mrs. Foley, a state senator, was following in the footsteps of her late mother who held the mayoral post more than 20 years before. The mother failed by one vote to get the senate seat her daughter later occupied. Like Miss Uccello, Mrs. Foley moved from the city council to serve as mayor, a largely honorary position. She is also a member of the city school board.

Mrs. Dorothy Nichols Dolbey was first elected to the Cincinnati City Council in 1953, after having been defeated in 1951, on the Charter Party ticket, a good-government group. She was re-elected for three consecutive terms before retiring in 1961. Mrs. Dolbey was the only woman ever re-elected to the council and the only woman to become vice mayor and acting mayor. She ran unsuccessfully for the council in 1963.

Mrs. Louis Reynold, an alderman and real estate dealer, served as acting mayor of Louisville, Kentucky, in January 1965, while the mayor and aldermanic president were briefly out of town. She was the first Negro and the first woman to hold the position. Also in 1965, the wife of the former mayor of Streater, Illinois, ran for his post. He was in jail following conviction for embezzlement.

A number of women have served as vice mayor. Mrs. Dorothy G. Allen served as vice mayor of Winchester, Virginia, for at least six years, beginning in 1956. Mrs. Helen Hale is Hawaii County superintendent, a post comparable to mayor. She taught English at Tennessee A. and I. College before moving to Hawaii in 1947 with her teacher-husband. He ran unsuccessfully in 1950 for the state constitutional convention. Later, he made speeches for his wife and took care of their six-year-old son. Mrs. Hale entered politics when she became the first woman member of the island's County Board of Supervisors. She won by only 212 votes. Mrs. Hale is active in civic organizations including the Business and Professional Women's Club. Her ancestry is an asset in the Hawaiian kaleidoscope. She is part Negro, part Indian, and a few other nationalities."[28]

Another post comparable to that of mayor is borough president of Manhattan. In 1965 Mrs. Constance Baker Motley was named to that position. When she ran later in the year for election to a full term, Mrs. Motley was paid the unusual tribute of receiving the nomination of the Democratic, Republican, and Liberal Parties.

The first woman to be a city manager was Mrs. R. E. Barrett, who served in that capacity in Warrenstown, Ohio, in the 1920's. Mrs. Betty A. Meagher was appointed city manager of New Rochelle, New York, after a 33-year administrative career in the city government. She started as a stenographer and moved to secretary to the city manager. She was administrative assistant to seven city managers and was acting city manager for six months before her appointment. After a nationwide appeal had been made for applicants, she was the unanimous choice of the council. Mrs. Meagher appointed a male assistant, considering it an advantage to have someone who could make field trips to construction sites. Her husband was an assistant comptroller of the United States Lines. [29]

As of December 1, 1963, only 11 municipalities, including New Rochelle, had female city managers.[30] Six of the 11 are in Maine. One of the Maine managers worked as town clerk, treasurer, and assistant manager prior to assuming the number one position. Only one of the 11 lady managers, an attorney, held a college degree.

Administration. In the 1964 elections in Wisconsin, 79 women were elected to county positions. All but two of the 79 were either registers of deeds, clerks of court, treasurers, or county clerks. In the 183 cities of Wisconsin, 55 women serve as city treasurers and 55 are either city clerks or deputy clerks. The majority of women village officials serve as treasurers (97 from 268 villages), as clerks (88), and as clerk-treasurers (16).[31]

In other states women serve as coroners, commissioners, criminal prosecutors, public administrators, members of election and tax boards, and boards of county welfare departments, and home demonstration agents.[32] A county recorder from Utah commented that in her state hers was an office which the parties recognized should be given to a woman.[33] It is quite acceptable for women to hold clerical posts, as opposed to policy-making posts.[34]

Miss Annie Matthews, a Democrat, served two terms as register of New York County in the 1920's. It was the highest paid public office in the county held by a woman up to that time. She was opposed in 1921 by Helen Varick Boswell, the first woman to attend a national political convention in an official capacity, and in 1925 by Mrs. Thomans L. Slack, former president of the New York City

Federation of Women's Clubs. Miss Matthews was succeeded in 1929 by Mrs. Rebecca F. Hoffman, the widow of a municipal court justice who was for two years the co-leader of her district political party. In the early 1930's Miss Martha Byrne became register.

In 1962 Mrs. Dorothy E. Cotter became the first woman to be elected city clerk of Yonkers, New York. She had been active in politics for more than 30 years and attended every state and national Republican convention since 1936. Mrs. Cotter was city Republican vice chairman, president of the GOP Federation of Yonkers, past president of the Crestwood Women's Club, and former administrative assistant to a congressman, as well as being chairman of the Heart Fund drive. She thought of her work of checking licenses for fishing, marriage, hunting, dogs, and myriad other duties as "strictly a man's job, but I like it." [35]

A number of cities now have women treasurers. Among these are Rochester, Buffalo, and New York City, in New York. According to Samuel Grafton, "women seem to be accepted as symbols of integrity." [36]

Gladys Miller became city treasurer of Minneapolis in 1939. She started out as a clerk and worked up to assistant treasurer. The city council appointed her to fill out the balance of the treasurer's term until 1941. She ran successfully for the full term and was twice re-elected.

Mrs. Hilda G. Schwartz was designated in 1958 by Mayor Robert Wagner to be New York City treasurer and head of the Department of Finance. Mrs. Schwartz is a graduate of New York University Law School. She is married to a lawyer who was twice chairman of the Greenwich Village Association. For the first 15 years of her married life, she had a private law practice. From 1946 to 1951 she was secretary of the Board of Estimate as well as trial commissioner of the board. Mrs. Schwartz was also vice president of the New York Young Democratic Club. In 1951 she was appointed a judge in the city magistrate's court. In her seven years as judge she sat on the following courts: Youth and Family, Home Term (family problems), Adolescents and Youth Term of Felony, Probation, Narcotics Term for Adolescents, and Women's. Mrs. Schwartz has been president of the New York Women's Bar Association and vice president of the National Association of Women Lawyers.

In 1914 and 1915 Dr. Katharine B. Davis was commissioner of corrections of New York City. Mayor Wagner, a sponsor of women, designated Magistrate's Court Judge Anna M. Kross to be his corrections commissioner when he took office in 1954. She had been an immigrant from Russia, a worker for the suffrage, and a union attorney. In 1918 she joined the staff of the Corporation Council of New York and was assigned to family court. In 1933 she moved from assistant corporation counsel to the magistrate's court where she served for 20 years. Her 50 years of public service were recognized in 1963 by her being named "Woman of the Year" by the American Association of University Women and in 1964 by her being given the first Eleanor Roosevelt Memorial Award. Mrs. Kross is married to a surgeon.

A third Wagner appointee was Dr. Leona Baumgartner, named in 1954 to be health commissioner. She served until 1962. Dr. Baumgartner was the daughter of a zoology professor and the wife of Nathaniel M. Elias, a well-known chemical engineer. She had served for 16 years in the Department of Health, for seven of those as director of the Bureau of Child Hygiene and for one year as assistant commissioner in charge of maternal and child health. In 1949 she became associate chief of the U.S. Children's Bureau. Dr. Baumgartner has taught at the Cornell Medical College, the Teachers College of Columbia University, and the Harvard School of Public Health.

Still another Wagner commissioner is Mrs. Hortense W. Gabel, city rent and rehabilitation administrator. Mrs. Gabel is a lawyer and the daughter of lawyers. She came from a politically oriented family. Her political activities have been supported by her husband, a dentist. At first she was repulsed by the New York Democrats' attitude toward women. Thursday was "women's night." The clubs would not let her join as an equal. Before the war, she was active in the American Labor Party, which was also unreceptive to women. Mrs. Gabel was assistant corporation counsel under LaGuardia. After the war, she found it difficult to get a post because of veteran's preference. She helped to found and became director of the National Committee Against Discrimination in Housing. Her career has been given boosts on a number of occasions by such men as Charles Abrams and Robert Weaver, both eminent in the public housing field. Under Governor Harriman she became general counsel to the Temporary State Rent Commission and rose to be first deputy administrator when Rockefeller became governor. At that point, she became assistant for housing to Mayor Wagner. She was asked to prepare the law giving the city control of rents and was the logical choice for the job. Mrs. Gabel is a believer in equal rights for women and gave women four of the 25 top jobs, including general counsel, in her agency.[37] Her advice to women in politics is: "You are far more conspicuous. You have to work hard and also be a lady. You are permitted no human sins, such as losing your temper. But you do have the advantage of standing out." [38]

A dozen years ago there were only three women community housing directors in the country. In 1964 there were 210 women among the 1,500 community housing posts. [39] Mrs. Marie McGuire, the first woman ever named public housing commissioner, urged more women to prepare for housing posts. Miss Elizabeth Wood, executive secretary of the Chicago Housing Authority, was the first woman to hold such a post in a large city. She previously taught English at Vassar and was a social worker. Miss Wood also worked for private and state housing boards.

Another Wagner woman was Mrs. Eleanor Clark French, New York City commissioner to the United Nations. Mrs. French taught school for 11 years in the Philadelphia area. After World War II she did social welfare work in France. From 1949 to 1955 she was women's news editor of the *New York Times.* In 1955 she was co-founder and vice president of the Democratic Women's Workshop, an ideas-and-issues approach to politics.[40] The next year she was asked to run for the state senate in a Republican district. From 1957 to 1960 Mrs. French was vice chairman of the Democratic state committee; she was appointed by Governor Harriman to fill an unexpired term and was elected the next year by the state committee. She resigned in 1960 in protest against the "old-fashioned" attitude of the state chairman who entrusted her with only "women's work." In 1964 she was asked to run for Congress against John Lindsay, a popular Republican in a Republican district. At first she turned down the proposal; after a man had rejected the nomination, she was asked to reconsider. She did so. Among her campaign supporters were Mrs. Hilda Schwartz and Mrs. Anna Kross.

Her husband, a non-gregarious lawyer, prefers to remain on the side-lines of politics.

One position where one would not expect to find a woman is that of sheriff. Yet even here women have made an appearance. Mrs. Jane Johnson, age 65, was elected sheriff of Roscommon County, Michigan, in 1920. Her husband had held the office for six years and she appointed him her deputy. Mrs. Adeline Grandle was elected sheriff of Hughes County, South Dakota, in 1955. Mrs. Donna Wilbright defeated three men to become sheriff of Clark County, Kansas. Her father was deputy sheriff in Colorado and her husband was her under-sheriff. They lived in a combination sheriff house and county jail. In addition to her administrative responsibilities at the jail, it was her duty to cook for the prisoners.[42] It was her husband's job to catch the occupants of the cells.

In 1951 four women were county sheriffs in Wisconsin. This curiosity is explained by the prohibition against sheriffs' serving more than two consecutive terms. The device for circumventing the regulation is to have the wife succeed to the office of sheriff and appoint her husband deputy. In the next election he runs for the sheriff's post.

Once again we encounter the phenomenon of widow's succession. Mrs. Daniel Leonard of Antigo, Wisconsin, was appointed sheriff in 1924 to fill the unexpired term of her late husband. Mrs. Kate Bolke became sheriff of Le Sueur County, Minnesota, in 1933 after the death of her husband. When the husband of Lierian Holley was killed in the line of duty, she succeeded him as sheriff of Lake County, Indiana.

Mrs. Barkley Graham was appointed sheriff of McCracken County, Kentucky, in 1949 to replace her husband who gave up the position to become police chief of Paducah.

Women also predominated on the local library boards of Wisconsin. In 1963, of 303 library boards, there were 1,059 women in a total of 1,865 members. [43]

The 1964 Report of the Governor's Commission on the Status of Women of Washington had the following comparison of the role of men and women in state and local government:

Elective Office	Number or Per Cent of Males	Number or Per Cent of Females
State Legislative		
(House and Senate)	99.04	.06
State Executive	100.00	.00
State Judicial	100.00	.00
School Boards	88.50	11.50
Library Boards	1.71	98.29
City Mayors	265	2
City Council Members	934	66
Treasurers, Treasurer-		
Clerks, and Finance		
Commissioners	128	139

Another position which is relatively more open to women and also of special appeal to them is that of school board member. There was a great increase in the number of women on such boards shortly after the suffrage amendment (1920-8.2 per cent, 1926-14.6 per cent) but the situation has reversed itself and the present figure given by the National School Boards Association is 9.7 per cent women. Schools with larger enrollments tend to have more women board members as do boards with larger memberships. Women constitute 23 per cent of big-city school boards. There is a larger proportion of women on boards in the northeast and southwest parts of the country. [44] More than half of the boards reported to the U.S. Office of Education that they had no women members at all and, of the remaining half, only 12 per cent had more than one woman sitting as a member. [45]

Judges. Mrs. Reah M. Whitehead was elected justice of the peace of Seattle in 1914 and held the position for 27 years. When she resigned in 1941 because of ill health, her spot was taken by another woman attorney, Mrs. Evangeline Starr, who still holds the office.[46]

The first woman magistrate of New York City was Jean Norris. She served from 1919 to 1931 on the women's court, the family court, and the district court. In 1931 she was dismissed for unfitness. Miss Norris had a financial interest in the bonding company active in relation to the business of her court, had altered court records, and had behaved unjudicially toward women offenders. Miss Norris's fall from grace did not deter Mayor LaGuardia from appointing Anna Kross to the court in 1933.

Other cities also took the plunge in the 1920's. Beginning in 1923 Mary B. Grossman of Cleveland was elected six times for terms of six years each to be municipal court judge. She had been admitted to the bar in 1912 and during World War I was chairman of the Office of Price Administration and Ration Board.

She was joined in 1931 by Lillian M. Westropp who was appointed to the Cleveland municipal court bench and was subsequently elected to four consecutive terms. Miss Westropp was a member of the executive committee of the state Democratic Party and was an organizer and first secretary of the Democratic Women of Ohio. She was also president of the Women's Federal Savings and Loan Association of Cleveland, a bank run by women for the general public.

The first woman judge of Cook County, Illinois, was Mary Bartelme, who was elected in 1923 to the Illinois juvenile court.[47] She was known for her enlightened treatment of juvenile delinquents. Miss Bartelme had been appointed in 1898 public guardian of Cook County and had served 11 years as assistant to the juvenile court judge. The second woman judge of Cook County was B. Fain Tucker, who was elected to the circuit court in 1956 with the help of business and professional women. She, too, was interested in juvenile delinquents.

At present, Edith S. Sampson, former social worker, assistant corporation counsel of Chicago, and twice a U.S. delegate to the U.N. General Assembly, is a Cook County judge. She filled a vacancy in 1962 and was elected to a full six-year term in 1964. Mrs. Sampson is one of five Negro woman judges in the country. The first was Juanita Kidd Stout, appointed a Philadelphia municipal court judge in 1959 by Governor David Lawrence. She was then elected to a 10-year term. In 1966 Judge Stout was a candidate for the state superior court, Pennsylvania's second highest tribunal.

Two women became presiding judges of San Francisco courts in 1955. Judge Theresa Meikle of the superior court of the city and county had had 25 years of judicial service. Prior to that she had been an assistant district attorney and an attorney for the State Division of Narcotics. Judge Lenore Underwood of the municipal court had been on the staff of the state attorney general from 1943 to her court appointment in 1951.

Neighboring Los Angeles could boast of having had the first woman police judge and justice of the peace in California. She was Mrs. Georgia P. Bullock who had been admitted to the bar in 1913 after studying law at night. She was a volunteer juvenile probation officer in Los Angeles and became deputy district attorney of the county. After serving as justice of the peace, she became a municipal court judge and was appointed to the superior court, being assigned to the children's court of conciliation. Judge Bullock was three times elected to this court.

The first woman municipal court judge in the District of Columbia was Mrs. Nadine Lane Gallagher who served from 1946 to 1957. She was president of the Woman's Bar Association of the District of Columbia and was co-editor of the *Federal Bar News* of the Federal Bar Association.[48]

Mrs. Libby E. Sachar became the first woman to hold a judgeship in New Jersey when she was appointed in 1946 to the juvenile and domestic relations court of Union County, New Jersey. Mrs. Sachar had practiced law with her husband and was active in the New Jersey Federation of Business and Professional Women and the National Council of Women.

For a number of years prior to her death in 1964, Judge Anna V. Levy held the elective post of judge of the first city court of New Orleans. Before this, Judge Levy was on the juvenile court. She was an outstanding public servant and the author of a book on family court problems. Her husband succeeded her on the bench.[49]

Most of the women judges in New York City are attached to the family court. There are five women among the 26 members of this court. Its administrative officer is Florence M. Kelley, a former public defender and granddaughter of Florence Kelley of the National Consumers League. Both her father and brother were lawyers. Mrs. Kelley was appointed in 1959 to be the city's first woman presiding justice of the domestic relations court. She had been attorney-in-charge of the criminal branch of the Legal Aid Society and was president of the Women's City Club from 1946 to 1948. She is married to David S. Worgan, executive assistant district attorney of New York County.

Mrs. Justine Wise Polier was the first woman in New York to hold a judicial post higher than magistrate when she was appointed by LaGuardia to the domestic relations court.[50] She is the daughter of Rabbi Stephen S. Wise, founder of the American Jewish Congress, and the wife of Shad Polier, a lawyer who is chairman of the governing council of the Congress. She became the first woman referee in the New York State Department of Labor and was counsel for LaGuardia's Emergency Committee on Relief. Mrs. Polier is one of the nation's leading experts on the problems of children and families.

Judge Sylvia Jaffin Liese of the New York family court went to law school while her son was in high school. Prior to that she was a housewife and settlement house volunteer. After she lost a housing fight in Westchester County, her dentist-husband told her that she should not have terminated her education with college but should have gone to law school. She was first in her class at Columbia Law School and was recommended by the school to the Manhattan district attorney's office. For 10 years she was assistant district attorney for New York County. After three years of working on appeals and arguing cases, she was assigned to working with youthful offenders. Mrs. Liese was recommended for the court opening in 1955 by civic and social agencies and the bar association.[51]

There are many communities where women have been given almost no opportunity to serve in any kind of judgeship. Of the 164 elected judgeships in Wisconsin, none in 1964 was filled by women. There were only four women justices of the peace in the 183 cities of the state and three woman J. P.'s in the 269 villages.[52]

Yet every year brings new opportunities. Denver, for example, recently acquired its first woman judge, Mrs. Zita Weinshienk. The young wife of a lawyer, she got her law degree at Harvard in 1958. Her performance as a municipal judge led to her promotion in January, 1965, to the county court.[53]

Women have failed to achieve anything resembling parity in local government. A larger proportion have attained legislative, executive, and judicial offices than at the state or federal level, but still relatively few. Women are frequently elected to clerical posts and far less frequently to policy-making positions.[54]

Footnotes and References

Chapter 1.
The Achievement of American Women in Politics Since 1920

1a. Suffrage Arguments and Their Aftermath

1. The National Woman Suffrage Association permitted women only to be members and concentrated upon getting a suffrage amendment to the constitution through Congress. The American Woman Suffrage Association enrolled men as officers and emphasized work in the states as a necessary prelude to federal action. These two groups merged in 1890 to form the National American Woman Suffrage Association. Dorothy Elizabeth Johnson, *Organized Women and National Legislation:* 1920-1941, unpublished Ph.D. dissertation, Western Reserve University, 1960, p. 8.

2. See Art Buchwald's column, *Milwaukee Sentinel,* September 22, 1964.

3. *Literary Digest,* September 4, 1920, p. 54.

4. George E. Howard, "Changing Ideals and Status of the Family and the Public Activities of Women," *The Annals,* November 1914, pp. 36-37.

5. Eleanor Flexnor, *Century of Struggle: The Woman's Rights Movement in the United States,* Cambridge: Belknap Press of Harvard University Press, 1959, p. 86.

6. Ella S. Stewart, "Woman Suffrage and the Liquor Traffic," *The Annals,* November 1914, p. 144.

7. Flexnor, *op. cit.,* p. 299.

8. V. O. Key, Jr., *Politics, Parties and Pressure Groups,* fifth edition, New York: Crowell, 1964, p. 615.

9. Maud Wood Park, *Front Door Lobby,* Boston: Beacon Press, 1960, p. 14.

10. Eugene H. Roseboom, *A History of Presidential Elections,* New York:

Macmillan, 1959, p. 384; Anne Firor Scott, "After Suffrage: Southern Women in the Twenties," *Journal of Southern History,* August 1964, pp. 298-318.

Literary Digest, August 28, 1920, p. 9. New Hampshirites finally amended their state constitution in 1958 to allow women to vote. Women had been voting in that state since the nineteenth amendment, so this was just a formality. *Congressional Quarterly Weekly Reports,* November 7, 1958, p. 1418.

12. *Literary Digest,* August 28, 1920, p. 11.

13. A. Maurice Low, "Women in the Election," *Yale Review,* January 1921, p. 321.

14. W. L. George, "Woman in Politics," *Harper's,* June 1919, p. 87.

15. *Literary Digest,* September 4, 1920, p. 54.

16. *Literary Digest,* August 28, 1920, p. 11.

17. The organization of the suffrage militants.

18. *Literary Digest,* August 7, 1920, p. 22.

19. North Dakota made the ladies use separate ballot boxes. Frank Graham, Jr., *Margaret Chase Smith,* New York: John Day, 1964, p. 32. When the Missouri legislature gave women the right to vote in presidential elections, it provided that they should use pink ballots in order to differentiate them. The state attorney general ruled that the "Pink Ballot Law" violated the right of secrecy. On the other hand, he ruled that the four women candidates for the state legislature in 1920 were not qualified to serve since the Missouri law required that, to be a member of the state legislature, one must be a male voter and a voter for two years before the elections. *The Woman Citizen,* October 30, 1920, p. 598. A constitutional amendment to allow women to hold any office in the state passed in 1921.

20. Franklin H. Giddings, *Studies in the Theory of Human Society,* pp. 186-189.

21. Marjorie Shuler, "Teaching Women Politics," *Review of Reviews,* September 1921, pp. 274-77; Charles E. Merriam, "The Chicago Citizenship School," *Journal of Social Forces,* September 1923, p. 600.

22. Scott, *op. cit.,* p. 315. In 1918 John W. Weeks, a bitter opponent of suffrage, was defeated for re-election to the U.S. Senate from

Massachusetts. *Ladies' Home Journal,* September 1923, pp. 159-60.

23. *Ladies' Home Journal,* September 1922, p. 12; August 1922, p. 8.

24. Harold Gosnell, *Democracy: The Threshold of Freedom,* New York: Ronald Press, 1948, p. 77.

25. Flexnor, *op. cit.,* p. 328. The New Jersey Democratic party platform for 1922 promised to enact a law giving equal guardianship rights to men and women in the care of minor children. "But the very law had been enacted a year before by the New Jersey legislature, and was in force when the Democrats promised it as a boon yet to be conferred upon mothers. The explanation is that they didn't care what, to catch women votes." "Fooling the Women in Politics," *Ladies' Home Journal,* September 1923, p. 29.

26. Valborg Esther Fletty, *Public Services of Women's Organizations,* unpublished Ph.D. dissertation, Syracuse University, #1952, p. 4. With equal rights went equal obligations in the 1920's. A Maryland law was repealed which said that a married woman was not responsible for a felony, other than treason or homicide, when committed in her husband's presence. Edna Kenton, "Four Years of Equal Suffrage," *The Forum,* July 1924, p. 44.

27. Eleanor Rowland Wembridge, *New Republic,* August 18, 1921, p. 328.

1b. Women as Voters.

1. Philip K. Hastings, "Hows and Howevers of the Woman Voter," *New York Times Magazine,* June 12, 1960, p. 14.

2. *Good Housekeeping,* September 1936, p. 156.

3. A Roper survey reported in *Editorial Research Reports,* February 20, 1956, p. 121.

4. Angus Campbell, Philip E. Converse, Warren E. Miller, and Donald E. Stokes, *The American Voter,* New York: John Wiley and Sons, 1960, p. 484.

5. Nona B. Brown, "Inquiry Into the Feminine Mind," *New York Times Magazine,* April 12, 1964, p. 17.

6. Brown, *op. cit.*, p.17. Measured in terms of population of voting age, however, 69 per cent of the Milwaukee men and 65 per cent of the women cast ballots.

7. *Washington Post,* December 9, 1964 p. A2.

8. "Women were allowed to register for local elections in Chicago as early as 1913; and yet, 10 years later, not half of the adult female citizens in the city had established voting habits." Charles E. Merriam and Harold F. Gosnell, *Non-Voting Causes and Methods of Control,* Chicago: University of Chicago Press, 1924, p. ix.

9. *Christian Science Monitor,* November 2, 1964, p. 1; Bernard R. Berelson, Paul F. Lazarsfeld, and William N. McPhee, *Voting: A Study of Opinion Formation in a Presidential Campaign,* Chicago: University of Chicago Press, 1954, p. 25. It was even said in the 1920's that some women would not vote because of fear that they would have to reveal their ages.

10. Men are more likely than women to feel that they can cope with the complexities of politics and to believe that their participation carries more weight in the political process. "Role beliefs pressure the woman to be a submissive partner. The man is expected to be dominant in action directed toward the world outside the family; the woman is to accept this leadership passively. She is not expected, therefore, to see herself as an aggressive agent in politics." Campbell, et al., *op. cit.,* p. 490.

11. Katherine Fullerton Gerould, "Some American Women and the Vote," *Scribner's Magazine,* May 1925, p. 450.

12. Eleanor Franklin Egan, "Women in Politics to the Aid of Their Party," *Saturday Evening Post,* March 22, 1920, p. 12.

13. Helena Huntington Smith, *Outlook and Independent,* January 23, 1929, p. 128.

14. Peter H. Odegard and Hans H. Baerwald, *The American Republic: Its Government and Politics,* New York-Evanston-London: Harper & Row, 1964, p. 148. In the West the differences between the sexes in voting was only one percentage point, according to a 1966 census study. Average differences in turnout proportions of the sexes: non-south metropolitan, 5 per cent; city and town, 20 per cent; village and rural, 28 per cent. Campbell, et al., p. 487. "It is possible that there are factors in these milieus that lend strength to clearer sex differentiation and that these factors are highly resistant to change." *Ibid.,* p. 488.

15. Robert E. Lane, *Political Life,* New York: Free Press, 1959, p. 214.

16. Brown, *op. cit.,* p. 17. Many Negro women look on politics as "man's business." The gap in the rate of political participation between Negro men and women is almost as great as the gap between Negroes and whites. Matthews and Prothro found, however, that as educational and income levels rise, Negro women as well as men become more interested in politics. Donald R. Matthews and James W. Prothro, *Negroes and the New Southern Politics,* New York: Harcourt, Brace & World, 1966.

17. *U.S. News and World Report,* May 8, 1953, p. 46, citing University of Michigan's Survey Research Center.

18. *Ibid.,* pp. 70-71.

19. Marguerite J. Fisher, "If Women Only Voted," *Christian Science Monitor,* October 30, 1948, p. 2. Arnold W. Green and Eleanor Melnick, "What Has Happened to the Feminist Movement," in Alvin W. Gouldner, ed., *Studies in Leadership; Leadership and Democratic Action,* New York: Harper, 1950, pp. 279-80. Campbell, et al., *op. cit.,* p. 487. Louise Young concluded that "women running for office stand a better chance of winning in a presidential election year, presumably because more of their sisters go to the polls." Louise M. Young, "The Political Role of Women in the United States," Report to the International Political Science Association, The Hague, 1953, p. 3.

20. See Appendix A in Berelson, et al., *op. cit.,*

21. Campbell, et al., *op. cit.,* p. 489.

22. Namely, what Campbell and his colleagues (p. 492) called D—No Issue Content, rather than A—Ideology, B—Group Benefit, or C—Nature of Times.

23. *Ibid.,* p. 493.

24. Neal Stanford, "The Woman's Vote," *Christian Science Monitor,* November 16, 1964.

25. Especially notable were the Good Citizenship Bureau of the *Woman's Home Companion* in the 1920's and the Pilgrim's Progress series of the *Ladies'*

Home Journal. The latter were begun by Margaret Hickey, Public Affairs Editor of the *Journal* since 1947 and a former president of the National Federation of Business and Professional Women's Clubs. The series presented case studies of women embarking on grass-roots political action. These campaigns resulted in such benefits as better parks and schools.

26. Lynn Stern, "Housewife in Politics," *American Magazine,* October 1954, p. 120. There was a hortatory tone in magazine stories aimed at getting women into politics—picturing them as "shining Joans of Arc leading the forces of righteousness" and wielding the "scrubbrush of reform." Young, *op. cit.,* p. 73.

27. The League of Women Voters pioneered in the use of radio as a medium of political education. In 1928 it joined with the National Broadcasting Company in presenting a weekly series of pre-election programs. Valborg Esther Fletty, *Public Services of Women's Organizations,* unpublished Ph.D. dissertation, Syracuse University, 1952, pp. 17-18.

28. See V. O. Key, Jr., *American State Politics,* New York: Knopf, 1956. Typical is the explanation of one usually Democratic female voter as to why she had voted for a Republican representative: "I like the way Heselton has voted; he takes a stand on issues without regard to politics." Hastings, *op. cit.,* p. 14.

29. Mrs. Katie Louchheim, former Democratic Woman's Division director, suggested that "the discreet wife, if she is at all clever, will not say that it was she who influenced her husband, but rather (will) go around saying: 'I voted the way my husband did.' A great many women do this even though it is they who have influenced their husbands," Hastings, *Loc. cit.*

30. Campbell, et al., *op. cit.,* p. 493. See also Lazarsfeld, et al., *The People's Choice* (on 1940 election), Campbell and Kahn, *The People Elect a President* (on 1948), and Campbell, Gurin, and Miller, *The Voter Decides* (on 1952).

31. Stuart A. Rice and Malcolm M. Willey, "American Women's Ineffective Use of the Vote," *Current History Magazine,* July 1924, p. 645.

32. Green and Melnick, *op. cit.,* p. 281.

33. *Ibid.,* p. 283.

34. Ethel Wadsworth Cortland, "Kitchen Statesmen." *Outlook,* March 17, 1926, p. 418.

35. Geoffrey Gorer, "Political Behavior of the Human Female," *New York Times Magazine,* May 30, 1948, p. 14.

36. William S. White, "Public Women," *Harper's,* January 1960, p. 86.

37. Eleanor C. French, "Key Political Force—The Ladies," *New York Times Magazine,* March 11, 1956, p. 34. On female activity in the 1928 campaign see Anna Steese Richardson, "Women in the Campaign," *Harper's,* April 1929, pp. 585-92.

38. It is interesting to speculate how women might have voted in the election of 1884. Cleveland had been accused of fathering an illegitimate child and Blaine of receiving a railroad bribe.

39. Mary Gray Peck, *Carrie Chapman Catt: A Biography,* New York: H. W. Wilson, 1944, p. 413.

40. Louis Harris, *Is There a Republican Majority?: Political Trends, 1952-56,* New York: Harper, 1954, p. 111.

41. Brown, *op. cit.,* p. 114.

42. Walter Davenport, "Where Men Go Wrong About Women," *Collier's,* September 14, 1956, p. 36. A similar comment was made in the 1920's: "Among local officers, where the election of one official may mean cleaner streets, or a better police force, or a lower gas rate, women can get excited; but they have not yet the habit of larger concerns." Gerould, *op. cit.,* p. 451.

43. Nona B. Brown, "Women's Vote: The Bigger Half," *New York Times Magazine,* October 21, 1956, p. 28.

44. Campbell, et. al., *op. cit.,* p. 485.

45. James G. March, "Husband-Wife Interaction Over Political Issues," *Public Opinion Quarterly,* Winter 1953-54, p. 468.

46. Brown ("Inquiry"), *op. cit.,* p. 114.

47. Sidney Shalett, "Is There a 'Women's Vote'?" *Saturday Evening Post,* September 17, 1960, p. 78.

48. Women consistently cite as important to them the candidate's age (preferably under 50), formal education, status as a family man and religious interests and practices. When queried, women voters are likely to emphasize the presidential candidates' character, personality, ability to inspire confidence, dexterity in handling politicans, intelligence. Hastings, *op. cit.,* p. 14.

49. Harris, *op cit.,* p. 116.

50. *Washington Post,* December 9, 1946, p. A2. Wilson won 10 of the 12 suffrage states in 1916. He lost Illinois, the only state where women's ballots were tabulated separately. Illinois women were stronger for Hughes than Illinois men.

51. *Newsweek,* September 21, 1964, p. 32.

52. When asked about the farm problem in the 1956 election, one housewife replied: "I really don't understand the whole thing, but I know that Eisenhower can handle it." Hastings, *op. cit.,* p. 14.

53. "In the GOP primaries against Nelson Rockefeller, Goldwater indeed showed to good advantage among women. But to a large extent he was the beneficiary of the silent issue of Rockefeller's divorce." *Newsweek,* September 21, 1964, p. 32. See also Brown ("Inquiry"), *op. cit.,* p. 114.

54. *Loc. cit.*

55. *Atlantic,* March 1964, p. 64. A similar poll taken in June 1958, had a 52 per cent "yes" response.

56. *U.S. News and World Report,* February 10, 1964, p. 34.

57. Brown ("Inquiry"), *op. cit.,* p. 114.

58. "Class consciousness is an easy thing to inject into politics, sex consciousness is not." Gerould, *op. cit.,* p. 450.

59. Harold W. Dodds, "Women's Place in Politics," *Ladies' Home Journal,* August 1952, p. 47.

60. Fred I. Greenstein, "Sex-Related Political Differences in Childhood," *Journal of Politics,* May 1961, p. 354.

1c. Women's Indirect Political Influence

1. This is the theme of James M. Barrie's play concerning a British politician, "What Every Woman Knows."

2. "The job descriptions of many leading positions presuppose the active participation of a wife. No couple—ambassadorial or company president—is paid a double salary, although the wife may give as much in her part as her husband in his." Edna G. Rostow, in *Daedalus,* Spring 1964, p. 752.

3. Ernestine Evans, "Women in the Washington Scene," *Century Magazine,* August 1923, pp. 509-10.

4. Perle Mesta, with Robert Cahn, *Perle: My Story,* New York-Toronto-London: McGraw-Hill, 1960, p. 130.

5. Among the other Washington female influentials are the members of the press corps. Some recent newswomen are Elizabeth May Craig, Ruby Black, Mary Hornaday, Sigrid Arne, Ruth Finney, and Bess Furman.

6. Robert S. Allen and Drew Pearson in *Washington Merry-Go-Round* (1931), quoted in *Current Biography,* 1943, p. 459. In Mrs. Longworth's home the fight against the League of Nations was decided upon and planned. Clare Ogden Davis, "Politicians, Female," *North American Review,* June 1930, p. 752.

7. W. Evans, *World's Work,* February 1929, p. 44.

8. Edmund A. Moore, *A Catholic Runs for President,* New York: Ronald Press, 1956, pp. 158-59.

9. *Time,* August 28, 1964, p. 20.

10. Marianne Means, *The Woman in the White House: The Lives, Times and Influence of Twelve Notable First Ladies,* New York: Random House, 1963, p. 154.

11. *Time,* August 28, 1964, p. 20.

12. Means, *op. cit.,* p. 136.

13. *Ibid.,* p. 169.

14. Dorothy Roe, *The Trouble With Women Is Men,* Englewood Cliffs, N. J.: Prentice-Hall, 1961, pp. 149-50. "This kind of energy might be admirable in a man. It was applauded among the qualities of her uncle, Theodore Roosevelt, whom in some ways she was said to resemble. But it was said to be unseemly in a woman who after all belonged at home, even if home happened to be the White House and the children for that very good reason were all away in school or college," Joan M. Erikson, "Notes on the Life of Eleanor Roosevelt," *Daedalus,* Spring, 1964, p. 782.

15. Means, *op. cit.,* p. 191.

16. Michael Amrine, *The Awesome Challenge,* New York: Putnam, 1964.

17. Ruth Montgomery, *Mrs. LBJ,* New York-Chicago-San Francisco: Holt, Rinehart, and Winston, 1964, p. 28.

18. *Time,* August 28, 1964, p. 23.

19. *U.S. News & World Report,* February 1, 1965, p. 33.

20. Marion K. Sanders, *The Lady and the Vote,* Boston: Houghton Mifflin, 1956, p. 157. See Charles L. Clapp, *The Congressman: His Work as He Sees It,* Garden City, N.Y.: Doubleday Anchor, 1963, Ch. 9.

21. Emily Newell Blair, "Wives in Politics," *The Forum,* October 1927, p. 581. Mrs. Blair thought we were coming to the phenomenon of the "co-candidate"—publicizing the charm of the wife to attract female votes for the husband.

22. Ellen Proxmire, *One Foot in Washington: The Perilous Life of a Senator's Wife,* Washington, D.C.: Robert B. Luce, Inc., 1963, pp. 160-61.

23. *Ibid.,* p. 2.

24. *Ibid.,* pp. 2-3. In 1952 Adlai Stevenson became the first divorced man to be

nominated for president. Opinion polls showed that his divorce was one important factor in his defeat in 1952 and in 1956. *U.S. News & World Report,* June 3, 1963, p. 44.

25. *Ibid.,* p. 79.

26. Mrs. Taft was national treasurer of the LWV in the 1930's.

27. Proxmire, *op. cit.,* p. 166. Jane Hart, wife of the Michigan senator, pilots her husband on campaign tours by plane or helicopter. She also acts as a one-woman lobby in Washington to get American women into the space program. She has passed the astronauts' difficult tests herself. *Ladies' Home Journal,* June 1964, p. 53. See also Mrs. Charles A. Halleck, "On Being a Politician's Wife," in James M. Cannon, editor, *Politics U.S.A.,* Garden City, New York: Doubleday, 1960, pp. 47-58.

28. Maurine Neuberger, in *McCall's,* September 1961, pp. 110-11, 166.

29. *Time,* September 4, 1964, p. 87.

1d. Women's Political Relationship to Men

1. Mrs. Mary Brooks, widow of Senator C. Wayland "Curly" Brooks, is also the daughter of a senator, the late John Thomas of Idaho. She is a member of the Idaho state senate in addition to heading up GOP women's activities nationally.

2. In the presidential election year of 1964 Hollywood gave its version of the plight of the man married to the first woman president. In "Kisses for My President," he runs the home while she runs the country. "As a husband he minds, but as a citizen he is too patriotic to protest." *Time,* September 4, 1964, p. 101.

3. Agnes De Mille, In Beverly Cassara, ed., *American Women: The Changing Image,* Boston: Beacon Press, 1962, p. 139.

4. Questionnaire returned after the 1964 Democratic Convention.

5. Interview in April 1964.

6. Questionnaire returned after the 1964 Democratic Convention.

7. Questionnaire returned after the 1964 Democratic Convention. The husband of Mrs. Charles H. Sabin, a GOP national committeewoman in the 1920's, was a prominent Democrat. *Saturday Evening Post,* May 22, 1920, p. 185.

8. In 1964 Ellen Proxmire replaced her husband, Senator William Proxmire, on the Wisconsin delegation to the Democratic Convention.

9. *Saturday Evening Post,* September 17, 1960, p. 79.

10. *Christian Science Monitor,* November 10, 1964, p. 11.

11. New York *Post,* February 25, 1964, p. 27.

12. She outpolled any other candidate, Republican or Democrat. In 1938 David N. Denman was elected to the Pennsylvania legislature, succeeding his wife who had become national legislation chairman of the National Federation of Business and Professional Women's Clubs.

13. Richard Neuberger, "My Wife Put Me in the Senate," *Harper's,* June 1955, pp. 40-46. "In politics Maurine and I operate in tandem. I make most of the decisions for us on what might be called cosmic issues. These are foreign policy, taxation, agriculture, conservation of natural resources, and civil liberties. Maurine sets the course where she is best informed—schools, public health, consumer problems, social welfare, recreation." *Ibid.,* p. 42.

14. *U.S. News & World Report,* December 12, 1958, p. 76. Said Congresswoman Catherine May: "I feel strongly that any woman who pursues a career outside the home without her husband's blessing is in for trouble. I would not have gone into politics if my husband had not wanted me to." *Current Biography,* 1960, p. 270.

15. Behind Josephine Roche, first woman assistant secretary of the treasury, was Senator Edward P. Costigan, Democrat, Colorado. Miss Roche was an unsuccessful candidate for governor of Colorado in 1934. John Gordon Ross, "Ladies in Politics," *The Forum,* November 1936, p. 210. Costigan was attorney for the United Mine Workers and became counsel of her Rocky Mountain Fuel Company. His wife, Mabel Cory Costigan, had been a leader in the suffrage movement and in the LWV. She was vice president of the Consumers League. In 1924 Mrs. Costigan was chief of the National Women's Division of the Progressive Party.

1e. The Political Impotence of American Women

1. *U. S. News & World Report,* February 10, 1964, p. 35.

2. "Man is God's honor and God's image." "Let your women keep silence in the churches."

3. "Men have broad and large chests, and small narrow hips, and are more understanding than women, who have but small and narrow chests, and broad hips, to the end they should remain at home, sit still, keep house, and bear and bring up children."

4. "A man cannot grant anything to his wife, or enter into covenant with her; for the grant would be to suppose her separate existence."

5. "Anatomy is destiny."

6. John Stuart Mill. Undoubtedly, men and women have physiological differences which affect their behavior; for example, the accident rate of women increases strikingly just before and during their menstrual periods. *New York Times,* December 20, 1964, p. 1. However, a cause-and-effect relationship will have to be established before women's social position can be attributed to their nature.

7. "Masculinity today is the salary a man makes, the title he holds, his success in climbing the status ladder on the job." Dr. Ethel J. Alpenfels, at First Governor's Conference on the Changing Status of Women, Madison, Wisconsin, January 1964, p. 63 of minutes.

8. Erik H. Erickson, "Inner and Outer Space: Reflections of Womanhood," *Daedalus,* Spring 1964, p. 585.

9. "The threat exists on many levels, challenging a man's comfort, his social life, his children's welfare, his sexuality, and his self- esteem. . . . In our society money and success have always been linked with the concept of masculinity. The poor provider has always been looked down upon by some men as being something less than a man. To the husband who is unsure of his maleness, a working wife may seem like a public announcement that his worst fears are true." Alvin Toffler in *Ladies' Home Journal,* June 1964, p. 26.

10. Talcott Parsons, "Age and Sex in the Social Structure of the United States," in Logan Wilson and William L. Kolb, editors, *Sociological Analysis,* New York: Harcourt, Brace, 1949, p. 596.

11. Robert C. Blood, Jr., and Donald M. Wolfe, *Husbands and Wives: The Dynamics of Married Living,* Glencoe: Free Press, 1960, pp. 246-47. "In recent decades a new definition of husband-wife roles is emerging: that of a partnership. . . . The partnership no less than the traditional relationship can be ethically consistent, provided each spouse accepts the duties which are logically linked to a given set of privileges. But this is precisely where the difficulty arises. With new and old patterns both in the air, it is all too human for each partner to reach out for the double dose of privilege, those of the old and those of the new role, leaving to the mate the double dose of obligations. So a wife who is vociferous in defending her right to a career may take it completely for granted that it is her husband's duty to provide for her." Mirra Komarovsky, *Women in the Modern World: Their Education and Their Dilemmas,* Boston: Little, Brown, 1953, pp. 88-89.

12. "Woman has always accepted with grace, with pride and satisfaction, her husband's interests and achievements, taking joy, without any sense of diminution and shame. Can the husband endure to learn this?" Agnes De Mille in Beverly Cassara, ed., *American Women: The Changing Image.* Boston: Beacon Press, 1962, p. 140.

13. Noticeable in reading the answers to a poll taken in 1964 on the Margaret Chase Smith candidacy was the ease with which both sexes resort to cliches: "It's a man's world." "Woman's place is in the home." An engineer's aide gave as his uniform answer to the question of whether he would vote for a woman for president, governor, senator, or congress-woman, "No—I'm a man." A mill worker replied: "I don't like women who try to feel so important." A farmer observed: "Men are not ready to surrender to a woman. They belong at home keeping kids out of trouble."

14. One New York leader was fond of saying, "Women belong in two places—at home and in bed."

15. Report of the Washington Governor's Commission on the Status of Women, December 1963, p. vi.

16. Reported by Marian Ash in her newsletter, "Skirting the Capitol," Volume 1, Number 1, July 24, 1967.

17. Questionnaire received after the Convention. The men may have resented treating women as equals or felt that the women were depriving men of the honor of serving.

18. Questionnaire received after the convention. The December 1964 Interim Report of the South Dakota Governor's Commission on the Status of Women noted: "Observations from political observers, not active politicians, are that women running for office against a man incumbent 'can not win.' Women are usually 'convinced' by political party heads or friends that they should not run for office, and that they do not have the competitive spirit, the campaign trail stamina, that a man has." Pp. 5-6.

19. Stated at Second Governor's Conference on the Status of Women, Madison, Wisconsin, March 6, 1965.

20. "Are Women Counting in Politics?" *Saturday Evening Post,* July 18, 1925, p. 7.

21. Jessie Bernard noted that whatever the mode of female role performance, neutral, sexy, feminine, or womanly, men are often uncertain how they should respond. This confusion is not encountered when dealing with other men. Bernard, *op. cit.,* pp. 198-99. If they are young and unmarried, women may be inhibited by the fear that initiation of a contact might appear to be a sexual advance.

22. *Saturday Evening Post.* July 18, 1925. p. 7. Compare the comment of the president of an advertising agency: "No woman can successfully deal on equal terms with men—and remain a woman. If she tries it, she becomes ridiculous or repulsive." Lee Graham, "Who's in Charge Here?": *New York Times Magazine,* September 2, 1962, p. 8.

23. Komarovsky, *op. cit.,* p. 204. One female politician, in replying to the complaint by women about not being consulted, said, "When the men find you in their way or when they need you, they will consult." *Saturday Evening Post,* July 18, 1925, p. 78.

24. Example of typical male conceit: "Woman gains from the expectation and acceptance of man's chivalry, his tolerance of her traditional weaknesses, his regard for her difficulties and deficiencies, physical and psychical. These privileges she can not retain simultaneously with the cheapening of man's regard that results from direct competition." Sir Adolphe

Abrahams, *Women: Man's Equal?* London: Christopher Johnson, 1954, p. 9. Compare the southern attitude: "There were inherent contradictions in the elements of women's role as the culture defined it: Women were supposed to be beautiful, gentle, efficient, morally superior, and at the same time, ready to accept without question the doctrine of male superiority and authority." Anne Firor Scott, *Journal of Southern History,* 1964, p. 299.

25. Ellen Proxmire quotes a political cartoon which depicts an irate wife accosting her husband over the evening paper with these words: "The trouble with you is that you live in a little world of your own—the Middle East crisis, the Far East Crisis, Berlin, the national economy, segregation, integration, government, Laos—just a little world of your own!" Ellen Proxmire, *One Foot in Washington: The Perilous Life of a Senator's Wife,* Washington, D.C.: Robert B. Luce, Inc., 1963, p. 82.

26. Amaury de Riencourt, "Will Success Spoil American Women?" *New York Times Magazine,* November 10, 1953, pp. 32, 98, 100-01. "By the time he has reached middle age, the American man realizes that it is too late, he can no longer recapture the power that has slipped out of his hands."

27. "There is some suggestion that the custody of moral values is often acquired as a consolation prize for exclusion from these activities which have the highest value in the society." Robert E. Lane, *Political Life,* New York: Free Press, 1959, p. 212.

28. "Equality is not synonymous with sameness. The plea for equality of women is by no means an emulation of masculinity, as some people fear. Women do not want to fit into a 'Man's World' by becoming more manly, but want instead to reshape that world so that as women they may assume a more mature, responsible part in it." *Wisconsin Women,* Report of the Governor's Commission on the Status of Women, Madison, Wisconsin, March 1965, p. 2.

29. Compare the other irrational prejudices of the sexes in America—a) that the wife should be younger than the husband, despite woman's greater longevity, and b) that the husband should be taller than the wife.

30. Komarovsky, *op. cit.,* p. 51. Feature story writers seem to delight in such anecdotes as the following: After Winifred Stanley's nomination for Congress at a Republican Convention, a woman rushed up to her and

exclaimed: "I'm so glad they have chosen you, my dear! The other woman they were considering wears such atrocious hats!" *Current Biography*, 1943, p. 730.

31. *The Nation*, July 9, 1924, p. 41.

32. The Sheppard-Towner Act, championed by the WJCC, was killed by the American Medical Association which was able in 1927 to bar any further federal appropriations. Valborg Esther Fletty, *Public Services of Women's Organizations*, unpublished Ph.D. dissertation, Syracuse University, 1952, p. 60.

33. "Conspicuous by their infrequency and in most cases by their complete absence—were articles dealing with the political participation of women." Earle R. Kruschke, *Female Politicals and Apoliticals: Some Measurements and Comparisons*, unpublished Ph.D. dissertation, University of Wisconsin, 1963, p. 2. Shortly before Senator John Kennedy's baby girl was born, he was asked on a television program: "If your child is a boy, would you want him to get into politics?" The Senator replied: "If it's a boy, certainly I'd want him to get into politics; and if we have a girl, I'd want her keenly interested in politics." *National Business Woman*, January 1958, p. 16.

34. This writer was one of a dozen men, half of them resource persons, among more than 200 women at the Second Governor's Conference on the Status of Women held in March 1965, in Madison, Wisconsin, and the only male among 150 registered for a conference on getting women into politics. "Antidote for Apathy," May 1965, Madison, Wisconsin. Over 95 per cent of those who came to hear Betty Friedan when she spoke at the Wisconsin State University campus were women.

35. Said Mary Anderson, longtime head of the Women's Bureau: "I always felt the men considered government as a man's business and did not want woman's intrusion there. Even if it was necessary to take up the question of women's employment and conditions of life, the men never felt that a woman could speak for women." Mary Anderson, *Woman at Work*, Minneapolis: University of Minnesota Press, 1951, p. 64.

36. *Fortune*, June 1956, p. 216. Morton M. Hunt, *Her Infinite Variety*, New York-Evanston: Harper & Row, 1962, p. 263. Colleges which admit the top 20 per cent of high school graduates, and who try to maintain a balanced number of men and women, are forced to relax the admission standards to admit men. Report of the Indiana Governor's Conference on the Status of Women, December 7, 1963, p. 32.

37. Komarovsky, *op. cit.,* p. 20.

38. Stuart A. Rice and Malcolm M. Willey, "American Women's Ineffective Use of the Vote," *Current History,* July 1924, p. 647. This discrimination may be less true in new fields, where women can get in without the disadvantages of being a latecomer.

39. *Good Housekeeping,* March 1940, p. 68. "The argument that bigoted white students delight in saying, 'I told you so,' when a Negro student does badly, was found easily offset by the fact that the biased also shrug off the Negro prize winner as 'just the exception.' " Finding of Fred M. Hechinger in a study of race relations in private schools, *New York Times,* April 5, 1964, IV.

40. Oliver Jensen, *The Revolt of American Women,* New York: Harcourt, Brace, 1952, p. 92.

41. A *Newsweek* study reported the results of a questionnaire sent to 521 women who had worked for both men and women. Of those answering, 99.81 per cent stated that they would prefer a male boss. Jensen, *op. cit.,* p. 92.

42. Of course, the men play favorites, too. An attractive woman gets the male assistance, whereas a plain woman has to fend for herself.

43. Taken from the cover jacket of Margaret Cussler, *The Woman Executive,* New York: Harcourt, Brace, 1958. "Women executives are a minority within a minority, for if there is one thing women are not supposed to be it is the 'boss.' Women executives are pictured often as cold chic statues, ruthless and calculating in their business techniques, yet apt to explode in a fiery tantrum or retire in a feminine pout. They are called too aggressive and too yielding, too feminine and too masculine, too emotional and too icy, too rigid and too indecisive, too personal and too impersonal. It makes little difference that these stereotypes contradict each other; to the person who fears the executive women, the contradiction seems logical." *Ibid.,* p. 3.

44. Komarovsky, *op. cit.,* p. 202. It is also said of women workers that they neither trust nor give credit to subordinates, are not ambitious enough to train themselves for bigger responsibilities, and have narrower interests than males.

45. Esther Peterson, "Working Women," *Daedalus,* Spring 1964, p. 692, and an interview with her in August 1964. Men tend to ask about economics. Women—in a women's audience—ask about foreign affairs, etc. Men are not used to hearing women discuss public affairs. In mixed groups women are either silent or restricted to small talk.

46. Quoted by Caroline K. Simon in a talk to the Brooklyn Management Club, May 8, 1962.

47. Sioux Falls, South Dakota, *Argus-Leader,* February 5, 1964, p. 6.

48. *Independent Woman,* April 1949, p. 102. The turnover rates in higher salary categories were less for women than for men. Report of the North Carolina Governor's Commission on the Status of Women, 1964, p. 6.

49. Margaret Chase Smith observed: "Whether or not there is a future in politics for women depends upon the women themselves. If they have the sufficient desire and determination to hold not only public office but to organize politically and vote in blocs and elect qualified women candidates, then there is most definitely a future in politics for women. The inescapable fact is that they hold the control of the public offices with their majority voting power." *U.S. News & World Report,* February 10, 1964, pp. 35-36.

50. The Report of the North Carolina Governor's Commission on the Status of Women, p. 42, contained a list of factors which keep women from running for office. These handicaps were named by 93 North Carolina women who did hold public office: (1) The attitude of men, or of husbands, (2) apathy of women in general, (3) antipathy toward the syndrome referred to as "politics"—conflict, misrepresentation, compromise, etc., (4) lack of the necessary "resources"—information, experience, knowledge, interest, encouragement, (5) home responsibilities, (6) lack of time, (7) fear of defeat, ridicule, or making decisions, (8) lack of self-confidence, (9) tradition, including the attitude of other women, and (10) other commitments in the community.

51. See, for example, Joseph Kirk Folsom, *The Family and Democratic Society,* 623-24; Gunnar Myrdal, *An American Dilemma: The Negro Problem and American Democracy,* New York-Evanston-London: Harper & Row, 1944, 1962, pp. 1073-78; Cornelius P. Cotter and Bernard C. Hennessy, *Politics Without Power: The National Party Committees,* New

York: Atherton Press, 1964, p. 151; Margery C. Leonard, ed., "Equal Rights Amendment," Senate Document No. 164, 87th Congress, Second Session, p. 13. This is also a theme of Simone De Beauvoir in *The Second Sex.*

52. See Helen M. Hacker, "Women as a Minority Group," *Social Forces,* October 1951, pp. 60-69. A minority group is any group of people who, because of their physical or cultural characteristics, are singled out from the others in the society in which they live for differential and unequal treatment, and who therefore regard themselves as objects of collective discrimination." *Ibid.,* p. 61.

53. Maurice Duverger, *The Political Role of Women,* Paris: UNESCO, 1955, p. 130.

54. *This Week Magazine,* February 9, 1964, p. 7.

55. Speech on "The Challenge of Women" delivered January 27, 1964, in which she announced her candidacy for president.

56. *Daedalus,* Spring 1964, p. 638. "Women will discriminate against women in the professions—doctors, lawyers, architects and dentists—more readily than men." *This Week Magazine,* February 9, 1964, p. 11.

57. See Ralph H. Turner, *The Social Context of Ambition: A Study of High School Seniors in Los Angeles,* San Francisco: Chandler, 1964, p. 7, for a discussion of the concept of "marginal man."

58. David Riesman in Bernard, *op. cit.,* pp. XVI-XVII.

59. *New York Times,* June 26, 1964. *Current Biography,* 1943, p. 633.

60. Questionnaire returned in November 1964.

61. Corra Harris, "Practical Politics for Gentlewomen," *Ladies' Home Journal,* September 1921, p. 16. A poll taken after Margaret Chase Smith's announced candidacy showed quite a bit of feminine animosity toward women who wished to change woman's roles.

62. One of the "scientific" books of the period which blamed feminism for much that was wrong in the world, George Lundberg and Marynia

Farnham's *Modern Woman: The Lost Sex,* New York: Harper, 1947, thought the suffrage was an ego-prop. "For now, from the point of view of the bruised female ego, women were politically 'just as good as men,' were the 'equal of men. . .' " P. 172.

63. *New York Times Book Review,* August 9, 1964, p. 14. The September 1964, issue of *Ladies' Home Journal* revealed reactions of their readers to Betty Friedan's June 1964 concept of four-dimensional women: "An almost equal percentage of wives were for and against Miss Friedan's 4-D vision, an almost equal percentage of single girls. The male correspondents did show a definite preference: Their letters ran about six to two against the 4-D woman." P. 34.

64. *Daedalus,* Spring 1964, p. 702.

65. Margaret Mead, *Male and Female: A Study of the Sexes in a Changing World,* New York: William Morrow, 1949, p. 234.

66. Komarovsky, *op. cit.,* p. 77. One girl said: "On dates I always go through the 'I-don't-care-anything-you-want-to-do' routine. It gets monotonous but boys fear girls who make decisions. They think such girls would make nagging wives." *Ibid.,* p. 80.

67. "Throughout her education and her development of vocational expectancy, the girl is faced with the dilemma that she must display enough of her abilities to be considered successful, but not too successful; enough ability to get and keep a job, but without the sort of commitment that will make her either too successful or unwilling to give up the job entirely for marriage and motherhood." Mead, *op. cit.,* p. 320.

68. "If the majority of women are little attracted to political careers, it is because everything tends to turn them away from them: if they allow politics to remain essentially a man's business, it is because everything conduces to this belief, tradition, family life, education, religion and literature. From birth, women are involved in a system which tends to make them think of themselves as feminine. The publicity which blazes around the few women who are outstandingly successful in non-feminine fields accentuates the fact that they are exceptions and the gulf which divides them from the normal woman's life." Duverger, *op. cit.,* p. 129.

69. Perhaps expressing sour grapes, Margaret Culkin Banning proposed in 1927

that women realize that they had no appetite for politics, that they are just figureheads and that politics is best left to men. *Independent,* December 3, 1927, p. 541. Wives of wage earners were asked in June 1948: "Do you approve of women's entering into politics as a career?" Forty-one per cent said yes: nearly 30 per cent no, and 31 per cent had no opinion. Louise M. Young, *Understanding Politics,* New York: Pellegrini & Cudahy, 1950, p. 182. A *McCall's* survey of political opinion among members of the General Federation of Woman's Clubs in 1964 found that only 56 per cent of the ladies balloted would vote for a woman for president. Fewer of the 34-years-old or younger were favorable. These young women also did not think it necessary to have laws guaranteeing equal business opportunity and pay for women. "The Women's Vote: How Will It Go?" *McCall's,* March 1964, pp. 7-72.

70. *Family Weekly,* April 12, 1964, p. 5.

71. *Independent Woman,* February 1947, p. 34.

72. Edward D. Eddy, Jr., "What's the Use of Educating Women?" *Saturday Review,* May 18, 1963, p. 67. Margaret Chase Smith put the problem squarely. "If women are to claim and win their rightful place in the sun on an equal basis with men, then they must not insist upon those privileges and prerogatives identified in the past as exclusively feminine." "The Challenge to Women," *op. cit.,* pp. 2-3.

73. *Columbia College Today,* Spring-Summer 1963, p. 6.

74. *Saturday Review,* May 18, 1963, p. 68.

75. Quoted in Bernard, *op. cit.,* p. 308.

76. In 1965 Phyllis McGinley's *Sixpence in Her Shoe* (New York: Macmillan, 1964) was on best-seller lists. Her book, which is a tribute to tradition-alism, sold over 100,000 copies in hard cover. Its message is that the world runs better when men and women keep to their own spheres. In her earlier work, *The Province of the Heart,* Miss McGinley (Mrs. Charles Hayden) distinguished between a job and a career. A job, she feels, can be subordinated to marriage and motherhood, but a career is a whole way of life and must inevitably, if followed by the married woman, imperil her home. (Argument summarized in Dorothy Dohen, *Women in Wonderland,* New York: Sheed & Ward, 1960, p. 114.)

77. As did Congresswoman Mary Norton in *Current Biography,* 1944, p. 500.

78. Ruth Benedict, the anthropologist, speaking of careers for women, wrote: "We know that we would lay it down with hallelujah in the height of our success, to make a home for the right man." Bernard, *op. cit.,* p. 27.

79. Margaret Chase Smith's mother asked her at the time of her first race for the Senate when she was "going to stop all this nonsense and get married." Helen Markel, "Twenty-four Hours in the Life of Margaret Chase Smith," *McCall's,* May 1964, p. 161.

80. Betty Friedan, *The Feminine Mystique,* New York: Norton, 1963, p. 233.

81. *Ibid.,* p. 237. Perhaps the picture is too bleak. George M. Low of the National Aeronautics and Space Administration summarized his wife's job in a more appreciative fashion: Mary, he said, is "program manager for one of the most challenging, yet thankless, projects in the Washington area. In this position Mary is in complete charge of a facility; maintains it and its surroundings; handles its budgets, expense accounts and liabilities; supervises its personnel; operates a motor pool; deals with the local and Federal Government on matters of taxation, and expertly handles numerous emergency problems." Her project was taking care of Mr. Low and their four children. Katherine B. Oettinger, "The Role of Women in Government," address before the Boston Council of Club Presidents, March 23, 1963, p. 11.

82. Komarovsky, *op. cit.,* p. 139.

83. "While it remains true that the majority of middle-class women, after marriage, never cease an eternal debate over whether they should attempt to 'do something better than housework,' this remains more a matter of vacillation than a purpose held above all other values." Arnold W. Green and Eleanor Melnick, "What Has Happened to the Feminist Movement," in Alvin W. Gouldner, ed., *Studies in Leadership: Leadership and Democratic Action,* New York: Harper, 1950, p. 297.

84. "The fact is that there are two conflicting tendencies in us all—one, an aspiration to independence; the other, a desire to let someone else make our decisions and fight our battles. Regardless of sex, one tendency can predominate in one individual; the other, in another." Elizabeth Lansing, in *Independent Woman,* April 1952, p. 297.

85. Even Mrs. Ruth Pratt, New York alderman and congresswoman, felt this. "In my term of service on the Board of Aldermen I was never conscious that I thought as a woman, except perhaps in one thing, and that was an extra degree of caution." *Outlook and Independent,* January 23, 1929, p. 126.

86. Seymour M. Farber and Roger H. L. Wilson, ed., *The Potential of Women,* New York-San Francisco-Toronto-London: McGraw-Hill, 1963, p. 179. "In addition to a lack of self-confidence, women place an overweening amount of importance on approval." *This Week,* February 9, 1964, p. 11.

87. *New York Times,* November 3, 1946, p. 56.

88. *Independent Woman,* July 1948, p. 196.

89. Margaretta Newell, "Must Women Fight in Politics?" *Woman's Journal,* January 1930, pp. 10-11, 34-35. Said Muriel E. Richter, president of the Women Lawyers Association of New York State and chairman of the Committee for Women for Public Office: "We don't want to be wooed for the women's vote. We want to do the job that the men are doing because we can do it—and because often we can do it better. We're going into every elective campaign from now on. We're not going to wait for backroom conferences where they grandly decide to give us something because they need us as a 'minority.' We're no longer a 'minority'—we're a power, financially and numerically, and we're now going to compete with the men for elective office, especially where a lawyer has to be considered, because we qualify as human beings." Gertrude Samuels, "Really a Man's World—Politics," *New York Times Magazine,* October 15, 1950, p. 51.

90. He made this statement as he received the first annual report of the Interdepartmental Committee on the Status of Women and the Citizens' Advisory Council.

91. For many years the city of Oshkosh, Wisconsin, was without a woman candidate for an aldermanic or council office. In January 1965 three women were among the 12 candidates who filed for four council positions. Appleton *Post-Crescent,* January 24, 1965, p. D1. All three were defeated.

92. Scott, *op. cit.,* p. 318.

93. Women in *Who's Who in America:* 1920—8.45 per cent of the listings;

1930-31—6.24 per cent; 1964—4.4 per cent. Green and Melnick, *op. cit.,* p. 292. Many of the women listed are in entertainment, society, or purely feminine areas.

94. This does not imply a battle of the sexes. Once the breakthrough occurs, women, like men, should be judged as individuals rather than as members of a group.

95. In 1920 the median years of schooling completed by women 25 years and older was 8.3 years. In the same year women received 34 per cent of the degrees conferred by institutions of higher learning. By 1962 the median years of schooling for women was 12 and the women earned 36 per cent of the degrees conferred. Esther Peterson, "Women and Policy Politics," address to Sixth Annual Alumnae Forum of Boston, April 4, 1964, p. 1. In 1961 women earned 38.8 per cent of all bachelor's degrees and 10.9 per cent of all first professional degrees. By 1965 the respective figures were 43.2 per cent and 13.2 per cent. *Report of Progress in 1966 on the Status of Women, op. cit.,* p. 13.

96. Herbert Hyman found that boys are more likely than girls to pick historic and public figures as their "ideal"; boys are also more likely to identify with men of affairs whereas girls tend to pick their ideals from among parents, teachers or acquaintances from their immediate environment. Herbert H. Hyman, *Political Socialization,* Glencoe, Ill.: The Free Press, 1959, pp. 30-33.

97. *Report on Four Consultations* of the President's Commission on the Status of Women, Washington, D.C., October 1963, p. 24. One *Ladies' Home Journal* reader wrote: "Why not the face of a woman political leader or scientist on your cover for a change? It would be nice if our daughters grew up thinking of these women as heroines, rather than television and screen stars." *Ladies' Home Journal,* September 1964, p. 34.

98. "Achievement need, workmanship and constructive aggression should be cultivated in girls and approved in women so that a female of any age should be similarly free to express these qualities in her social relationships." Alice S. Rossi, "Equality Between the Sexes: An Immodest Proposal," *Daedalus,* Spring 1964, p. 608.

99. This is a proposal of the New York Governor's Committee on the Education and Employment of Women. *New York Women,* Dec. 1964, p. 36.

100. Seven out of ten of the top students in Wisconsin high school graduating classes are women. *Wisconsin Women,* Report of the Wisconsin Governor's Commission of the Status of Women, Madison, Wisconsin, March 1965, p. 13. (See also Report of Indiana Governor's Conference on the Status of Women, December 7, 1963, p. 31.) Of the top 40 per cent of U.S. high school graduates, only half went on to college: of the half who stopped, two out of three were girls. See Dael Wolfe, *America's Resources of Specialized Talent,* New York: Harper, 1954. Of those who go to college, the women drop out at a faster rate, leaving only 37 per cent who graduate in contrast to 55 per cent of the men. Opal D. David, ed., *The Education of Women—Signs for the Future,* Washington, D.C.: American Council on Education, 1959, pp. 14-15. The two major reasons for coed dropouts are discouragement and marriage.

101. "Nationally there are now three and a half million college educated women with free time during each day, with 35-40 years of healthy, active life ahead after their last child is in school, who hear from many sides the pleas for educated personnel to cope with the new knowledge and to fill the areas of need." Kathryn F. Clarenbach, "University Education of Women," *Annual Report,* University of Wisconsin, October 1964, p. 3.

102. Women today face "retirement" 20 years before their husbands. Carl Degler, *Daedalus,* Spring 1964, p. 666. When mothers reach the "empty nest" period, when their children are adults or nearly so, their employment and community participation may be at a low level unless prior to that time they have kept active. If married women take a job at 30 and have no more children, they can expect to average 23 years of work. Esther Peterson, *Daedalus,* Spring 1964, p. 674.

103. "The greater economic demands on the family—in higher cost of educating children, the higher cost of health care, and the cost of the greater variety of goods and services considered essential to meet the American standard of living—increasingly require a 'two pay-check' household." *Wisconsin Women, op. cit.,* p. 33.

104. "A woman's goal, like that of men, is to develop a life style that uses her energies and capacities in such a way that she functions in her various roles efficiently and productively, with sufficient integration among these roles to give her at least some personal satisfaction in each." Lotte Bailyn, *Daedalus,* Spring 1964, p. 701.

105. "Are women to be seen as individuals with special capacities and

possibilities, or primarily as wives and mothers? Are we to continue to provide an education for girls that is comparable to an education for boys and then reward with praise and approval the girl who makes no use of her education, and ignore the one who does?" Margaret Mead, in Cassara, *op. cit.,* p. xiii.

106.   In 1890 less than one American wife in 20 held a job; in 1950, one in four; in 1960; one in three.

107.   In 1920 the average woman worker was single and 28 years old. In 1963 the average woman worker was married and 41 years old. *Wisconsin Women, op. cit.,* p. 33. "The main trouble with a large percentage of today's women workers is that they seldom plan on a full-scale career, never intend to take a job that is more than temporary, then find themselves in a rut." Dorothy Roe, *The Trouble With Women Is Men,* Englewood Cliffs, N.J.: Prentice-Hall, 1961, p. 90. "Few of them show any hard-driving careerism, but more wives than ever before would like to work, more actually do work both before and after rearing their children, and more work even while their children are young." Hunt, *op. cit.,* p. 252.

108.   *Fortune,* June 1956, p. 116. The chances that a woman will seek paid employment tend to increase with the amount of education she has received. For example, more than half of the women with a college degree were working in 1959, but less than one-third of the women who had left school after the eighth grade. *1962 Handbook on Women Workers,* Women's Bureau Bulletin No. 285, 1963, p. 109.

109.   *Job Horizons for College Women in the 1960's,* Women's Bureau Bulletin No. 288, 1964, p. 64; Report of the Washington Governor's Commission on the Status of Women, 1963, p. 25; Alice S. Rossi, "Equality Between the Sexes." *Daedalus,* Spring 1964, p. 638.

110.   Part-time work exists most frequently among private-household workers, farm workers, and sales workers. Relatively few women workers are employed part time in five occupational groups: craft, managerial, operative, clerical, and professional. *Handbook on Women Workers, op. cit.,* p. 57.

111.   Clarenbach, *op. cit.,* p. 7. Bruno Bettelheim, "Women: Emancipation Is Still to Come," *New Republic,* November 7, 1964, pp. 56-57. Betty

Friedan noted that bowling alleys and supermarkets had nursing facilities but schools, colleges, scientific laboratories, and government offices did not. Friedan, *op. cit.,* p. 374.

112. In *Life Stress and Mental Health,* Langner and Michael make the point that "children exhibit the best mental health if their mother worked part time rather than full time or not at all." Quoted in the Report of the North Carolina Governor's Commission on the Status of Women, 1964, p. 12. See also Glenn V. Ramsey, Bert K. Smith, and Bernice M. Moore, *Women View Their Working World,* Austin: University of Texas Hodge Foundation for Mental Health, 1963, pp. 8-9.

113. See the report of "Women in Volunteer Activities" by Constance F. Threinen to the Wisconsin Governor's Conference on the Changing Status of Women, January 31, 1964. "There is fierce competition, to be sure, for the busy housewife's leisure—from the PTA, the Cerebral Palsy Drive, folk dancing, the garden club, the Mental Health Association and the Girl Scouts—to name only a few." Marion K. Sanders, *The Lady and the Vote,* Boston: Houghton Mifflin, 1956, p. 30.

114. Robert E. Lane, *Political Life: Why People Get Involved in Politics,* Glencoe, Ill.: The Free Press, 1959, pp. 160, 355.

115. Roe, *op. cit.,* p. 23.

116. N. C. Report, *op. cit.,* p. 9.

117. Cussler, *op. cit.,* p. 25.

118. Of the women in a recent *Who's Who in America,* 40 per cent were unmarried and 41 per cent of those who were married had no children. Jensen, *op. cit.,* p. 99.

119. Bernard, *op. cit.,* p. 83.

120. Wendell Bell, Richard J. Hill, and Charles R. Wright, *Public Leadership,* San Francisco: Chandler, 1961, p. 41; *Time,* March 20, 1964, p. 85; *Handbook on Women Workers, op. cit.,* p. 16.

121. *Handbook on Women Workers, op. cit.,* p. 16. The total number, though, of women professional and technical workers was 87 per cent more than in 1940.

122. Katherine Hamill, "Women as Bosses," *Fortune,* June 1956, p. 106.

123. *Time,* March 20, 1964, p. 85; *Handbook on Women Workers, op. cit.,* p. 18; Roe, *op. cit.,* p. 99.

124. Cussler, *op. cit.,* p. 15.

125. Women constitute 85 per cent of the elementary school teachers and 47 per cent of the secondary school teachers. *Saturday Review,* May 18, 1963, p. 70.

126. *This Week,* February 9, 1964, p. 7. In 1950 women constituted 45 per cent of those in the professions; today only 36 per cent. Wilbur J. Cohen, "Womanpower Policies for the 1970's," *Seminar on Manpower Policy and Program,* U.S. Department of Labor, 1967.

127. Men now comprise 59 per cent of elementary school principals. *New York Times,* December 6, 1964, p. E7. In 1964 there were no female superintendents of schools in Minnesota and only four per cent of the members of the Minnesota Association of Secondary School Principals were women and only 37.6 per cent of the Minnesota Association of Elementary School Principals. *Minnesota Women! Report of the Governor's Commission on the Status of Women,* 1965, p. B-11.

128. The proportion of women in college teaching has not increased. In 1920, women constituted 26 per cent; in 1930, 27 per cent; in 1940, 28 per cent, and in 1964, 22 per cent. *Report of Progress in 1966 on the Status of Women, op. cit.,* p. 14. In the 1950's, out of the 120 women college presidents, only 20 were in coeducational institutions. Bernard, *op. cit.,* p. 180. By 1963 there were 155 female presidents of four-year colleges and universities, out of 1,447 positions. All but 15 were heads of Catholic women's colleges. *Saturday Review,* May 18, 1963, p. 70. The share of all doctoral degrees awarded to women has declined from a high of 15 per cent in 1920 and 1930 to 11 per cent in 1963. *Wisconsin Women, op. cit.,* p. 34. Women receive 39 per cent of all master's degrees.

129. 1910—558 women lawyers; 1940—4,447; 1950—6,271; 1960—7,434. This represents three per cent of the total. *Job Horizons for College Women in the 1960's, op. cit.,* p. 67. The Human Engineering Laboratory of Stevens Institute made a study of the primary characteristics common to various professions. In the case of lawyers it found five important traits: a

subjective personality, capacity for inductive reasoning, an aptitude for account, a large English vocabulary, and creative imagination. The report concluded that "in every aptitude of a lawyer which the laboratory can measure, women average higher than men." Dorothy Kenyon, "Case (By One of Them) for Women Lawyers," *New York Times Magazine,* February 19, 1950, pp. 54-55.

130. Donald R. Matthews, *The Social Background of Political Decision-Makers,* New York: Random House, 1954, p. 30. Lawyers are only one-tenth of one per cent of the labor force.

131. *Minnesota Women, op. cit.,* p. A-18. Those women who do choose law as a career generally have family connections with lawyers. Women are hired by law firms for the "non-visible" research and library work.

132. *Ibid.,* p. A-19.

Chapter 2.
Women as Political Party Members

1. Emily Newell Blair, "Women at the Conventions," *Current History,* October 1920, p. 26.

2. *Literary Digest,* April 26, 1930, p. 11.

3. *The Outlook,* January 23, 1924, p. 148. In 1966 at least one male was so concerned at the inroads women were making into the two major parties that he urged the formation of a third party, conservative enough to keep women in their place. *New York Times,* August 30, 1966.

4. Jessica Weis in James M. Cannon, editor, *Politics U.S.A.,* Garden City, N. Y.: Doubleday, 1960, p. 187.

5. Interview made at the 1964 Republican Convention.

6. Mrs. Mae Geraghty, a New York Democratic leader, was also "born into" politics. Her father was a Democratic district captain and her forebears were Sinn Feiners and political activists in Ireland. Her husband came from a similar background. They worked together for the Suffrage Amendment during courtship and early years of marriage. (Interview at 1964 Democratic Convention.)

7. Eleanor Roosevelt and Lorena A. Hickok, *Ladies of Courage,* New York: Putnam's Sons, 1954, p. 290. Said one Democratic national committeewoman: "After pioneering in the field of mental retardation and having helped found the local state Association for Retarded, it became apparent that help from the State House was greatly needed to help remedy the awful and disgraceful conditions that existed in our own institutions. I hoped to gain political power that could help change the status quo in this field." (Interview at 1964 Democratic Convention.)

8. Interview at the 1964 Republican Convention. Another woman delegate told me that she felt an obligation to work for the Republican Party in Oklahoma after completing the Practical Politics Course offered by the United States Chamber of Commerce.

9. Roma Connable, "Politics—A New Wide-Open World for Women," *Mademoiselle,* March 1964, p. 165. Another young pro was Patt Shannon, paid executive secretary at 17 of the Lenox Hill Democratic Club of New York City, a reform association of 400 members. During the school year she spent about six hours a day in the club headquarters; at other times she worked up to 14 hours a day. She aspires to a U.S. Senate seat. *New York Times,* August 23, 1964, p. 72.

10. Emily Newell Blair, "New Styles in Feminine Beauty," *Outlook and Independent,* June 26, 1929, p. 330.

11. Interview at 1964 Republican Convention. Another national committeewoman agreed. "I feel that if women show that they are not self-seeking and have mature, objective judgment, they will be consulted for their views and ideas."

12. Emily Newell Blair, *Outlook and Independent,* June 26, 1929, p. 330.

13. New York *Post,* February 24, 1964, p. 19.

14. Marion K. Sanders, *The Lady and the Vote,* Boston: Houghton Mifflin, 1956, p. 141; Weis, *op. cit.,* p. 174.

15. Ernestine Evans, "Woman in the Washington Scene," *Century Magazine,* August 1923, pp. 512-13. This charge that women are suspicious of the motives of other women and are jealous of their advancement is echoed in Roosevelt and Hickok, *op. cit.,* pp. 304-05.

16. "Politicians will cheerfully continue to exploit women's genius for dreary detail. Over 8,000,000 dedicated ladies will toil in this year's campaign for long hours, no wages and no visible rewards. But let a woman talk strategy or policy, issues, patronage or money, and men's faces freeze; they are repelled by any such presumption of political equality." Barbara Wendell Kerr, "Don't Kid the Women," *Woman's Home Companion*, October 1956, p. 4.

17. *Independent Woman*, January 1951, p. 5.

18. Hugh D. Scott, Jr., *How to Go into Politics*, New York: John Day, 1949, p. 148; Maurice Duverger, *The Political Role of Women*, Paris UNESCO, 1955, p. 129.

19. Interview at 1964 Republican Convention.

20. Alice Curtice Moyer-Wing,, "The Vote: Our First Comeback," *Scribner's Magazine*, September 1928, pp. 261, 263.

21. Stella E. Barker, *Independent Woman*, January 1951, p. 28.

22. "Gina Allen," *Ladies' Home Journal*, November 1962, p. 138.

23. Louise M. Young, *Understanding Politics*, New York: Pellegrini & Cudahy, 1950, p. 170.

24. Samuel Grafton, "Women in Politics: The Coming Breakthrough," *McCall's*, September 1962, pp. 102-03.

25. *Woman's Home Companion*, July 1955, p. 18; John Gordon Ross, "Ladies in Politics," *The Forum*, November 1936, p. 213.

26. Ann Hard, "Are Women Making Good in Politics?" *Pictorial Review*, June 1928, p. 79.

27. Sanders, *op. cit.*, p. 120. An estimated 6,000,000 women did some sort of volunteer work in the presidential campaign of 1960.

28. *Ibid.*, p. 31. Women also constitute a majority of the staff in the various national and state committee headquarters. Hugh A. Bone, *Party Committees and National Politics*, Seattle: University of Washington Press, 1958, p. 107.

29. Interview at 1964 Republican Convention.

30. Cornelius P. Cotter and Bernard C. Hennessy, *Politics Without Power: The National Party Committees,* New York: Atherton, 1964, p. 54.

31. *Democratic Campaign Manual,* 1964, pp. 17-18. Senator Henry Cabot Lodge was reputed to have said after his loss to John F. Kennedy in 1952: "It was those damned *Kaffeeklatches* that beat me!" *Saturday Evening Post,* September 17, 1960, p. 78.

32. Marion K. Sanders, "Issues Girls, Club Ladies, Camp Followers," *New York Times Magazine,* December 1, 1963, p. 65.

33. Interview with a delegate to 1964 Democratic Convention.

34. "It is perfectly logical for the doorbell ringer to be a woman, because the person who *answers* the doorbell is likely to be a woman." Comment of Esther Peterson to a meeting of the Democratic National Committee. January 18, 1963, p. 4.

35. William Hettinger, deputy state chairman of the Michigan Democratic Party, observed: "Because of the women, we now keep records and have filing systems in the precincts." *McCall's,* September 1962, p. 156.

36. Sonya Forthal, *Cogwheels of Democracy: A Study of the Precinct Captain,* New York: William-Frederick Press, 1946, pp. 21, 24-25.

37. Scott, *op. cit.,* p. 147 Coke and rummage sales are penny ante as far as the parties' needs are concerned.

38. Marybeth Weston, "Ladies' Day on the Hustings," *New York Times Magazine,* October 19, 1958, p. 91.

39. *Ladies' Home Journal,* May 1952, p. 168.

40. Duverger, *op. cit.,* p. 110, noted that auxiliary organizations may present a problem to a party because of two conflicting objectives: (a) the object of preventing the development within the party of more or less autonomous groups which might lead to rivalry and division, and (b) the object of winning as many supporters as possible by demonstrating the party's interest in the particular problems of each social group.

41. Quoted from a Republican leaflet of the time. E. F. Egan, "Women in Politics to the Aid of Their Party," *Saturday Evening Post,* March 22, 1920, p. 13. This view was presented by Will H. Hays, chairman of the Republican National Committee. Mrs. Egan "wanted to ask if that was the basis on which the 21- to 24-year-old boys are admitted to the party, but I hardly liked to risk being impertinent, so I kept quiet."

42. *Esquire,* July 1962, p. 93. For an early criticism of party auxiliary organizations for women, see Esther Evereth Lape, "When Are Equal Suffragists Equal?" *Ladies' Home Journal,* July 1920, p. 82.

43. Sanders, *op. cit.,* p. 143.

44. Interview of a delegate to 1964 Democratic Convention.

45. Elizabeth Green, "I Resign from Female Politics," *New Republic,* April 22, 1925, p. 234. A letter to the editor, *New Republic,* June 10, 1925, p. 76, commented that many of her accusations of make-work and inefficiency were equally applicable to male political organizations. The writer recommended quota representation for party offices as a way to give women their chance.

46. Mrs. Corrine Roosevelt Robinson, T. R.'s sister, had declined the post of woman leader because of an eye condition. Harding thereupon suggested Mrs. Upton as being "safe and sane." *Random Recollections of Harriet Taylor Upton,* Committee for Preservation of Ohio Woman Suffrage Records, 1927, Ch. XXV, p. 6.

47. Eunice Fuller Barnard, "Madame Arrives in Politics," *North American Review,* November 1928, p. 553; Ann Hard, "Are Women Making Good in Politics?" *Pictorial Review,* June 1928, p. 79; *North American Review,* June 1930, p. 754.

48. The woman's movement in the Democratic Party had passed its peak by the beginning of F.D.R's third term. Bess Furman, *Washington By-Line: The Personal History of a Newspaperwoman,* Knopf, 1949, p. 284. The memoirs of Farley and Edward Flynn give scant credit to the work of their party's Women's Division. Assisting Miss Dawson in the thirties were Mrs. James H. Wolfe, wife of a Utah Supreme Court justice, and Mrs. Dorothy McAllister, wife of a Michigan Supreme Court justice.

49. Gladys Tillett has been president of the North Carolina League of Women Voters (1933-34). Her father was a North Carolina Supreme Court judge and her husband was a lawyer. In 1940 she became vice chairman of the Democratic National Committee. She served under six male chairmen. Later, in 1955, she became a member of the Advisory Political Committee of the Democratic National Committee and in 1961 was named an alternate delegate to the U.N.

50. Between terms as Connecticut secretary of state and U.S. Congresswoman.

51. A veteran of 22 years on the *Chicago Tribune.*

52. *Saturday Evening Post,* July 7, 1951, p. 109. Mrs. Edwards asked President Truman: "Don't you think it would be a good idea to have a woman on the FCC? Women are very concerned about radio and its influence on the home." The president appointed Frieda Hennock to the Federal Communications Commission. Tris Coffin, "India Edwards: Queen-Maker of Washington," *Coronet,* April 1951, p. 126.

53. The GOP alternately called the head of its women's division "assistant chairman" and "assistant to the chairman." It is an unwritten law that she must be a member of the Republican National Committee.

54. Miss Adkins, a dean of women at Maryland College, was a national committeewoman from 1948 to 1958. Mrs. Anne Wheaton, who had served from 1940 to 1957 as director of women's publicity for the Republican National Committee, became associate press secretary to the President. Her father had been a New York state assemblyman and labor commissioner under five governors. From 1924 to 1939 she was a public relations consultant for such groups as the Cause and Cure of War Conference, Women's Organization for Prohibition Reform, and LWV. Mrs. Wheaton prepared an annual survey of women in the public service, first for the LWV and then for the Republican National Committee.

55. Some argued that this was a realization that women were coming of age politically. Paul P. Van Riper, *Handbook of Practical Politics,* Second Edition, Evanston, Illinois: Row, Peterson, 1960, p. 128-29.

56. Her husband was a lawyer with the Securities and Exchange Commission since 1934. In 1961 she became deputy assistant secretary of state, Bureau of Public Affairs.

57. *Saturday Evening Post*, September 17, 1960.

58. In approaching the local party organizations, the Women's Divisions in the national headquarters always try to operate through the committeewomen if they can. Bone, *op. cit.*, p. 18.

59. A New York County Democratic Woman's Workshop attempted for three years in the 1950's to raise the level of political literacy. It was criticized within the party organization for duplicating the LWV and was ended.

60. Cotter and Hennessy, *op. cit.*, p. 1952; Bone, *op. cit.*, p. 53.

61. Democratic Congressional Wives Forum, *History of Democratic Women*, 1960, p. 29; and other party publications.

62. Paul T. David, Ralph M. Goldman, and Richard C. Bain, *The Politics of National Party Conventions*, Brookings Institution, 1960, pp. 327-29, 515-16.

63. *Christian Science Monitor*, July 11, 1964.

64. The Maryland United Democratic Women's Clubs and the Republican Federation of Women's Clubs campaigned intensively for greater representation of their sex at the 1964 national conventions. Lists were compiled and interested women were urged to contact their city and county leaders to let it be known they wished to be delegates. *Report of the Maryland Commission on the Status of Women*, 1966-67, p. 37.

65. Each state delegation is to select a male and female delegate to serve on each committee. Failure to select a woman could result in the loss of 50 per cent of that state's voice and vote. In 1944 the practice began of naming a woman co-chairman of each major convention committee.

66. Marion Sanders, "Woman in Politics," *Harper's*, August 1955, p. 56.

67. Frank Graham, Jr., *Margaret Chase Smith: Woman of Courage*, New York: John Day, 1964, p. 91.

68. According to Margaret Mead: "There are two aspects of American campaign politics that have little appeal for most women. One is the element of play—an interest in the game for its own sake, regardless of the

stakes. The other is the sense of personal involvement in a struggle for power—the thrill of taking part in a contest." Margaret Mead, "Must Women Be Bored With Politics?" *Redbook,* October 1964, p. 20.

69. Emily Newell Blair, "Men in Politics," *Harper's,* May 1926, pp. 704, 706. Mrs. Blair concluded: "Whether politics will make women into a fighting animal or whether women will make politics into a club—that remains to be seen." P. 709.

70. Mrs. Blair said of her position on the National Committee: "I was simply stage furniture and nothing more." *Harper's,* October 1925, p. 521.

71. Mrs. Vredenburgh, whose husband was in the lumber business, had been active in the Young Democratic Clubs. She was elected national committeewoman of the Alabama Young Democrats in 1941 and in 1943 became vice president of the Young Democratic Clubs of America, the highest office that a woman could hold in that organization. *Current Biography,* 1948, p. 659.

72. John W. Bush is chairman of the Interstate Commerce Commission.

73. Josephine L. Good, *The History of Women in Republican National Conventions and Women in the Republican National Committee,* Washington, D.C.: Women's Division of Republican National Committee, 1963, p. 27. Mrs. Hay was a national committeewoman from 1942 to 1948. She was succeeded as secretary in 1948 by Mrs. Katherine Howard of Massachusetts. Mrs. Howard, a national committeewoman from 1945 to 1953, was named by President Eisenhower in 1953 to be assistant administrator of Civil Defense. Other secretaries have included Mrs. George Knowles, Montana; Mrs. Wesley M. Dixon, Illinois and Mrs. Elizabeth E. Heffelfinger, Minnesota.

74. Plus a bonus of one, invariably a man, granted by the Republicans to states which tend to vote Republican.

75. Roosevelt and Hickok, *op. cit.,* pp. 15, 38. "But the framework is there. It's up to the woman to use it effectively."

76. Seymour M. Farber and Roger H. L. Wilson, ed., *The Potential of Women,* New York-San Francisco-Toronto-London: McGraw-Hill, 1963, p. 178. Edward J. Flynn, a Democratic national chairman under Roosevelt, once

listed his specifications for the ideal national committeewoman: "She must be handsome, a lady, able to introduce the President gracefully, and wear orchids well; she must have an acceptable bank account—and she must never, never, interfere with party policy." Barbara Wendell Kerr, "Don't Kid the Women," *Woman's Home Companion,* October 1956, p. 4.

77. *Fortune,* February 1964, p. 82.

78. Cotter and Hennessy, *op. cit.,* p. 59. Frank R. Kent, in *The Great Game of Politics* (quoted in Sanders, *op. cit.,* p. 22) wrote in 1923, "Two-thirds of the women on national committees are muddy-minded. Apparently they were selected by the local machine leaders to avoid friction."

79. *Ibid.,* p. 22. "The mores of the patriarchal society work against the political woman in this way as in many others; she cannot so easily tie her family to her political career as is possible for—as, indeed, is the common practice of—the male."

80. Interview at 1964 Democratic Convention.

81. Cotter and Hennessy, *op. cit.,* p. 45.

82. Interview at the 1964 Democratic Convention.

83. Interview at the 1964 Republican Convention.

84. Interview at the 1964 Republican Convention.

85. *Life,* July 4, 1960, p. 75.

86. *Milwaukee Journal,* January 24, 1965, p. 10. By 1967 there were four females out of 37 coordinating committee members—Senator Margaret Chase Smith, Mrs. Brooks, Mrs. Collis P. Moore of Oregon, national committee vice chairman, and Mrs. J. Willard Marriott of Washington, D.C., national committee vice chairman.

87. Louis Harris, *Is There a Republican Majority?: Political Trends,* 1952-1956, New York: Harper, 1954, p. 106.

88. Roosevelt and Hickok, *op. cit.,* p. 303.

89. Interview after 1964 Democratic Convention.

90. Interview of a former Democratic state chairwoman after the 1964 convention.

91. *McCall's,* September 1962, p. 156.

92. Interview at 1964 Democratic Convention.

93. Interview after 1964 Democratic Convention.

94. An article in the *New York World* in 1923 said of Mrs. Moskowitz's influence on Governor Smith: "He has consulted with her about appointments, big and small; action upon bills sent by the Legislature, messages, proclamations, public addresses and all manner of political matters." Denis Tilden Lynch, "Friends of the Governor," *North American Review,* October 1928, p. 425.

95. Her husband was also a social worker in politics. He had run as a Bull Moose candidate for Congress in 1912 and 1914, and had been civil service commissioner of New York City.

96. Roosevelt and Hickok, *op. cit.,* p. 205. The national chairman in 1928 was John J. Raskob, a "Tyro in Politics" Lynch, *op. cit.,* p. 421. See also *Dictionary of American Biography,* Volume XI, p. 568.

97. Maria Falco, "The Day the Bosses Fumbled," in Rocco J. Tressolini and Richard T. Frost, ed., *Cases in American National Government and Politics,* Englewood Cliffs, N. J.: Prentice Hall, 1966, p. 62.

98. In 1964, New Jersey passed a law specifically allowing women to become chairmen. Some women had charged that the previous political nomenclature, "vice chairlady," was discriminatory because it implied that the post of chairman could be held only by a man. *New York Times,* May 3, 1964, IV, p. 2.

99. *New York Times,* January 17, 1965, p. 63; *Milwaukee Sentinel,* February 24, 1965, part 3, p. 4. Mrs. Kate Powell is chairman of the Missouri GOP. The Democrats in California have a woman chairman of the state's southern division, Mrs. Carmen Warschaw of Los Angeles. She is the daughter of the head of the Harvey Aluminum Company. In 1966 she was an unsuccessful candidate for state chairman.

100. Interview with Democratic vice chairman.

101. Interview with the Democratic national committeewoman from North Carolina.

102. There is no male equivalent to the Federation of Republican Women. Past state presidents of this organization are sometimes promoted to the post of state chairwoman.

103. Said one former state chairwoman: "For the most part, you find great jealousy; a woman nice and plump, about 60 or over, not aggressive along the work line, just a fine meeting attender, is always accepted much better than a neat, attractive, younger woman, who is a hard worker."

104. Esther Everett Lape, "When Are Equal Suffragists Equal?" *Ladies' Home Journal,* July 1920, p. 82.

105. Mrs. Arthur L. Livermore, a member of the National Suffrage Board and an officer during the four-year fight for suffrage in New York State, became chairman of the New York Executive Committee of the Republican Women after they got the vote.

106. In 1930, his daughter, Miss Sarah Schuyler Butler, became vice chairman of the New York Republican State Committee.

107. Colorado, Florida, Indiana, Iowa, Kansas, Missouri, Montana, New Jersey, Oregon, South Dakota, Utah, and West Virginia. The unofficial party organizations in Wisconsin give 50-50 representation on their state executive committees.

108. Delaware, Massachusetts, New Mexico, North Carolina, Oklahoma, and Pennsylvania.

109. Michigan, Nebraska, Texas, and Wyoming.

110. *Editorial Research Reports,* February 20, 1956, p. 125.

111. *McCall's,* September 1962, p. 158. Mrs. St. George got the county campaign committee chairmanship in 1942 as a consolation prize after being unable to win her party's endorsement for the State Assembly. She was the first woman in the state to hold such a post. Next year she became

county chairman. *Current Biography*, 1947, p. 560.

112. Interview at 1964 Democratic Convention.

113. One colleague noted that Mrs. Spiegel improved etiquette at meetings of the executive committee: "It's harder to be rude to a woman than to a man." *New York Times,* November 15, 1964, IV, p. 2. She was the first woman elected as chairman of the executive committee.

114. *New York Times,* December 12, 1964, pp. 1, 22. It is curious that no one considers it contrary to propriety for a father and son or brothers similarly to be engaged in politics and law.

115. Interview in Spring 1964.

116. James Q. Wilson, *The Amateur Democrats: Club Politics in Three Cities,* Chicago: University of Chicago Press, 1962, p. 63.

117. Dan Wakefield, "The Outriders," *Esquire,* July 1962, p. 92.

118. *New York Post,* February 25, 1964, p. 27.

119. The traditional co-leaders were usually housewives with little education who were simply picked because a woman had to be in the job and because her husband asked her to do it. Carmine De Sapio's co-leader, Mrs. Elsie Mattura, was interviewed on television in 1959 just before a primary election. She claimed that women had a voice in Mrs. De Sapio's club and that they were independent. When asked if she had ever voted against De Sapio in Tammany Hall, she looked shocked and exclaimed, 'God forbid!' " Wilson, *op. cit.,* p. 236.

120. Example: Representative Charlotte Reid was opposed in 1964 by a woman, Poppy X. Mitchell, a housewife who had never run for office, but who had had experience as a platform speaker.

121. Comment of Annabel Williams-Ellis in John H. Cutler, *What About Women?* New York: Ives Washburn, 1961, p. 192. This idea is echoed by Richard Neuberger. "Demagoguery ill suits a woman. A male politician may get by with stem-winding speeches that sound like a steam calliope. Such a performance from a woman would be regarded as practically a vaudeville act." *Adventures in Politics,* New York: Oxford University Press, 1954, p. 50.

Chapter 3
Women's Political Achievements in Other Countries

1. There have also been the female grey eminences like Catherine di Medici, Lady Wu, and the Empress Tzu-Hsi and the kings' mistresses, especially those who dominated French diplomacy in the reign of Louis XV. The Renaissance women rulers were as talented in intrigue as their male counterparts.

2. Carl Degler, "The Changing Place of Women in America," *Daedalus,* Spring 1964, p. 664. In several southern states, Republican women seem more steadily active than Democratic women, partly because their party is "new" to the region. *McCall's,* September 1962, p. 158. Women found it easier to succeed politically in the western United States than in the long-settled states.

3. Women's Bureau of U.S. Department of Labor, *Women in the World Today: Women in High-Level Elective and Appointive Positions in National Governments,* February 1963, p. 1. Statistics in this chapter come from this source unless otherwise stated.

4. Helen Gregory McGill, "These Women in Politics," *Canadian Magazine,* May 1934, p. 40.

5. *Reader's Digest,* July 1963, pp. 154-57; *New York Times,* December 6, 1964.

6. Alice Frazer, "You Are Losing Ground," *McCall's,* August 1947, p. 44.

7. Gosnell thought that the single-member district system made it harder for women to secure seats. Harold F. Gosnell, *Democracy: Threshold of Freedom,* New York: Ronald Press, 1948, p. 74.

8. *Louise M. Young, Understanding Politics,* New York: Pellegrini and Cudahy, 1950, p. 215. Women were 6.2 per cent of the French Chamber of Deputies, 10.7 per cent of the Danish Rigstag, and 5.4 per cent of the first Japanese Diet elected after the war.

9. Vera Brittain, *Lady Into Woman: A History of Women From Victoria to Elizabeth II,* London: Andrew Dakers Ltd., 1953, pp. 47-48, 51.

10. Miss Margaret Herbison, minister of Pensions and National Insurance; Miss Alice Bacon, minister of state for the Home Office; Jennie Lee (Mrs. Aneurin Bevan), parliamentary secretary to the Minister of Public Buildings and Works; Mrs. Eirene White, parliamentary secretary to the Colonial Affairs Ministry; Mrs. Judith Hart, parliamentary under secretary of State for Scotland; Mrs. Harriet Slater, a government whip. Note that Britain has a larger proportion of unmarried women holding key political posts than the U.S. Miss Patricia Hornsby-Smith, when she was 38 years old, was named parliamentary secretary to the Ministry of Health and became the youngest woman minister in British history. Miss Hornsby-Smith, now Dame Patricia, served as a minister from 1951 to 1961. She has been in Parliament since 1950. *New York Times,* June 26, 1964, p. 13. Most of the women who have reached ministerial rank have gone to education, health, or food. Marjorie Tait, *The Education of Women for Citizenship: Some Practical Suggestions,* Basle: UNESCO, 1954, p. 74. In 1955 Dame Evelyn Sharp became permanent secretary of the Ministry of Housing and Local Government.

11. *New York Times,* October 25, 1964.

12. *New York Times* June 26, 1964, p. 13. Said Dame Patricia Hornsby-Smith, "I'm always looked at as if I'm crackers when I mention to my American friends the possibility of a woman chairman at the Republican or Democratic conventions."

13. Britain, *op. cit.,* p. 48.

14. *Ibid.,* p. 59.

15. Denmark—15 out of 179 in the Folketing; Finland—34 out of 200 in Parliament; Norway—15 out of 150 in the Storting; Sweden—14 out of 151 in the First Chamber, 34 out of 232 in the Second Chamber. *Women in the World Today, op. cit.,* pp. 2, 5-6.

16. *Ibid.,* p. 6. In the early 1950's, 17 per cent of the Supreme Soviet were women. Maurice Duverger, *The Political Role of Women,* Paris: UNESCO, 1955, p. 76. There were 366 women among the 1,378 deputies in the Supreme Soviet, 26.4 per cent, in 1958. Several of the Republics in the U.S.S.R. have had Supreme Soviets which included one-third female membership. In 1959, 32.2 per cent of the Russian S.S.R. deputies were women as were 33.9 per cent in the Ukraine and 32.4 per cent in Kazakhstan.

17. *Ibid.,* p. 4. European women vote more for conservative and religious parties than European men. These parties believe that women belong in the home. It seems likely that most of the women legislators in Europe are put foward by the liberal and leftist parties. In such traditionalist countries as Portugal and Spain, women legislators are rare. Portugal had three in the 120-member National Assembly; Spain had three out of 586 members of the Cortes. There were more women elected under the Spanish republic than subsequently. Neither country had women in high-level administrative positions.

18. "This, in spite of the fact that at the time she actually was the powerful head of the party's committee in San Juan." Henry La Cossitt,"The Mayor Wears Flowers in Her Hair," *Saturday Evening Post,* May 22, 1954, p. 39. One observer described her as "an astute politician who looks like Queen Victoria." *American City,* May 1964, p. 39.

19. The first Diet after the war had 39 women among the 716 positions.

20. *Time,* February 10, 1967, pp. 31-32.

21. This "stems from a Moslem tradition of male privilege in the home, separation of the sexes in school, and perpetuation of a 'racist' notion that women are 'objects' worthy only of disdain. A 'good' girl in men's eyes, wears the veil, stays home, works hard, lets her father and her brother decide her life and pick her husband, and later lets her husband do all outside chores including the shopping." *New York Times,* January 24, 1965.

22. *Women in the World Today, op. cit.,* p. iii. A U.N. report prepared for the February 1965 meeting of the Commission on the Status of Women reported that the number of women serving in parliamentary, judicial, or foreign service posts appeared to be on the increase. Forty-seven of the 54 countries supplying data had women serving in the national legislatures. Twenty-three of these countries had women ministers and 14 had women ambassadors. *New York Times,* January 24, 1965, p. 2.

Chapter 4
A Survey of Women's Organizations in America.

1. Figures used by Gertrude Atherton, *Can Women Be Gentlemen?* Boston:

Houghton Mifflin, 1938, p. 17. Pretty much the same statistics are employed in the 1965 report of the Illinois Commission on the Status of Women.

2. According to Cathleen Schurr, "The real control of America's vast assets is, unforgettably, where it always was, in the hands of men, with the banks, investment brokers, insurance companies, trust administrators, executors and assorted businessmen who still happen to run our economy." *New York Times Magazine,* November 24, 1957, p. 24. "Of 20 industrial corporations—public utility, railroad, oil, motors, food products, and so on—chosen at random in 1960, listing 419 officers and 298 directors, only two names of women appeared, and both for internal reasons. One was an assistant secretary and one an assistant treasurer." Mildred Adams, *The Right To Be People,* Philadelphia-New York: J. B. Lippincott, 1966, p. 219.

3. Maurice Duverger, *The Political Role of Women,* Paris, UNESCO, 1955, pp. 114-15.

4. In the old days, welfare legislation was attacked as "the uplift stuff with which the lady politicians were trying to save the world," proposed by old maids "meddling with other people's children." This line of attack has subsided now that most of the crusading is handled by married women who are mothers. Olive A. Colton, "Adventures of a Woman Voter," *Survey,* September 1, 1928, pp. 534, 561.

5. "Bouquets to the power of women for good were presented in an editorial *after* the law was passed," wrote one woman activist, "but there were no wayside flowers to pick during the legislative siege." *Ibid.,* p. 535.

6. Arnold M. Rose, "The Role of Voluntary Associations in American Democracy," *The American Review,* December 1961, p. 83.

7. One such organization is the Woman's Municipal League of Boston which has worked in the following areas: city cleanup campaigns, community education, naturalization and citizenship training, adult education, social welfare, art and music activities, public health, and morality. See Dorothy Worrell, *The Woman's Municipal League of Boston: 1908-1943,* Boston: Privately published, 1943.

8. Mary Gray Peck, *Carrie Chapman Catt: A Biography,* New York: H. W.

Wilson, 1944, p. 309. What may have been disturbing the New York Republican women was the League's campaign against the re-election of New York Republican Senator James W. Wadsworth, the only instance in which the National LWV took a specific stand on a candidate in an election. Dorothy Elizabeth Johnson, *Organized Women and National Legislation: 1920-1941,* unpublished Ph.D. dissertation, Western Reserve University, 1960, p. 311. Wadsworth received 800,000 fewer votes than the head of his ticket, Harding.

9. One conservative GOP congressman called the League "a very insidious organization." "It parades around as a non-partisan, good-government group, but the truth of the matter is that all of its policy positions are very liberal . . . . If their staff people presented both sides of an issue and encouraged the local groups to form their own positions, I'd say the League was a very good thing. As it is, though, the organization sucks in a lot of civic-minded women who lack political orientation, then deluges them with Democratic propaganda." *Wall Street Journal,* October 17, 1968, p. 8.

10. Sara Barbara Brumbaugh, *Democratic Experience and Education in the National League of Women Voters,* New York: Teachers College Bureau of Publications, 1946, p. 38.

11. *Woman's Day,* May 1964, p. 114.

12. LWV, *Forty Years of a Great Idea,* Washington, D.C.: Publication #266, 1960, p. 16.

13. *New York Times,* February 23, 1936, IV, p. 12; Valborg Esther Fletty, *Public Services of Women's Organizations,* unpublished Ph.D. dissertation, Syracuse University, 1952, pp. 73-76.

14. *Forty Years of a Great Idea, op. cit.,* p. 16.

15. See p. 948ff of the House Foreign Affairs Committee Hearings on the Foreign Assistance Act of 1964.

16. LWV, *The Member and the League,* Washington, D.C., Publication #264, March 1960, pp. 2-3.

17. See Fletty, *op. cit.,* pp. 37, 39. The New York City LWV also campaigned

successfully for the abolition of the county form of government and for elimination of the residence requirement for city employees.

18. *Wall Street Journal,* October 17, 1963, p. 1.

19. Among these is the *Handbook for Citizens,* 1963, prepared by the LWV of Raleigh, North Carolina. It is sent to tourists, businesses, and prospective residents.

20. Among these is *Man and the River: The Story of the Delaware River Basin,* prepared in 1959 by the LWV's of Delaware, New Jersey, New York, and Pennsylvania.

21. A number of women in political party positions fail to recognize this and insist that the League was non-partisan because it feared losing tax-exempt status. The Internal Revenue Service considers it a lobbying group.

22. See, for example, the brochure "Who Writes to Congressmen?" prepared by the New York State LWV in behalf of the 1963 foreign aid bill.

23. Hilda Cole Espy, "The League of Women Voters," *Woman's Day,* May 1964, p. 45. The legislative agent for Michigan's AFL-CIO, which opposed the League's drive for a new state constitution, complained: "To differ with the League is to differ with motherhood and the flag. You try to debate with them and the woman comes in late. She says she's sorry but she had to change the baby or see her daughter married. After this, it's hard to argue the merits of the issue." *Wall Street Journal,* October 17, 1963, p. 1.

24. *Wall Street Journal,* October 17, 1963, p. 8. George Romney told the LWV National Convention in 1962 to be less leisurely and less feminine and to become more active in politics. *New York Times,* May 3, 1962, p. 5.

25. *Century Magazine,* August 1923, p. 514.

26. *The Member and the League, op. cit.,* pp. 14-15.

27. Marion K. Sanders, *The Lady and the Vote,* Boston: Houghton Mifflin, 1956, p. 119.

28. *Illinois Voter* (LWV of Illinois), July-August 1964, p. 1.

29. LWV, *Facts About the League of Women Voters,* Washington, D.C., Publication 221, June 1964. The "Voteless League of Women Voters" of Washington, D.C., studies legislation affecting that city and testifies before congressional committees in behalf of stronger school attendance laws, mothers' pensions, minimum wages for women and for adequate appropriations for municipal institutions. Green, *op. cit.,* p. 318.

30. *Wall Street Journal,* October 17, 1963, p. 1.

31. Johnson, *op. cit.,* p. 51.

32. League officers are usually chosen from a single slate of candidates. This is a not uncommon practice among national organizations.

33. Philip Hastings, "How and Howevers of the Women Voter," *New York Times Magazine,* June 12, 1960, p. 14.

34. *The Member and the League, op. cit.,* p. 2.

35. A few men are accepted, along with girls and aliens, as associate members and have no vote and no voice in policy. They pay dues in order to obtain the League's stream of fact sheets, pamphlets, leaflets and reports.

36. June 6, 1962, news release of the New York Department of State.

37. Brumbaugh, *op. cit.,* p. 4.

38. Often the arguments resemble those justifying separate colleges for women. The former president of Vassar predicted, however, that women's colleges would either become coeducational—since their programs are as suitable for men as for women—or cease to exist. Jessie Bernard, *Academic Women,* University Park: Pennsylvania State University Press, 1964, p. 99.

39. Betty Friedan, *The Feminine Mystique,* New York: W. W. Norton, 1963, p. 390.

40. American Legion Auxiliary (membership, approximately 1,000,000), Ladies Auxiliary to the Veterans of Foreign Wars of the United States (membership, 355,000), Disabled American Veterans Auxiliary (membership, 50,000).

41. Daughters of the American Revolution (membership, 185,000), Daughters of Union Veterans of the Civil War (membership 15,000), United Daughters of the Confederacy (membership 36,000).

42. The April 1964 issue of the American Legion Auxiliary magazine, *National News,* reminded members that Section 2 of Article II of the ALA Constitution read: "The American Legion Auxiliary shall be absolutely non-political and shall not be used for the dissemination of partisan principles nor for the promotion of the candidacy of any person seeking public office or preferment," p. 14. The January 1964 DAR circular to members contained a similar declaration of non-political status.

43. The patriotic organizations were not among the backers of woman's suffrage. One of the early leaders of the DAR, Mrs. Flora Adams Darling, widow of a Civil War general and a magazine editor, said she believed in "men for offices—women for pleasure." Martha Strayer, *The DAR: An Informal History,* Washington, D.C.: Public Affairs Press, 1958, p. 1.

44. Peck, *op. cit.,* pp. 440-41.

45. Among the other female peace lobbyists were former Representative Jeannette Rankin (National Council for the Prevention of War), Josephine Schain (National Conference on the Cause and Cure of War), Estelle Sternberger (World Peaceways). For many years Dorothy Detzer served as national secretary, lobbyist, of WIL. See her account, *Appointment on the Hill,* New York: Henry Holt, 1948. The present Washington representative of the WIL is Mrs. Annalee Stewart, an ordained Methodist minister.

46. Mrs. Hedgeman was the first Negro woman appointed to the Social Security Agency and the first in the New York mayor's cabinet. See her *The Trumpet Sounds: A Memoir of Negro Leadership,* New York: Holt, Rinehart and Winston, 1965. In 1965 she was an unsuccessful candidate for president of the New York City Council.

47. A group called MOMS (Mothers Opposed to Meddling in Schools) was organized in Chicago in 1965 to support Superintendent Benjamin Willis. They attended meetings of the Board of Education and knitted while listening.

48. See John B. Keeley, "Moses on the Green," Inter-University Case Program #45, 1959, for an example of how a small group of outraged and

determined mothers were able to "fight City Hall" and win.

49. Friedan, *op. cit.*, p. 375.

50. Lobbying was attacked by "George Madden Martin," a woman, as "both a moral and political crime." George Madden Martin, "The American Woman and Representative Government," *Atlantic,* March 1925, p. 369.

51. For an article on the WJCC with a most misleading title see Charles A. Selden, "The Most Powerful Lobby in Washington," *Ladies' Home Journal,* April 1922, pp. 5, 93-96.

52. Fletty, *op. cit.,* p. 51. The NWTUL legislative chairman was often chairman of WJCC subcommittees created to support particular measures.

53. There were annual fluctuations in the number of working subcommittees and in the number of member organizations: 1920, 10 members; 1925, 21 members; 1929, 18 members. In 1928 the General Federation of Women's Clubs withdrew. By 1951 the National Federation of Business and Professional Women's Clubs and the League of Women Voters had also withdrawn and the National Women's Trade Union League was extinct.

54. Eudora Ramsey Richardson, "The Ladies of the Lobby" *North American Review,* June 1929, p. 652.

55. The National Association Opposed to Woman Suffrage opposed the Sheppard-Towner bill. Josephine Goldmark, *Impatient Crusader: Florence Kelley's Life Story,* Urbana: University of Illinois Press, 1953, p. 108. The DAR at first supported the measure, but later reversed its stand.

56. Eleanor Flexnor, *Century of Struggle: The Women's Rights Movement in the United States,* Cambridge: Belknap Press of Harvard University Press, 1959, p. 325.

57. *Congressional Quarterly Weekly Reports,* April 7, 1961, pp. 624-25. Some of these groups acted in a quid pro quo arrangement. That is, they were not vitally concerned with the issue but their allies on other matters were.

58. Miss Paul earned an M.A. and Ph.D. from the University of Pennsylvania, and LL.B. from Washington College of Law, an LL.M. and D.C.L. from American University.

59. Elizabeth Jordan, "Women in the Presidential Campaign," *Ladies' Home Journal,* October 1920, p. 4.

60. Mrs. O. H. P. Belmont, "Women as Dictators," *Ladies' Home Journal,* September 1922, p. 7.

61. Smith told a NWP representative: "You will never turn me against these protective laws . . . . I believe in equality, but I cannot nurse a baby." Johnson, *op. cit.,* p. 144.

62. Thanks to the NWP, the Federation of Women's Clubs, the LWV, the Wisconsin Women's Progressive Association, and other groups, Wisconsin in 1921 passed an Equal Rights Law: "Women shall have the same rights and privileges under the law as men in the exercise of suffrage, freedom of contract, choice of residence for voting purposes,* jury service, holding office, holding and conveying of property, care and custody of children, and in all other respects. The various courts, executive and administrative officers shall construe the statutes where the masculine gender is used to include the feminine gender unless such construction shall deny to females the special protection and privileges they now enjoy for the general welfare."** Mabel Raef Putnam, *The Winning of the First Bill of Rights for American Women,* Milwaukee: privately published, 1923.

63. In the 1960's it was supported by the Ladies Auxiliary to the Veterans of Foreign Wars. In 1943 the NWP and its allies formed a Women's Joint Legislative Committee for Equal Rights to coordinate work for the amendment.

64. Said Holmes: "It will take more than the nineteenth amendment to convince men that there are no differences between men and women."

65. They contend that every statute affecting the relation of women in society would be subjected to constitutional attack. They note that the passage of the nineteenth amendment was used by the conservative majority in the

---

*The fact that a wife could not establish a separate legal domicile might prevent her from being able to vote if her husband maintained as his residence his place of business in a different community. Johnson, *op. cit.,* p. 75.

**William Bradford Smith, a Madison attorney, prepared a fact paper for the First Wisconsin Governor's Conference on the Status of Women, 1963, entitled "Equal Rights—In Favor of Women." He contended that in the area of wage and hours legislation, inheritance, property disposal, and divorce, especially if children were involved, Wisconsin women enjoyed better than equal rights.

Supreme Court to justify their attitude in the Adkins case, which declared the Washington, D.C., women's minimum wage law unconstitutional. Justice Sutherland stated that the grant of suffrage had improved the status and bargaining power of women so that limiting their freedom of contract was a violation of the due process clause of the fifth amendment of the constitution.

66. Fletty, *op. cit.,* pp. 270-72.

67. According to Perle Mesta, she went to the convention as a National Women's Party lobbyist. The chairman of the platform committee was an old friend of hers. She suggested he use the NWP proposal. Perle Mesta, with Robert Cahn, *Perle: My Story,* New York-Toronto-London: McGraw-Hill, 1960, p. 79. In 1944, after switching her registration to the Democrats, Perle, an alternate delegate, helped Emma Guffey Miller get the NWP equal rights plank added to the Democratic platform, despite the opposition of Mrs. Roosevelt and Secretary of Labor Frances Perkins. *Ibid.,* p. 98.

68. President Truman endorsed the amendment in 1945. By 1947, 30 state governors had come out for it.

69. Republicans: "(We pledge) continued opposition to discrimination based on race, creed, national origin or sex. We recognize that the elimination of any such discrimination is a matter of heart, conscience, and education, as well as of equal rights under law." Democrats: "We will support legislation to carry forward the progress already made toward full equality of opportunity for women as well as men."

70. Lyndon Johnson: "Regarding the Equal Rights for Men and Women Amendment,—as I am sure you know, I have consistently supported this resolution, and I intend to continue with this support." October 19, 1960, letter to National Woman's Party. Barry Goldwater: "I will be very glad to help you in any way that I can on the Equal Rights for Women Amendment. I felt certain that it would be approved by now, but the ways of amending the constitution prove long and difficult. But I believe, as you must also, that this is a wise way." November 13, 1963, letter to National Woman's Party. Henry Cabot Lodge: "Concerning the issue of the Equal Rights for Women Amendment—during my time in the Senate, I supported legislation of this nature, and my position has not changed." October 31, 1960, letter to National Woman's Party. Richard M. Nixon: "It is my hope

that both major parties will include a declaration in behalf of the Equal Rights Amendment to the constitution in their platforms. With this kind of bi-partisan support we can finally achieve the objective of equality between the sexes." December 30, 1963, letter to National Woman's Party. Nelson A. Rockefeller: "As the Woman Suffrage Amendment to the constitution completed the first step in the emancipation of women, so the present step, the removal of every remaining discrimination against women under the law, through the adoption of the Equal Rights Amendment, seems a logical conclusion to women's effort to achieve equality and justice." August 23, 1959, statement to National Woman's Party.

71. William Goodman, *The Two-Party System in the United States,* third edition, Princeton, N. J.: Van Nostrand, 1964, p. 366.

72. The headline in the *Independent Woman,* publication of the pro-amendment National Federation of Business and Professional Women's Clubs, for August 1953, p. 300, reflected the chagrin of the proponents: "Senate Scuttles Full Partnership." Senator Hayden's amendment stated: "The provisions of this article shall not be construed to impair any rights, benefits or exemptions now or hereafter conferred by law upon persons of the female sex." The language resembles the escape clause in the 1921 Wisconsin statute.

73. One of its backers, Senator Margaret Chase Smith, has accused the NWP of being overzealous and alienating senators, of talking too long and too hard. Sanders, *op. cit.,* pp. 17-18.

74. Like the Women's International League for Peace and Freedom and the National Woman's Party, the National Council is the U.S. section of an international association.

75. Among its prominent members are Mary P. Lord, a former member of the U.S. delegation to the U.N. and chairman of the New York Governor's Committee on the Employment and Education of Women. Eleanor Clark French, former vice chairman of the New York State Democratic Party and New York City's UB Commissioner, Marietta Tree, former member of the U.S. U.N. delegation, Dr. Persia Campbell, adviser to the New York State and U.S. governments on consumer problems, and Judge Libby E. Sachar. Many of the members are the capable wives of prominent political, academic and business men, for example, Mrs. Robert Meyner, Mrs. Lloyd

K. Garrison, Mrs. Quincy Wright, Mrs. Birch E. Bayh, Mrs. Abe Fortas, Mrs. Brooks Hays, and Mrs. John J. McCloy.

76. N. C. W. Bulletin, October-November 1964, p. 2.

77. *Ibid.,* p. 6.

78. Interview with Mrs. Louis J. Robbins.

79. Johnson, *op. cit.,* pp. 95-96.

80. *Literary Digest,* October 26, 1935, p. 38.

81. Miss Rock, whom the author interviewed, seems to be the only activist in it.

82. Marion Ash, *Skirting the Capitol,* Vol. I, No. 3, August 3, 1967, pp. 1-2.

83. Thomas J. Fleming, "Sex and Civil Rights," *This Week,* March 19, 1967.

84. The NFBPWC, sensitive to a charge of being special-interest oriented, changed the name of its magazine in 1956 from *Independent Woman* to *National Business Woman* and made stylistic changes in its 1956 platform in 1957 so as to make clear that the organization supported equality of treatment for men and women. See *National Business Woman,* March 1957, pp. 6-7.

85. The League and the General Federation of Women's Clubs were responsible for the establishment of the Food and Drug Administration. Goldmark, *op. cit.,* p. 90.

86. It is apparently up to women to speak for the under-represented consumers. Consumer legislation has been backed by the LWV, the General Federation of Women's Clubs, the National Women's Trade Union League, the AAUW, the American Home Economics Association, and the YWCA. The Tennessee Valley Authority was endorsed by the LWV, the GFWC, and the NWTUL. The LWV, the AAUW, the AHEA and NCW sent representatives to public hearings of the National Industrial Recovery Act to promote the consumer point of view. The AHEA and the AAUW opposed the Miller-Tydings Act of 1937, legalizing price-fixing agreements. The LWV, the GFWC, the NWTUL, the AAUW, and the YWCA opposed high tariffs.

87. The League can be credited with bringing the notion of a minimum wage to the United States. Louis Brandeis and Felix Frankfurter worked with the League in litigation involving the constitutionality of state wage and hour laws.

88. Johnson, *op. cit.,* pp. 37-38.

89. *Ibid.,* pp. 40-43.

90. Louise M. Young, "The American Women at Mid-Century," *The American Review,* December 1961, p. 137.

91. Hazel Davis and Agnes Samuelson, "Women in Education," *Journal of Social Issues,* Volume VI, Number 3, 1950, p. 34; *New York Times,* July 4, 1965, Section 4, p. 5.

92. R. Joseph Monsen, Jr., and Mark W. Cannon, *The Makers of Public Policy: American Power Groups and Their Ideologies,* New York-St. Louis-San Francisco-Toronto-London-Sydney: McGraw-Hill, 1965, Ch. 6.

93. Example: A few women's religious groups felt the state had no business requiring prayers in schools. After the Engel vs. Vitale decision, other organizations complained about outlawing religious observances. The campaign for the Becker Amendment to permit school prayers brought groups with both viewpoints into the political arena.

94. The liquor interests opposed the woman's vote because of this connection. Carrie C. Catt attributed the defeat of a suffrage referendum in 1916 to the fact that the campaign was led and staffed by active WCTU members. Flexnor, *op. cit.,* p. 185.

95. Joseph R. Gusfield, *Symbolic Crusade: Status Politics and American Temperance Movement,* Urbana: University of Illinois Press, 1963, pp. 76-77, 79.

96. There has been a corresponding consistent increase in the percentage of WCTU membership from the South and Midwest. Gusfield *(Ibid.,* pp. 161-62) estimated that there were 195,000 members in 1960. The WCTU claimed 300,000.

97. *Good Housekeeping,* July 1924, p. 184.

98. *Collier's,* May 21, 1932, p. 22.

99. Inez Haynes Irwin, *Angels and Amazons: A Hundred Years of American Women,* Garden City, N. Y.: Doubleday, Doran, 1933, pp. 332-33. "Membership in the anti-Prohibition organization merely means the signing of a card. There are no dues, no obligatory attendance at meetings, no committee work, whereas WCTU membership means both financial and personal sacrifice and untiring zeal." Malvina Lindsay, "Mrs. Grundy's Vote," *North American Review,* June 1932, p. 489.

100. This new ingredient undoubtedly precipitated the new amendment fight. Repeal promised jobs for the unemployed and tax revenues for bankrupt communities.

101. In the 1930's the organization opposed the Child Labor Amendment to the constitution and the bills to sterilize the "socially unfit." John Gordon Ross, "Ladies in Politics," *The Forum,* November 1936, p. 214.

102. A 1929 study revealed that of about a thousand members of the DAR living in 10 cities in five scattered states, more than a fourth belonged to the GFWC. Both organizations supported the quota system of immigration and internal security measures. Johnson, *op. cit.,* p. 513.

103. The GFWC and NFBPWC have also campaigned for uniform marriage and divorce laws.

104. "The nation is so vast, has so many sectional differences, that General Federation delegates find it difficult to agree at convention time and have been known to vote one way one day and reverse the vote the day after." *Woman's Home Companion,* April 1955, p. 68. According to another critic, whose criticism is just as valid for many men's organizations: "It would be a joy to report that the directives given its representatives by the General Federation of Women's Clubs on legislative matters are based on thorough schooling of its affiliated groups. Unfortunately, this is an exaggeration which could not be sustained in fact. While it has a hard-working legislative department whose national chairmen are selected with care and who are themselves almost invariably capable, only a small proportion of the club delegates can be said to have weighed carefully some of the most important matters on which votes are called during convention sessions. The brief time permissible for debate on programs crowded with reports from additional departments, as well as the lengthy

musical attractions and addresses customary at such events, is not conducive to exhaustive examination of such matters." Kathleen McLaughlin, "Women's Impact on Public Opinion." *The Annals,* May 1947, p. 109.

105. V. O. Key, *Politics, Parties, and Pressure Groups,* fifth edition, New York: Crowell, 1964, p. 105.

106. This is not just the case with women's groups. See Samuel H. Stouffer, *Communism, Conformity and Civil Liberties,* 1955.

107. Duverger, *op. cit.,* p. 115.

108. Johnson, *op. cit.,* p. 395. Example: Oshkosh, Wisconsin, had a city manager repeal referendum campaign in 1965. The local LWV scheduled a debate. When it could not get a representative from the anti-manager group, it announced it would hold an informational meeting. But it soon withdrew its sponsorship, fearing this would be interpreted as LWV endorsement.

109. Julia Lathrop, first head of the U.S. Children's Bureau, "learned to explore women's organizations for that moral enthusiasm which she constantly needed to back her official undertakings." Jane Addams, "Julia Lathrop at Hull House: Women and the Art of Government," *Survey Graphic,* September 1935, p. 434.

110. Johnson, *op. cit.,* p. 266. "Congress would have voted upon the bill in question long before the membership of any one of the groups had studied the principle involved and had given its endorsement through a national convention, as its regulations required." The constitution of the NWTUL permitted officers to act on emergency measures which they believed the membership would support. *Ibid.,* pp. 266-67.

111. Hugh D. Scott, Jr., *How To Go into Politics,* New York: John Day, 1949, p. 454. Scott also noted that women's organizations invite men to speak to them—much more frequently than vice versa, p. 155. Men's groups are more apt to have debates; women's groups prefer panels.

112. Miss Charl C. Williams, vice chairman of the Democratic National Committee from 1920 to 1924, eventually became president of both the NEA and the NFBPWC. Judge Florence E. Allen was active in the LWV,

the NFBPWC, and the AAUW. Mrs. Ellis A. Yost was a leader in the WCTU and the Republican Party. Mrs. Robert Lincoln Hoyal, director of the Women's Division of the Republican Party from 1935 to 1937, was president for two years of the Arizona State Federation of Business and Professional Women's Clubs and was national president of the American Legion Auxiliary. Congresswoman Ruth Bryan Owen was affiliated with the LWV, the NFBPWC, the AAUW, and the YWCA. Congresswoman Chase G. Woodhouse was national president of the Altrusa Clubs, 1933-37, and was also active in the NFBPWC, the LWV, and the American Home Economics Association.

Julia Lathrop was a member of the GFWC, the NWTUL, and the LWV. After her return from Washington, Miss Lathrop became president of the Illinois LWV, 1922-24, and later served as vice president and counsellor in public welfare of the national league. She spoke at citizenship schools and appeared at Illinois legislative committee hearings advocating protection of maternity and infancy, restrictions on child labor, the shorter working day, the minimum wage, women on juries, women in political parties, and educational measures. She even addressed hostile audiences of manufacturers, associations and medical societies. Mary G. Hay, New York State Republican vice chairman in 1920, was president of the Women's City Club of New York. Dr. Mary E. Wooley, president of Mount Holyoke College, was the national head of AAUW and a member of the YWCA Board, the LWV, the NFBPWC, and the NWTUL. She was appointed by Hoover as a delegate to the Geneva Disarmament Conference.

113. Our culture expects men to be aggressive and take the lead. Masculinity is made synonymous with assertiveness; femininity with quiescence. The male is instrumentally oriented, basically concerned with getting the task done. The female is expressively oriented, keeping human relations harmonious. In mixed company these qualities are projected to the point of exaggeration, whereas in segregated groups each sex feels free to perform both functions. The Wisconsin Governor's Commission on the Status of Women, *Wisconsin Women,* p. 26, reported in 1965 that women "hold a small percentage of top positions in the organizations having both male and female membership, and they spend limited time on the action or legislative programs."

Chapter 5.
Women in Government Since 1920

5a. Women in National Government

1. Democratic National Committee, *History of Democratic Women,* 1960, p. 15. Women hold numerous postal positions today. In Wisconsin, for example, there are 255 women among the 823 postmasters, 31 per cent. Mrs. Mary D. Briggs was appointed acting postmaster of Los Angeles in 1937 following the death of her husband. Another postmaster who "earned" her job at Fall River, Massachusetts, through widowhood was Mrs. Louis M. Howe, wife of Roosevelt's mentor. Mrs. Joseph T. Robinson, widow of the Senate leader, was made postmaster of Little Rock, Arkansas, in 1938

2. There are three commissioners. Miss Boardman was the chief organizer of the Women's Volunteer Services of the American Red Cross and was one of Washington's wealthy social elite. Constance McLaughlin Green, *Washington: Capital City: 1879-1950,* Princeton: Princeton University Press, 1963.

3. In 1964, only 14 women ran for 13 of the 435 congressional seats. Two ran for the same seat. Ten won. It was the lowest feminine total in years. Since 1917, women have constituted less than two per cent of those in Congress.

4. Anne Hard, "The Three Ruths in Congress," *Ladies' Home Journal,* March 1929, p. 13. There are few occasions where congresswomen act as a bloc. These circumstances usually involve the status of women. In 1964 Representative Edith Green objected to the practice of selecting only male congressional pages. She accused Congress of violating the section of the 1964 Civil Rights Act outlawing discrimination in employment based on sex. Another instance of discrimination on Capitol Hill, where the women legislators are as guilty as the men, is in the selection of personal staffs. Usually, men are appointed to the major positions, and women to minor ones. Undoubtedly, this reflects the sex ratio in the schools of law and political science. But these, in turn, reflect the job opportunities. Only five senators have female administrative assistants: Bartlett of Alaska, Church of Idaho, Mansfield of Montana, Curtis of Nebraska, and Randolph of West Virginia. Several representatives, such as Steiger of Wisconsin, have female administrative aides.

5. When Miss Rankin arrived in Washington, the reporters sent to interview her

were instructed to ask her if she could make pie. *Independent Woman,* January 1931, p. 3.

6. Louise M. Young, *Understanding Politics,* New York: Pellegrini and Cudahy, 1950, p. 199.

7. *The Outlook,* January 23, 1924, p. 150. James M. Burns, in his *Congress on Trial,* 1949, described the background of the average congressman: about 56; the son of someone who was reared on a farm but moved to town and into a business career, owning his own business; active in his high school student government or debate team; a lawyer; a member of the Masons, Elks, and Kiwanis; a veteran and member of the American Legion; previously elected to local government posts, town committeeman, county assistant attorney, or prosecuting attorney. In short, the logical choice for congressman when a vacancy developed on the death of the incumbent.

8. The Washington *Evening Star* called the practice "strange nepotism." Mrs. LaFollette preferred that her 31-year-old son, Bob, Jr., succeed her husband in the Senate, thereby keeping the seat in the family. *Literary Digest,* July 18, 1925, p. 13.

9. Grace Adams, "Women Don't Like Themselves." *North American Review,* June 1939, p. 291.

10. *Woman's Home Companion,* November 1922, p. 81. She lost again in 1924. In 1930 she ran unsuccessfully for a seat from New York. In 1928 a bereaved lady in Pennsylvania was also defeated for Congress. *American Mercury,* October 1929, p. 157.

11. *Outlook and Independent,* January 23, 1929, p. 126. Sometimes the right name is more important than the "heredity and training." Mrs. Caryl Kline, an unsuccessful candidate for Congress from New York, was the sister of Senator Wayne Morse, the daughter of a close friend of the LaFollettes, and the granddaughter of a founder of the Republican Party. However, the "Kline" name did not ring a political bell. Her husband, a Syracuse University geography professor, was her campaign manager. Marybeth Weston, "Ladies' Day on the Hustings." *New York Times Magazine,* October 19, 1958, pp. 32, 91-95. Not that a familiar name always brings victory. Mrs. Shirley Temple Black, as a candidate for Congress to fill a vacancy in 1967, received much more publicity than the other nine candidates, but was defeated in the primary. Analysts thought there had been a "Hollywood backlash."

12. Mrs. Mary Norton, a 13-termer who did not rise from her husband's ashes, was the only other congresswoman to head a major committee, the Labor Committee from 1937 to 1947.

13. Page H. Dougherty, "It's a Man's Game, But Woman Is Learning," *New York Times Magazine,* November 3, 1946, p. 54. This is true for congressmen as well. Said one, "There are 40 different ways for a member of Congress to solve the problem of keeping the family together, none of them any good." *McCall's,* September 1962, p. 160.

14. Marion K. Sanders, *The Lady and the Vote,* Boston: Houghton Mifflin, 1956, pp. 156-57.

15. *New York Times,* November 3, 1946, p. 54. Mrs. Kathryn Granahan wore a hat for her first appearance in the House of Representatives in 1956, but was told by the parliamentarian that an 1831 House rule forbade the wearing of hats during sessions. *Current Biography,* 1959, p. 158. It is also not proper for congresswomen to wear gloves when the House is in session. *New York Times,* January 8, 1959, p. 13.

16. Compare the treatment of female faculty members. "I wish hostesses would let me stay with the men, whose talk is interesting," complained one academic woman in words echoed by Senator Maurine Neuberger, "rather than insisting on including me among the women, most of whose talk is not interesting to me." Jessie Bernard, *Academic Women,* University Park: Pennsylvania State University Press, 1964, p. 188.

17. According to an ex-congresswoman, "Gradually all the femininity she may have had will be squeezed out of her. She will have to take to frills to hide the fact that she is becoming 10 times the man the male congressman is." Dougherty, *op. cit.,* p. 54. One congresswoman that the author interviewed mentioned, however, that when a woman makes a speech or asks a question, it is quieter in Congress. Another congresswoman claimed that a smart lobbyist will not approach a woman.

18. According to Representative Hansen: "A political career is developed, not inherited, and you don't usually arrive at zenith without some preparation more than being able to cook a good stew."

19. Seven states have had one woman senator: Alabama, Arkansas, Georgia, Louisiana, Maine and Oregon. Two states, Nebraska and South Dakota,

have had two. Of the 10 women senators, five were Republicans and five Democrats. Seven were on the job less than one year. Senator Neuberger served two terms, Senator Caraway three, and Senator Margaret Chase Smith, five. Donald Matthews found that almost half of the post-war senators achieved their first public office before they turned 30 and three-quarters of them before they were 40. Eighty-seven members of the 88th Congress, 1964, had held other public offices. David S. Broder, "What Makes a Great Senator?" *New York Times Magazine,* June 14, 1964, p. 15.

20. She polled 27,000 more votes than the man running for governor on the same ticket. Mrs. Hooper was also chairman for International Relations of the General Federation of Women's Clubs.

21. Willie Snow Ethridge, "The Lady from Georgia," *Good Housekeeping,* January 1923, p. 122; Ida Clyde Clarke, "A Woman for the Senate," *Century Magazine,* June 1929, p. 130.

22. The Louisiana Kingfish supplied a sound truck for Mrs. Caraway and persuaded her to wear widow's weeds. *Time,* September 5, 1960, p. 14.

23. Young, *op. cit.,* p. 204. *Ladies' Home Journal,* May 1933, p. 114.

24. Drury, *op. cit.,* p. 19.

25. *Ibid.,* pp. 224-25.

26. *Literary Digest,* September 4, 1937, p. 6.

27. Graduate of Huron, South Dakota, College. A teacher who later went into life insurance and farm management. An organizer and officer of the LWV. State Representative, 1923-26. Secretary of State, 1927-31. Member, State Securities Commission, 1931-33. Delegate to the 1940 Republican Convention. Appointed in 1941 to the South Dakota Board of Charities and Correction.

28. Mrs. Bushfield studied at Stout Institute, Wisconsin, Dakota Wesleyan University, and the University of Minnesota.

29. Asked about her courtship by Clyde Smith, she said: "Mostly we went campaigning. Anyone who ever spent any time with him ended up going

campaigning." Frank Graham, Jr., *Margaret Chase Smith: Woman of Courage,* New York: John Day, 1964, p. 26.

30. *Ibid.,* pp. 38-40. Mrs. Smith is quite effective in bringing home the groceries for her constituents. The military is one of the five top industries in Maine. *Ibid.,* p. 92. Atomic submarines were later constructed at Kittery, B-52 bombers were stationed at Loring Air Force Base, and missiles were installed in Aroostook County. *Ibid.,* pp. 130-31.

31. *Ibid.,* pp. 48-50.

32. *Saturday Evening Post,* April 18, 1964, p. 31.

33. This Lou Gehrig performance was compared by a colleague to "being in jail." *Saturday Evening Post,* April 18, 1964, p. 31. Most congressmen are kept busy off the floor and are often absent from minor votes or pair with colleagues who wish to be announced as "Voting" the opposite way.

34. *U.S. News & World Report,* February 10, 1964, p. 36.

35. Graham, *op. cit.,* pp. 74-77.

36. One of her first votes in Congress was an endorsement of the critical draft bill of 1940.

37. His death in 1944 left her owner and operator of a 10,000-acre ranch.

38. Donald R. Matthews attributes their designation to a factional fight within the Republican Party. They were "temporary, compromise senators. No doubt their lack of officeholding experience and political ambitions were among their major qualifications for the job." *U.S. Senators and Their World,* Chapel Hill: University of North Carolina Press, 1960, p. 13.

39. She studied at Oregon College of Education, the University of Oregon, and UCLA, and taught school for a dozen years. She became interested in politics through her activity in the LWV and the AAUW.

40. Widows have not always been consoled by a Senate seat. The widow of Senator H. Styles Bridges of New Hampshire was passed over for appointment by the governor in November 1961, and she was unsuccessful in the special election to choose someone to complete his term. It had

been expected that Governor Wesley Powell, Republican, would appoint Dolores Bridges to the vacant Senate seat; instead he selected his attorney general. *Congressional Quarterly Weekly Reports,* December 1, 1961, p. 1909. Mrs. Bridges ran against Representative Perkins Bass in the September 1962 primary. She accused Representative Bass of "Bass chivalry" for announcing ahead of her. *Congressional Quarterly Weekly Reports,* August 31, 1962, p. 1459. The ten-month delay between Bridges' death and the primary cost the widow much of the sympathy vote. In 1966 Mrs. Bridges made another unsuccessful bid for the nomination.

41. Graham, *op. cit.,* p. 66.

42. *Ibid.,* p. 164. Stories appeared of chilliness between the two women senators. *Saturday Evening Post,* April 18, 1964, p. 32. The male tendency to put the two in the same category, despite their being of different parties, ages, and orientations could be a source of friction.

43. "The electoral college of Indiana, having first cast its vote for Cleveland, changed its mind and cast it over again for Mrs. Lockwood. She subsequently petitioned Congress demanding credit for the Indiana vote." J. Miller, "She Chose to Run," *Christian Science Monitor Magazine,* November 2, 1940, p. 14. Mrs. Lockwood ran in 1884 and 1888 under the banner of the Woman's National Equal Rights Party of California.

44. Fred Greenstein, *Journal of Politics,* May 1961, p. 357. In October 1963, 55 per cent said they would vote for a qualified woman in their own party. The Gallup Poll in 1945 on the question "If your party nominated a woman for president and she seemed best qualified for the job, would you vote for her?" showed that 33 per cent would vote for a woman. In 1937 the Gallup Poll figure was 27 per cent. Hadley Cantril and Mildred Strunk, *Public Opinion: 1935-1946,* Princeton: Princeton University Press, 1951, pp. 1052-54. Evidently the public is becoming more receptive to the possibility of a female chief executive.

A survey of opinion in February 1964, in Winnebago County, Wisconsin, showed that only 36.2 per cent of approximately 200 polled would support a woman for president, 31.7 per cent of the men and 42.3 per cent of the women. Half of those interviewed would not support a woman for governor, 45.6 per cent would, 46.1 per cent would not; 59.3 per cent would support a woman for senator and 63.1 per cent a woman for representative.

45. *New York World-Telegram and Sun,* February 25, 1964, p. 31.

46. In Gore Vidal's play, "The Best Man," the outgoing president said one day there will be a Jewish and a Negro president—and eventually a president from the majority, a woman.

47. Kathleen Norris, "If I Were President," *Delineator,* January 1929, p. 9.

48. David Lawrence concluded: "There is no inherent reason . . . why a woman shouldn't serve as president of the United States. But there is a reason why most of the celebrities—men or women—who aspire to high office should not be named. They lack the necessary training." *U.S. News & World Report,* February 17, 1964, p. 108.

49. *Ladies' Home Journal,* February 1947. Helen Jepson concurred, "The largest number of successful women are found in jobs which were once relegated to the home and are now performed outside—nursing, education, interior decoration, and so on. The woman department store president, political leader or diplomat is still the exception rather than the rule. When women become accepted in these latter jobs so matter-of-factly that there will no longer be any news value attached to their succession, they will have acquired the background necessary for the job of being president." *Loc. cit.*

50. *The Wisdom of Eleanor Roosevelt,* New York: McCall, 1962, p. 94.

51. *McCall's,* June 1964. One writer argued that Senator Smith came close to winning the nomination in 1952. "Taft was threatening to support Mrs. Smith. It was conceivable that she could have won the nomination on the first ballot." New York *News,* June 28, 1964, p. 4.

52. *U. S. News & World Report,* February 10, 1964, p. 35.

53. *Saturday Evening Post,* April 18, 1964, p. 32.

54. Perle Mesta, with Robert Cahn, *Perle: My Story,* New York-Toronto-London: McGraw-Hill, 1960, p. 180.

55. Compare the 1940 election: Democrats argued in favor of a third term and for an experienced politician; Republicans found just as many arguments against the third term and in favor of a political amateur with business experience. In 1964 the Republican choice of William Miller, a Catholic, seemed to make political sense in the light of Kennedy's 1960 victory.

56. W. Lloyd Warner, Paul P. Van Riper, Norman H. Martin, and Orvis F. Collins, *The American Federal Executive,* New Haven and London: Yale University Press, 1963, p. 177. In 1964 there were 184,308 men in government positions paying $10,000 and over, as compared with 8,872 women.

57. *Ibid.,* p. 180. "When we recall that, at the lower white collar levels, up to three-fourths of the total employees are women, it is clear that movement up out of white collar ranks is, with few exceptions, not possible for women in government." *Ibid.,* p. 187.

58. Proportionately more women came from the ranks of the professions and fewer from business. Over one out of five women began as a public school teacher. *Ibid.,* pp. 183-84.

59. Two-thirds of the women executives studied by Warner were unmarried, compared with less than five per cent of the men. *Ibid.,* p. 187.

60. When comparisons were made by age groups, salary levels, and occupations, women's rates, while still higher, were much closer to men's.

61. *American Women: Report of the President's Commission on the Status of Women,* 1963, p. 33.

62. *Ibid.,* pp. 33-34. In 1923 a thousand male postal employees in Washington held a protest meeting when a woman employee was promoted above them at a higher wage. Ernestine Evans, "Women in the Washington Scene," *Century Magazine,* August 1923, pp. 508-09.

63. Warner, *op. cit.,* p. 180.

64. "These two agencies are most intimately concerned with the problems in which women, in their traditional roles in the home, have always taken keen interest." *Loc. cit.* Even in Health, Education and Welfare, there were only 16 women among the top 278 officials. Peter Lisagor and Marguerite Higgins, "L.B.J.'s Hunt for Womanpower," *Saturday Evening Post,* June 27-July 4, 1964, p. 86.

65. Philadelphia *Bulletin,* November 24, 1963, p. 4.

66. *Independent Woman,* May 1955, p. 162; *American Woman, op. cit.,* p. 51.

Seventy-nine women of 3,273 upper level posts in 1951-52; 84 of 3,491 in 1958-59; and 93 of 3,807 in 1961-62. A comparison of employment opportunities for women in the federal service in 1939 and in 1959 concluded that women made the least gains, in terms of numbers of percentage of total workers, in the categories of administrator, doctor, engineer, and lawyer. U.S. Department of Labor, Women's Bureau, *Women in the Federal Service, 1939-1959,* 1962, p. 5.

67. Lisagor and Higgins, *op. cit.,* p. 86. On still another occasion he said: "Providence has distributed brains and skills pretty evenly over our people. To conclude that women are unfitted to the risks of our historic society seems to me the equivalent of closing male eyes to female facts." Mary Booth, "If You're a Man," *This Week,* January 10, 1965, p. 12.

68. "Most people are either courtin' me or cussin' me," he says. "But women tend to tell me exactly what they think." Lisagor and Higgins, *op. cit.,* p. 87.

69. India Edwards has said that a man's attitude toward women is conditioned by the kind of wife he has.

70. Another newswoman whom Johnson has favored is Nancy Dickerson, White House correspondent of the National Broadcasting Company. She met him in the early 1950's when she worked for the Senate Foreign Relations Committee. Steven V. Roberts, "Another First for Nancy," *New York Times,* January 3, 1965, II, p. 16.

71. Mrs. Esther Peterson, assistant secretary of Labor, is also consulted by the President in the selection of women, Nadine Ullman, *Newsday,* May 1, 1964.

72. Booth, *op. cit.,* p. 12. This article is guilty of a misleading orientation, an assumption that men are out and women are in. "Men who leave their government jobs find they have been replaced by women. One male job hunter actually was told, 'With your record, we'd hire you in a minute, if only you were a woman.' " *Ibid.,* p. 10. This is sheer fantasy.

73. As Mrs. Carpenter observed, "The outstanding business or professional woman who is free to take a full-time government job is still unique."

74. Lisagor and Higgins, *op. cit.,* p. 87.

75. Among those appointed to full-time positions were: Katharine A. White, ambassador to Denmark; Marguerite Tibbetts, ambassador to Norway; Mary I. Bunting, member, Atomic Energy Commission; Virginia Mae Brown, member, Interstate Commerce Commission; Mary Gardiner Jones, member, Federal Trade Commission; Jane Hanne, deputy assistant secretary of Defense for Civil Defense; Dorothy Jacobson, assistant secretary of Agriculture for International Affairs; Elizabeth S. May, member, Board of Direction, Export-Import Bank; Katherine Goodwin, special assistant to the commissioner, Welfare Administration, H.E.W; Lee Walsh, deputy assistant secretary of State for evaluations; Mary Keyserling, head of Women's Bureau, Department of Labor; Rose McKee, information director, Small Business Administration; Ruth Van Cleve, director, Office of Territories, Interior Department; Gladys M. NaDeau, Food for Peace Office, AID; Leona Baumgartner, assistant administrator, AID; Esther B. R. LaMarr, assistant for Intergroup Relations to VA Administrator; Helen Iliff, medical officer, Division of Chronic Disease, Bureau of State Services, Public Health, H.E.W; Joy R. Simonson, chairman, Alchoholic Beverages Control Board, D.C; Marie D. Gadsen, Peace Corps Volunteer Development Office; Mrs. Herbert Stats, consultant to the Office of Aging, H.E.W; Eleanor Poland, executive secretary, Medical Study Section, H.E.W; Barbara Bolling, special assistant to U. S. chief of Protocol, State Department; Charlotte M. Hubbard, deputy assistant secretary of State for Public Affairs; Frances Hall, head, International Trade Analysis Division, Commerce Department; Dr. Penelope H. Thunberg, member, U.S. Tariff Commission; Dr. Regina Goff, assistant commissioner of Education; Irene Parsons, first assistant administrator of the Veterans' Administration; Aileen Hernandez, member, Equal Employment Opportunity Commission.

76. Katherine Brownell Oettinger, "The Role of Women in Government," p. 13. See Bibliography, Government Publications. Mrs. Oettinger, the present chief of the Children's Bureau, is a descendant of Susan B. Anthony.

77. Furman, *op. cit.,* p. 70.

78. In her first ten years, Dr. Eliot commuted between Washington and New Haven, Connecticut, where she was professor of pediatrics at Yale. In 1947 she was elected the first woman president of the American Public Health Association.

79. *Current Biography,* 1957, p. 419.

80. She was the second woman to hold the New York Industrial Commission post, the first being Frances Perkins.

81. She was used to working with men because of her union background. At first she was treated deferentially at meetings in the Department of Labor but soon was treated as one of the team.

82. Mrs. Peterson is a longtime board member of the National Consumers League. Her husband is a retired Foreign Service officer who is a professor of international labor relations at American University. He encouraged her participation in government.

83. A brother served in the New York legislature. Through him she met a number of New York State politicians including Al Smith, Robert Wagner, Sr., and Franklin Roosevelt.

84. She was discharged by the secretary of the new Department of Health, Education, and Welfare, Mrs. Oveta Hobby.

85. She is in private life Mrs. Wayne W. Parrish, wife of an aviation magazine publisher.

86. She succeeded Mrs. Gladys Morelock, the first woman superintendent of the mint, who served from August 1, 1952, to February 8, 1953.

87. The directorship of the mint was held by two men during the Eisenhower years.

88. Appointed to the post of assistant treasurer was Catherine B. Cleary, a Wisconsin lawyer, who was president of the Association of Bank women. She later became assistant to the secretary of the Treasury.

89. In 1922 she was an unsuccessful candidate for Congress.

90. It was alleged that since the Democrats had had a woman assistant attorney general from California, the Republicans thought they should have one, too. Helena Huntington Smith, "Mrs. Willebrandt," *The Outlook and Independent,* October 24, 1928, p. 1006.

91. Eleanor Roosevelt, "Women in Politics," *Good Housekeeping,* January 1940, p. 19.

92. Smith, *op. cit.*, p. 1008.

93. Wainwright Evans, "When Lovely Woman Votes 'Thumbs Down,' " *World's Week,* February 1929, p. 43.

94. Edmund A. Moore, *A Catholic Runs for President,* New York: Ronald Press, 1956, p. 190.

95. Smith, *op. cit.*, pp. 1007-08.

96. *Ibid.,* p. 1045.

97. President Johnson appointed Mrs. Jane Hanna in 1964 to be deputy assistant secretary for Civil Defense. Eisenhower had named Mrs. Katherine G. Howard to be deputy administrator of Civil Defense. Mrs. Howard commuted on weekends between Washington and Boston to be with her lawyer-husband.

98. Mayor LaGuardia of New York said of her: "She knows more about human relations than any man in the country." *Independent Woman,* January 1951, p. 30. "At 19 she already had settled her first strike and had sold nearly $10,000 worth of Thrift Stamps and Liberty Bonds on a corner of Broadway, and worked as a volunteer nurse, had organized 1,000 high school girls for women's suffrage, led a big delegation to a meeting of the New York Board of Aldermen, acted as its spokesman, won her point." *Ibid.,* p. 8.

99. *Loc. cit.* Mrs. Rosenberg later became a member of the New York City Board of Education.

100. She had been an active Democrat in New York for some years prior to her appointment. Said the FCC chairman when Miss Hennock was sworn in: "We've had rectitude, fortitude, and solemnitude, but never before pulchritude." *Current Biography,* 1948, p. 279.

101. She received her law degree at 19, but had to wait until 21 before she could be admitted to the New York bar.

102. Both women took the lowest ranking Cabinet posts of their day. Compare with Barbara Castle, whose position in the British Labour Cabinet is Number 23 out of 23 positions.

103. She admitted her lack of warmth to the newspaper people. Frances Perkins, "Eight Years as Madame Secretary." *Fortune,* September 1941, p. 78. Furman, *op. cit.,* p. 165. In her desire for privacy she resembled Herbert Hoover. "In her personal life she is kindly, straightforward, truthful and loyal. In her public life she is often rattled, unreliable, confused and scared, and when scared enough she can be both cruel and unfair." Benjamin Stolberg, "Madame Secretary: A Study in Bewilderment," *Saturday Evening Post,* July 27, 1940, p. 9. Stolberg accused her of that worst of all feminine sins, incessant talking.

104. Mary Anderson, *Woman at Work:* Minneapolis: University of Minnesota Press, 1951, p. 148. "She made mistakes a woman inexperienced in the masculine milieu of politics might be expected to make. She kept senators waiting, for example." Margaret Cussler, *The Woman Executive,* New York: Harcourt Brace, 1958, pp. 186-87. Miss Perkins told one congressman that his statement "didn't make sense" and begged another to be "realistic." Ray Tucker, "Fearless Frances,"*Collier's,* July 28, 1934, p. 16.

105. *Parade,* June 21, 1964, p. 8. "A woman secretary of Labor is about as sound psychologically as a male nurse in a gynecologist's office." Irene Corbally Kuhn, "Women Don't Belong in Politics," *American Mercury,* August 1953, p. 5. Miss Perkins invited the labor leaders to have tea with her. They did not appreciate the invitation. John C. O'Brien, "Women Bid for Politics," *The Sign,* January 1959, p. 19. A 1945 Gallup Poll asked: "Would you approve or disapprove of having a capable woman in the President's cabinet?" Thirty-eight per cent approved; 48 per cent disapproved.

106. Many of the women's associations which had favored the creation of a Department of Education objected to its inclusion in a Department of Welfare. Dorothy Elizabeth Johnson, *Organized Women and National Legislation: 1920-1941,* unpublished Ph.D. dissertation, Western Reserve University, 1960, p. 359. Harding proposed in 1920 a cabinet level Department of Public Welfare. It was said that he favored a woman to head such a department. *The Woman Citizen,* December 4, 1920, p. 729.

107. She served as parliamentarian from 1925 to 1931 when she got married. She served again in the same position from 1939 to 1941. Mrs. Hobby studied at the University of Texas Law School. She was an unsuccessful candidate for the Texas legislature at 24.

108. *Current Biography*, 1944, p. 524.

109. Note that our first three women ministers were appointed to Scandinavian countries. Two of President Johnson's appointments were also to Scandinavia. Mrs. Anderson's husband's Scandinavian name may have accounted for her assignment. After her designation, she studied Danish.

110. *New York Times*, December 6, 1964, p. 9. Symptomatic of the mutual coolness was the status of minister rather than ambassador.

111. She was the first American minister ever appointed to Luxembourg. Mesta, *op. cit.*, p. 136. Her friend, Supreme Court Justice Fred Vinson, doubted that Luxembourg really needed a minister. *Ibid.*, p. 130. There were only four other resident ministers. *Ibid.*, p. 139.

112. In 1953 Eisenhower, an old friend, was under heavy pressure from the Women's Division of the Republican National Committee to get rid of her. They did not want a Democratic appointee to be representing the U.S. Government at the coronation in England in May 1953. *Ibid.*, p. 182.

113. John Kobler, "The First Tycoon and the Power of His Press," *Saturday Evening Post*, January 16, 1965, p. 44. "In effect, Italy got two ambassadors for the price of one."

114. Dorothy Detzer, *Appointment on the Hill*, New York: Henry Holt, 1948, pp. 104-08. Dr. Mary Wooley's appointment as a delegate to the Geneva Conference was at first viewed with apprehension by the U.S. Minister to Switzerland, Hugh Wilson, who feared she might be "finicky" and, not a smoker herself, object to "our nicotinized caucuses." *Democratic Digest*, 1934, p. 9.

115. *New York Times*, December 13, 1964, p. 87.

116. Mrs. Roosevelt considered her "the country's most distinguished woman lawyer" when appointed. Eleanor Roosevelt and Lorene A. Hickok, *Ladies of Courage*, New York: Putnam's Sons, 1954, p. 195.

117. Judge Allen once remarked: "The other judges are not expected to be responsible for selecting the dining room draperies or entertaining at a luncheon. Why, just because I am a woman, should I?" *Current Biography*, 1941, p. 18.

118. She commented on her nomination by Kennedy: "State federations and local Business and Professional Women's Clubs all over the country as well as the National Federation wrote the attorney general and the President in my behalf, and undoubtedly were an effective force in the nomination. I am very grateful." *National Business Woman,* November-December, 1961, p. 11.

119. *McCall's,* September 1962, p. 158. Only one woman has ever been a clerk of a Supreme Court justice, in Justice Douglas's office in the 1940's.

5b. America's Congresswomen, 1917 to 1967

1. A legend has developed, fostered by the press, that Miss Rankin was in tears when she cast her vote. This has been used to illustrate a contention that women approach political decisions emotionally.

2. But Frank Hague ran the party! Reinhard H. Luthin, *American Demagogues: Twentieth Century,* Gloucester, Mass.: Peter Smith, 1959, p. 139.

3. She received letters from women criticizing what they regarded as her betrayal of the cause of women. *Literary Digest,* March 30, 1935, p. 24.

4. Congresswoman Mary Norton and Senator Hattie Caraway had their nieces as secretary-companions. Huey Long's daughter served as Mrs. Long's secretary when she was in the Senate. Representative Buchanan's daughter also served for a time as her secretary.

5. At least five of the women representatives won via this difficult route.

6. One article said: "Women do not like her, and she knows it perfectly well. Men are afraid of her, and she knows that, too." Ida Clyde Clarke, "A Woman in the White House," *Century Magazine,* March 1927, p. 595. Another factor contributing to her defeat was that State Representative Lottie Holman O'Neill ran for the Senate as an independent, splitting the vote.

7. She was reputed to be the best speaker among the congresswomen. Clare Ogden Davis, *North American Review,* June 1930, p. 754.

8. She then had to plead her case for the House seat, which was contested on the claim that she had lost her American citizenship by reason of her marriage to a foreigner. Bess Furman, *Washington By-Lines: The Personal History of a Newspaperwoman,* New York: Knopf, 1949, p. 90.

9. Her daughter, Mrs. Rudd Brown, wife of Dr. Harrison Brown, the noted geochemist, campaigned unsuccessfully for a House seat from California in 1958 and 1960.

10. Miss O'Loughlin was known as one of the few women broncobusters.

11. Allen Drury, *A Senate Journal: 1943-1945,* New York-Toronto-London: McGraw-Hill, 1963, p. 251.

12. "Asked if she would seek re-election in two years, when she will be approaching 82, Mrs. Bolton replied: 'Heavens, yes, I'll stay here till I die.' " *New York Times,* March 28, 1965, p. 54.

13. When in 1944, the Republicans featured ex-playwright, Mrs. Luce, as a convention spellbinder, the Democrats countered with ex-actress Helen Gahagan Douglas.

14. One of her students, Jessie Sumner, was also in Congress.

15. Mrs. St. George's first choice of committees in 1947 was Foreign Affairs. Her second was Agriculture, and her third was Military Affairs. The Republican Committee on Committees, however, assigned her to the Post Office and Civil Service Committee.

16. Mrs. Kelley does not believe in a career in politics for a woman when her husband is in politics, especially if they have children.

17. Marion K. Sanders, *The Lady and the Vote,* Boston: Houghton Mifflin, 1956, p. 66.

18. In an interview she said that she took on the job during World War II because it was difficult to get and keep help.

19. A territorial delegate is a non-voting member of the House but has the right to offer legislation, to speak at congressional sessions, and to serve on committees.

20. She lost the first time she ran for the legislature.

21. When Mrs. Griffiths was a judge, she was the examining magistrate in the 1953 Michigan criminal conspiracy case involving Teamster Leader Jimmy Hoffa and the jukebox rackets. She received a lot of threatening letters but never reported them or asked for protection, "because being a woman, I was afraid it would look silly," she said. Boston *Herald,* January 28, 1962.

22. She also succeeded her late husband as a Democratic ward leader in Philadelphia. However, unlike her husband who provided the traditional barrel of beer for ward meetings, she served cookies and tea to the 72 district committeemen. *Current Biography,* 1959, p. 157.

23. Her husband was a year from retirement when she first ran for Congress. He urged her to run, although it meant commuting each weekend.

24. Her husband died in July 1958; although he was not in Congress, she profited from sympathy for the widow.

25. His father had served in Congress for 12 years.

26. She pledged to carry out her husband's program, but in her campaign she would not discuss issues or her opponent. *New York Times,* March 1, 1964.

27. In 1959 she lost out in a primary bid for Congress.

5c. Women in State Government

1. *New Republic,* February 11, 1920, p. 319.

2. *Democratic Digest,* April 1937, p. 23.

3. "It was a shock to find that some of the women I loved most were Democrats, because this meant a parting of the ways. I began to scan anxiously the ranks of my own party and was happy to find others of my good friends in the Republican fold." Alice Curtice Moyer-Wing, "Men Only," *Scribner's Magazine,* September 1926, p. 294.

4. Anne Martin, "Woman's Vote and Woman's Chains," *Sunset Magazine,* April 1922, p. 13.

5. Wendell Bell, Richard J. Hill, and Charles R. Wright, *Public Leadership,* San Francisco: Chandler, 1961, p. 37. In Wisconsin, minor legal limitations prohibited women from serving as clerks of legislative committees or as other employees of the state legislature.

6. *Literary Digest,* October 5, 1935, p. 7. The only elective office open to women was commissioner of Charities and Corrections. Mrs. Mabel Bassett held this office from 1923 to 1947. Mrs. Bassett ran unsuccessfully for Congress in 1940.

7. According to the report *American Women,* of the President's Commission on the Status of Women, there were 234 women in state legislatures in 1962, p. 21. Accurate figures are hard to obtain. Some legislatures are elected in odd years, others in even. Some women are elected or appointed to fill vacancies. Constitutional changes alter the total number of seats.

8. *History of Democratic Women,* Democratic Congressional Wives Forum, 1960, p. 17.

9. Harold F. Gosnell, *Democracy: Threshold of Freedom,* New York: Ronald Press, 1948, p. 72.

10. Louise Young, *Understanding Politics,* New York: Pellegrini and Cudahy, 1950, p. 210. This writer claimed that women are often nominated for "forlorn hope" districts, for example, Republicans in Democratic areas.

11. In 1929 there were 149 women in 33 legislatures. By 1939 there was a decline to 129 in 28 states. Eleanor Roosevelt, "Women in Politics," *Good Housekeeping,* January 1940, p. 18.

12. There were 34 women in the upper house of 18 states. There were 328 women out of 7,900 seats. *The Book of the States, 1964-1965,* Chicago: The Council of State Governments, 1964, p. 436. Women in the upper houses are a rarity. In 1966 Mrs. Mildred Hughes was sworn in as the first woman senator in New Jersey history. She had served eight years in the state Assembly before her election to the Upper House.

13. *New York Times,* December 6, 1964, p. 168. Within the state there are

some counties with a large percentage of women legislators and others with very few. Rutland County, Vermont, had only one woman (single) among the 28 elected to the 1965 House, whereas Orleans County had six (all married or widowed) out of 19. Essex County had seven women out of 13 positions but Lamoille had none out of 10, Franklin had one in 15, Chillenden 2 in 17, Washington 3 out of 20, and Windsor 3 out of 24.

14. *New York Times,* January 31, 1965. Starting with the 1966 election, there were 177 Representatives selected from districts reapportioned on the "one-man, one-vote" principle enunciated by the Supreme Court.

15. "New Hampshire Legislators," *Ladies' Home Journal,* November 1951, p. 222. Vermont legislators receive $2,550. *The Book of the States, 1964-65, op. cit.,* p. 39.

16. Small legislative districts, however, make it easier to campaign, a factor which itself may help more women to serve.

17. See John C. Wahlke, Heinz Eulau, William Buchanan, and LeRoy E. Ferguson, *The Legislative System: Explorations in Legislative Behavior,* New York-London: Wiley, 1962, Part Two: The Legislative Career.

18. "Occupations of State Legislators, 1949" Belle Zeller, editor, *American State Legislatures,* New York: Crowell, 1954, p. 71. An attorney is prohibited from advertising but political campaigning is a very effective form of publicity. A legislative office can be combined with a lawyer's business better than most occupations.

19. There is often a family "lien" upon a legislative office. Mrs. Flora M. Vare, widow of the late Senator Edwin H. Vare, was elected in 1924 to be the first and only woman in the Pennsylvania State Senate. She was the fourth member of the Vare family to hold in direct succession the state Senate seat. The Vare organization controlled the Philadelphia Republican Party.

20. According to Gosnell, *op. cit.,* pp. 72-73, over 80 per cent of the early women state legislators had had college or university training. Nearly 80 per cent of the women in the 1948 legislatures were married.

21. "Only exceptional women among those pursuing professional careers have

time to run for office. Many women who have the time, lack the money." Young, *op. cit.,* p. 233.

22. *Pictorial Review,* October 1924, p. 2. For a reason best known to a male, the five women members of the Connecticut Assembly in 1920-21 were given seats together. *The Woman Citizen,* July 30, 1921, p. 11.

23. "These are questions which primarily concern women, yet they have been decided by a legislative body overwhelmingly made up of men." Maurine Neuberger, "Footnotes on Politics by a Lady Legislator," *New York Times Magazine,* May 27, 1951, p. 18.

24. "Vermont Ladies Are Taking Over," *Life,* April 6, 1953, pp. 21-23.

25. Mrs. Howorth, a law partner of her husband, went to Washington in 1934 and served for 16 years with the Veterans Administration. In the 1950's she became general counsel of the War Claims Commission. She was on the national boards of directors of the AAUW and the NFBPWC.

26. The chief clerk of the Assembly did not know whether to address her as "the lady from Marathon County" or Assemblywoman Barber. "Political Pioneer," *Milwaukee Sentinel,* February 24, 1965, Part 3, p. 1.

27. *Mademoiselle,* January 1964, p. 73.

28. Helen Worden, "Pretty Good Politicians," *Collier's,* January 14, 1950, p. 18.

29. "Indiana's Coed Legislator," *Life,* February 28, 1949, pp. 101-04.

30. *Mademoiselle,* March 1964, p. 236.

31. Questionnaire returned after the 1964 Democratic Convention.

32. Questionnaire returned after the 1964 Democratic Convention.

33. *Mademoiselle,* May 1956, pp. 163, 188.

34. Marion K. Sanders, *The Lady and the Vote,* Boston: Houghton Mifflin, 1956, p. 21.

35. *Ladies' Home Journal,* November 1951, p. 222.

36. Mrs. Smith was the lone woman when first elected. Her colleagues assumed that she would welcome being placed on the Education and Medical Affairs committees, supposedly within the competence of a woman. Male legislators called her speeches "sob stuff" and said she was "peddling sugar." One exclaimed, "You do bring out the screwiest bills." A proposal to put women on juries turned into a battle of the sexes. Despite the men's patronizing behavior, her work won their grudging admiration. Eudochia Bell Smith, *They Ask Me Why* . . . . Denver: World Press, 1945.

37. Questionnaire returned after the 1964 Democratic Convention.

38. Despite her busy life, Mrs. Lawrence still found time to earn a pilot's license.

39. Much of this material was obtained in an interview with Mrs. Lawrence.

40. Among those who have served are Doris L. Byrne, former Democratic state vice chairman and now a criminal court judge, Jane H. Todd, a longtime assemblywoman and Republican state vice chairman, and Genesta Strong, who duplicated Mrs. Neuberger's stunt of demonstrating to male legislators the nuisance of coloring oleomargarine. *New Yorker*, May 5, 1956, p. 140.

41. She defeated a Republican Negro woman lawyer, Cora Walker. Mrs. Motley has stated that Negro women are more used to leadership than white women because in the Negro community the service and church groups are largely led by women. She feels that the only way to improve the civil rights picture in the North is through legislation in such areas as housing, employment, and quality education. The Negroes' lack of power in the North is a result of their low participation in politics.

42. New York *Post*, February 24, 1964, p. 19.

43. *The California State Employee*, September 29, 1967, p. 15.

44. In 1947 Fern Ale of Indiana was the first woman secretary of a state senate.

45. "As Maine Goes . . . ." *Time*, September 5, 1960, pp. 13-14.

46. A state-by-state list of women who have held major positions may be found at the end of this chapter.

47. The percentage of women in government jobs paying over $10,000 per year in New York State is 9.2 per cent in competitive or non-competitive, and 5.9 per cent in exempt and unclassified service. *New York Women and Their Changing World,* Report of the Governor's Committee on the Education and Employment of Women, 1964, p. 52.

48. Dr. Potter was succeeded in 1927 by Mrs. E. S. H. McCauley as Pennsylvania secretary of Welfare. Mrs. Eleanor G. Evans served as Pennsylvania secretary of Public Assistance from 1951 to 1955. She had taught physical education and was active in charities. Mrs. Evans had been twice elected recorder of deeds of Delaware County. Sophia M. R. O'Hara was Pennsylvania secretary of the commonwealth from 1939 to 1943 when she was appointed to a four-year term as secretary of Welfare. Following this, she was named to the Board of Parole.

In 1937 Rose Schneiderman was appointed secretary of the New York State Department of Labor. She was an honorary vice president of the United Hatters, Cap and Millinery Workers International Union and president of the National Women's Trade Union League. Mary Donlon, who is now a Federal Customs Court Judge, was appointed chairman of the New York State Industrial Board in 1944 and of the Workmen's Compensation Board in 1945. She had run unsuccessfully for U.S. congressman-at-large from New York State in 1940. The highest cabinet position in New York which is presently held by a woman is that of president of the Civil Service Commission. Miss Mary G. Krone has been active in Republican politics, becoming vice president of the State Young Republicans.

Governor Robert Meyner of New Jersey appointed Mrs. W. Howard Sharp, the widow of a judge-assemblyman-senator and former Democratic state vice chairman and national committeewoman, to be president of the New Jersey Civil Service Commission. Governor Richard J. Hughes reappointed her and she is still serving. In 1965 women were serving as president of the Public Utilities Commission in New Jersey, director of Industrial Relations in Ohio, commissioner of Welfare in Tennessee, and chairman of the Workmen's Compensation Commission of New York. Mrs. C. Frank Scott, the Tennessee commissioner of Health, Education, and Welfare, was appointed to the governor's cabinet after serving as a state representative and senator. At present, she is serving as commissioner of Employment Security.

Miss Marion Martin of Maine, a lawyer, former state legislator, and director of the Women's Division of the Republican National Committee, was named state commissioner of Labor. It was said that she had the distinction of being invited to speak to men's groups in Maine and in many other parts of the country just as often as to women's groups. *Independent Woman*, January 1942, p. 6. Esther D. Hawley is chairman of and only woman on the six-member Maine Personnel Board. Aside from the state librarian, she is the only major female officeholder in the state government.

Mrs. Rebecca Laing Rainey, now Mrs. Sims Garrett, Sr., of Georgia became a member of the state Pardon and Parole Board in 1948 and its chairman in 1961. Previously, she had served in the State Senate (1945-46) and House (1947-48). When County Judge Vera Binks was appointed by Illinois Governor William Stratton in 1953 to be director of Registration and Education, it was said that she was the first woman in the 130 years of Illinois history to receive a cabinet appointment.

49. In 1937 Miss Grace Reany, a suffrage leader who had been for eight years the executive deputy secretary of state, became president of the New York Civil Service Commission.

50. Questionnaire returned after the 1964 Democratic Convention.

51. *New York Women and Their Changing World, op. cit.,* pp. 52-53.

52. One woman is required by law to be on the Board of Regents of the Wisconsin State Universities. Women regents might be expected to be concerned with counseling, security guards at night, and student health whereas men would become specialists in finance and organization.

53. Eleanor Roosevelt and Lorena A. Hickok, *Ladies of Courage,* New York: Putnam's Sons, 1954, p. 111. The Iowa Governor's Commission on the Status of Women reported that a comparison of the 1949 Iowa Official Registry indicated fewer women serving on state-wide boards and commissions in 1964. *First Report on the Status of Women,* September 1964, p. 11.

54. Gosnell, *op. cit.,* pp. 71-72. One of these was Mrs. Mary C. C. Bradford, who was elected for a fifth time in 1922. She was a former president of the State Federation of Women's Clubs and National Education Association. In 1908 she was a delegate to the Democratic Convention. The last

holder of the elective office of Colorado superintendent of Public Instruction became the first appointed commissioner of Education in 1950 under an elected state Board of Education composed of five members of which three are currently women. Mrs. Bernice S. Frieden of the Colorado State Board of Education is president of the National Association of State Boards of Education.

55. In Wyoming the secretary of state, currently Mrs. Thyra Thomson, becomes acting governor when the governor is absent from the state.

56. Mrs. Maria de la Soledad Cahves y Baca de Chacon, New Mexico's first woman secretary of state (1923-26), was a descendant of five governors of New Mexico. She appointed her husband, Ireno Chacon, her assistant.

57. Miss Pool is presently a member of the Alabama Public Service Commission.

58. Including Mrs. Bettye Frink who attained the post at 26. Miss Alice Lee Grosjean was only 24 when she became Louisiana's secretary of state in 1930. This was after six years as Governor Huey Long's private secretary. *The Woman Journal,* November 1930, p. 5. Miss Grosjean later became supervisor of Public Accounts. Mrs. Frink subsequently became state auditor and was defeated by Mrs. Baggett in 1966 in a primary contest for state treasurer.

59. Although there are only a few cases to go by in Alabama and elsewhere, it would seem that the political progression is from secretary of state to treasurer and from treasurer to auditor.

60. She first found out about her appointment as vice chairman from the local newspaper. *Ladies' Home Journal,* May 1927, p. 194.

61. Democrat Harriet S. Mills ran unsuccessfully for secretary of state of New York in 1920. In 1921 she was appointed associate chairman of the State Democratic Committee. At one time she was president of the New York State Suffrage Association. Another New York State suffrage leader who was asked to run for secretary of state was Gertrude Foster Brown. She declined the honor. Mildred Adams, *The Right to Be People,* Philadelphia-New York: J. B. Lippincott, 1966, p. 162.

62. In private life she is Mrs. Irving Halpern, wife of the former chief probation officer of the New York Supreme Court.

63. Information obtained by the author in an interview.

64. *Christian Science Monitor,* October 15, 1964, p. 14. Mrs. Sloan said she got interested in politics partly because her husband was interested in it.

65. In private life she is Mrs. Irwin A. Swiss, the wife of a lawyer.

66. Wyoming is proud of its title, The Equality State. Both the Republican state vice chairman and the Democratic national committeewomen wrote the author that women were very much to be seen in Wyoming politics. Two women candidates, one a Republican and one a Democrat, led their tickets in running for legislative posts. One woman was elected to her fifth term and three to their second. One woman in the State Senate had been mayor of her city. The state had a woman secretary of state and auditor.

67. A feminist magazine said of "Ma" Ferguson: "An untrained woman is nominated for governor by anti-suffragists and wets on a professed issue of religious liberty." *Woman Citizen,* September 6, 1924.

68. Mrs. Ferguson appointed Mrs. Emma Meharg in 1925 to be secretary of state.

69. "The ranchers and mountaineers refused to believe that any woman could have as much ability as any man." *Current Biography,* 1941, p. 725. Miss Roche had been Denver's first policewoman. Roosevelt appointed her assistant secretary of the Treasury. In 1939 she became president of the National Consumers League.

70. Mrs. Frohmiller defeated the incumbent governor, Dan E. Garvey, in the Democratic primary. During her 22 years as state auditor, Mrs. Frohmiller had signed her name to millions of old-age and relief checks. The startled organizational leaders offered her their support but were told that she wanted no strings attached to either her campaign or her election. These professional politicians, rather disgruntled, resolved to let her sink or swim on her own. All other Democratic candidates were easily re-elected. James Retchley, *States in Crisis: Politics in the American States: 1950-1962,* Chapel Hill: University of North Carolina Press, 1964, pp. 43-44.

71. In 1937 Governor Bill Graves of Alabama appointed his wife to a U.S. Senate vacancy.

72. In 1934 after Governor William Langer of North Dakota was convicted of levying political assessments on Federal officeholders, thereby being disqualified for renomination, the Nonpartisan League, which had control of the Republican machinery, substituted his wife's name as the gubernatorial candidate. She was defeated by less than 20,000 votes. Mrs. Johnson Murray ran unsuccessfully in 1954 for governor of Oklahoma to succeed her husband, who was constitutionally barred from a second consecutive term.

73. Mrs. Hazel K. Barger, Republican national committeewoman from Virginia, was an unsuccessful candidate for lieutenant governor in 1962.

74. *Time,* January 29, 1965, p. 41.

75. 1922 was a year of judicial breakthrough. That year the first woman clerk of a state Supreme Court, Grace K. Davis of Minnesota, was elected. She was re-elected for four-year terms from 1926 to 1942. Also in 1922 Mrs. Fannie C. Scott was elected to succeed her late husband as probate judge, the first woman to hold such office in South Carolina. She ran for re-election.

76. *Democratic Digest,* November 1937, p. 22.

77. Miss Sharp became North Carolina's first woman Supreme Court judge in 1962. She and her father were active in Democratic politics and were in law partnership from 1929 to 1949. Miss Sharp was city attorney of Reidsville, North Carolina, from 1939 to 1949. From 1949 to 1962 she was judge of the Superior Court, the first woman ever appointed.

78. She was defeated in the election. Miss Alpern had reportedly been passed over several times for appointment to the Federal bench because her service as Pittsburgh solicitor and Pennsylvania attorney general had made enemies. *New York Times,* July 27, 1961, p. 14.

79. *Time,* January 29, 1965, p. 41. Men also have to overcome an emotional reaction. Wisconsin's chief justice in 1875 flatly rejected a woman lawyer's application to practice by saying: "It would be shocking to man's reverence for womanhood that women should be permitted to mix professionally in all the nastiness of the world which finds its way into courts of justice." *Loc. cit.* Today the male's dilemma is: "Should a woman judge be treated with the respect due a judge or the gallantry

accorded a woman?" Helen Hacker, *Social Forces,* October 1951, p. 66.

5e. Women in Local Government

1. *American City,* June 1922, p. 543.

2. Wendell Bell, Richard J. Hill, and Charles R. Wright, *Public Leadership,* San Francisco: Chandler, 1961, p. 37; Eleanor Roosevelt and Lorena A. Hickok, *Ladies of Courage,* New York: Putnam's Sons, 1954, pp. 101-02. Reports of women in government are compiled by the General Federation of Women's Clubs and the National Federation of Business and Professional Women's Clubs.

3. *National Business Woman,* July 1960, p. 20.

4. Kanab, Utah, had a five-woman council from 1910 to 1912. They could not retain a male marshal, who was ribbed by the men for being bossed by women. *The Woman Citizen,* June 26, 1920, pp. 104-05. Other cities to have women governments before 1940 were Valley Center, Kansas; Jewett, Texas; and Umatilla, Oregon.

5. *The Independent,* September 11, 1920, p. 300.

6. *Literary Digest,* December 4, 1920, p. 52.

7. *Woman's Home Companion,* October 1922, p. 22.

8. *Literary Digest,* June 21, 1924, p. 50.

9. *American City,* June 1922, p. 544.

10. *American City,* July 1936, p. 77.

11. Now Mrs. Wyman. Her husband, a lawyer, is Democratic national committeeman from California.

12. Interview in Spring 1964.

13. *Wisconsin Women,* Report of the Governor's Commission on the Status of Women, March 1965, p. 23. Mrs. Robert Stillings of Appleton, Wisconsin,

was defeated in 1965 after 12 years as the only woman on the 20-member council. Her opponent advertised that it was a *man*-sized job. Mrs. Stillings contended, in an analysis of her defeat, that men rarely ran clean campaigns. While she ran "on the truth," men resorted to falsehoods and money. She felt that there was one alderman who always voted "no" when she voted "yes" and vice versa. Statements made at May 1, 1965, "Antidote for Apathy" conference at Madison, Wisconsin.

14. *Ibid.,* p. 22. The only woman on the 54-member Winnebago County Board of Supervisors, Mrs. Virginia Nolan, is the daughter of Frank B. Keefe, congressman from 1939 to 1951. She served on the board since 1951. Both Mrs. Nolan and her husband are lawyers.

15. Questionnaire returned after 1964 Republican Convention.

16. Marion K. Sanders, *The Lady and the Vote,* Boston: Houghton Mifflin, 1956, p. 119.

17. A possible counterargument could run: Men *do not* find it easy to talk over *their* problems with a woman.

18. Questionnaire returned in January 1965.

19. Questionnaire returned in November 1964.

20. Some men insisted on calling her "alderwoman," a title she persisted in correcting. "The woman label follows her around like a faithful dog, so much so that it would seem the world regards her identity as incomplete without it. Thus she is the woman candidate, not merely a candidate. If elected, she becomes the woman alderman, not simply an alderman." Ruth Pratt, "The Lady or the Tiger," *Ladies' Home Journal,* May 1928, p. 8.

21. Ruth Pratt, "Men Are Bad Housekeepers." *Harper's Monthly,* May 1927, p. 682.

22. Roosevelt and Hickok, *op. cit.,* p. 76.

23. Mrs. Norma S. Fleisch, "Chit Chat," *Montana Municipal League Newsletter,* November 1964. Most were in communities of less than 5,000. A questionnaire was mailed to each of the 112 women mayors by the Montana Municipal League asking for their viewpoints on women in public

office. Those responding felt that women mayors were more apt to follow through on details. They maintain a closer personal contact with their constituents, are more meticulous and study problems in detail. Some reported resentment toward a woman in office, especially in the deep South. One mayor pointed out that if women in office would stay away from the words "beautification" and "civic betterment" they might be better accepted by men in politics.

24. Mrs. Landes was president of the Seattle Federation of Women's Clubs, the Women's Century Club, and the Women's City Club. Her husband was dean of the College of Science at the University of Washington. He said of her political activities: "There is nothing revolutionary about a woman in office; it is simply an enlargement of her sphere. Men are too busy to go into politics, and women are better fitted temperamentally and by training."

25. Mrs. F. F. Powell, who served on the Seattle Council from 1935 to 1955, was chosen its president in 1941.

26. Said the *Seattle Post-Intelligencer,* quoted in *Woman's Journal,* April 1928, p. 22: "We suspect that Mrs. Landes was defeated solely because Seattle wishes to be known as a he-man town."

27. Richard L. Neuberger, *Adventures in Politics,* New York: Oxford University Press, 1954, p. 191. Mrs. Landes and Mrs. Lee met the fate of most reform mayors, ingratitude from voters. Mrs. Lee's opponents labeled her "Dotty-do-good" and "Mrs. Air-wick."

28. "Hawaii's Top Woman Politician," *Ebony,* April 1963, p. 51.

29. *National Business Woman,* January 1959, p. 15.

30. Al Stewart, "Feminine City Managers," *The American City,* May 1964, p. 154.

31. *Wisconsin Women, op. cit.,* pp. 22-23.

32. In New Orleans women are serving as city decorator, administrator of cemeteries, secretary of the Department of Streets, and director of the Department of Welfare. Miss M. Z. Eggert, who was active in the suffrage movement and was the first woman to serve on a jury in Harris County,

Texas, served under one Houston mayor as chairman of the city Board of Censors. She received a jury summons by mistake and insisted on serving. All directors of Houston's Public Library, at least since 1903, have been women. In Washington, D.C., a woman is chairman of the Alcoholic Beverage Control Board.

33. Questionnaire returned after the 1964 Republican Convention.

34. "Participation of Women in Politics," a fact-sheet prepared for the first Governor's Conference on the Changing Status of Women, Wisconsin, 1963, p. 2. "Pay at the county level is not high enough to encourage heads of families to be deputies. In the top counties there are 240 appointive jobs, and the majority of these are held by women." Interim Report of South Dakota Governor's Commission on the Status of Women, 1964, p. 6.

35. New York *Daily News,* February 21, 1964, p. BW7.

36. *McCall's,* September 1962, p. 160.

37. Interview with Mrs. Gabel in June 1964.

38. *Mademoiselle,* March 1964, p. 238.

39. Sioux Falls, South Dakota, *Argus-Leader,* February 5, 1964, p. 6.

40. Women were given a secondary role in Tammany politics. Implicit admission of this was their being charged half the dues paid by men.

41. Interview with Mrs. French, June 1964.

42. *National Business Woman,* January 1958, p. 20.

43. *Wisconsin Women, op. cit.,* p. 23.

44. Supplement to the 1963 Wisconsin report on "Participation of Women in Politics." Statistics available for 385 Wisconsin school districts out of 674 covering 90 per cent of the school children in the state, showed 186 school boards with women members, and a total of 257 women. *Wisconsin Women, op. cit.,* p. 23; *New York Times,* November 7, 1965, p. E11.

45. Jack Sessions, "Who Runs the Public Schools?" *The American Teacher,* January 1964, p. 12.

46. *Seattle Times,* October 16, 1960, p. 4.

47. This was a logical breakthrough position. Camille McGee Kelley of Memphis, Tennessee, and Mrs. Dorothy Young of Tulsa, Oklahoma, were other early women juvenile court judges. Judge Kelley was appointed in 1920, the second woman juvenile court judge in the U.S. and the first in the South. She was elected in 1922 and continued in office until her retirement in the early 1940's.

48. At present there are three women judges in the District of Columbia. Mary C. Barlow was appointed legal assistant to the judges of the Municipal Court, now the Court of General Sessions, in 1947. In 1950 she was appointed to the court by President Truman. Catherine B. Kelly was appointed by President Eisenhower in 1957 to take Judge Gallagher's place. Judge Marjorie M. Lawson of the Juvenile Court was appointed by President Kennedy in 1962. She was the first Negro woman ever to be approved by the U.S. Senate for a statutory appointment. Her predecessors include Fay L. Bentley and Edith H. Cockrill.

49. Usually, it is the woman who inherits political office. When William S. Untermann, a Newark, New Jersey, magistrate, died in 1944, his wife, Esther, was appointed to his position. She served till 1955. Mrs. Sophie Cooper, also of Newark, was appointed to the City Council in 1958 to serve out the term of her late husband. She was subsequently elected and served until 1962. About 20 years ago, Mrs. Ella Bailey succeeded to a vacancy caused by the death of her husband, who had been a member of the Baltimore City Council. About 15 years ago, Mrs. Arthur was similarly chosen by the City Council to fill the vacancy caused by the death of her husband. Subsequently, Mrs. Arthur ran in her own right and was elected.

50. New York *Post,* March 5, 1964. Six years later she set another precedent by taking the first maternity leave of absence in the state courts. Under the 1964 court reorganization, she is now in the juvenile division of the new Family Court.

51. Interview with Judge Liese, June 1964.

52. *Wisconsin Women, op. cit.,* pp. 22-23.

53. *Time*, January 29, 1965, p. 41.

54. On the other hand, the nonpartisan character of much of local government often makes women more willing to participate. Campaigning is not considered appropriate for certain offices such as the school board. Sometimes, though, there is disguised partisanship; the parties encourage and work for candidates.

Bibliography

BOOKS

Abrahams, Sir Adolphe, *Women: Man's Equal?*, London: Christopher Johnson, 1954.

Adams, Mildred, *The Right To Be People*, Philadelphia—New York: J. B. Lippincott, 1966.

Aldrich, Darragh, *Lady in Law: A Biography of Mabeth Hurd Paige*, Chicago: Ralph Fletcher Seymour, 1950.

Amrine, Michael, *The Awesome Challenge*, New York: Putnam, 1964.

Anderson, Mary, *Woman at Work*, Minneapolis: University of Minnesota Press, 1951.

Atherton, Gertrude, *Can Women Be Gentlemen?*, Boston: Houghton Mifflin, 1938.

Beard, Mary R., *Woman as Force in History: A Study in Traditions and Realities*, New York: Macmillan, 1946.

Bell, Wendell, Hill, Richard J., and Wright, Charles R., *Public Leadership*, San Francisco: Chandler, 1961.

Berelson, Bernard R., Lazarfeld, Paul F., and McPhee, William N. *Voting: A Study of Opinion Formation in a Presidential Campaign*, Chicago: University of Chicago Press, 1954.

Bernard, Jessie, *Academic Women*, University Park: Pennsylvania State University Press, 1964.

Blood, Robert C. Jr., and Wolfe, Donald M., *Husbands and Wives: The Dynamics of Married Living*, Glencoe: Free Press, 1960.

Blumenthal, Walter H., *American Panorama: Patterns of the Past and Woman-hood in Its Unfolding,* Worcester (Mass.): Achille J. St. Onge, 1962.

Bone, Hugh A., *Party Committees and National Politics,* Seattle: University of Washington Press, 1958.

Boone, Gladys, *The Women's Trade Union Leagues in Great Britain and the United States of America,* New York: Columbia University Press, 1942.

Borgese, Elisabeth Mann, *Ascent of Woman,* New York: George Braziller, 1963.

Breckinridge, Sophonisba P., *Women in the Twentieth Century: A Study of Their Political, Social, and Economic Activities,* New York and London: McGraw-Hill, 1933.

Brittain, Vera, *Lady into Woman: A History of Women from Victoria to Elizabeth II,* London: Andrew Dakers Ltd., 1953.

Brumbaugh, Sara Barbara, *Democratic Experience and Education in the National League of Women Voters,* New York: Teachers College Bureau of Publications, 1946.

Burns, James M., *Congress on Trial,* New York: Harper, 1949.

Campbell, Angus, Converse, Philip E., Miller, Warren E., and Stokes, Donald E., *The American Voter,* New York: John Wiley & Sons, 1960.

Cantrell, Hadley, and Strunk, Mildred, *Public Opinion: 1935-1946,* Princeton: Princeton University Press, 1951, pp, 1052-54.

Cassara, Beverly, ed. *American Women: The Changing Image,* Boston: Beacon Press, 1962.

Cotter, Cornelius P., and Hennessy, Bernard C., *Politics Without Power: The National Party Committees,* New York: Atherton, 1964.

Cussler, Margaret, *The Woman Executive,* New York: Harcourt, Brace, 1958.

Cutler, John H., *What About Women?,* New York: Ives Washburn, 1961.

David, Opal D. ed, *The Education of Women—Signs for the Future,*

Washington, D.C.: American Council on Education, 1959.

David, Paul T., Goldman, Ralph N., and Bain, Richard C., *The Politics of National Party Conventions,* Brookings Institution, 1960.

Detzer, Dorothy, *Appointment on the Hill,* New York: Henry Holt, 1948.

Dohen, Dorothy, *Women in Wonderland,* New York: Sheed & Ward, 1960. ·

Drury, Allen, *A Senate Journal: 1943-1945,* New York-Toronto-London: McGraw-Hill, 1963.

Duverger, Maurice, *The Political Role of Women,* Paris: UNESCO, 1955.

Farber, Seymour M., and Wilson, Roger H. L., ed., *The Potential of Women,* New York-San Francisco-Toronto-London: McGraw-Hill, 1963.

Flexnor, Eleanor, *Century of Struggle: The Woman's Rights Movement in the United States,* Cambridge: Belknap Press of Harvard University Press, 1959.

Forthal, Sonya, *Cogwheels of Democracy: A Study of the Precinct Captain,* New York: William-Frederick Press, 1946.

Friedan, Betty, *The Feminine Mystique,* New York: W. W. Norton, 1963.

Furman, Bess, *Washington By-Line: The Personal History of a Newspaper-woman,* New York: Knopf, 1949.

Goldmark, Josephine, *Impatient Crusader: Florence Kelley's Life Story,* Urbana: University of Illinois Press, 1953.

Goldsen, Rose K., Rosenberg, Morris, Williams, Robin Jr., and Suchman, Edward, *What College Students Think,* Princeton: Van Nostrand, 1960.

Good, Josephine L., *The History of Women in Republican National Conventions and Women in the Republican National Committee,* Washington, D.C.: Women's Division of Republican National Committee, 1963.

Goodman, William, *The Two-Party System in the United States,* 3rd ed., Princeton, N. J.: Van Nostrand, 1964.

Gosnell, Harold F., *Democracy: The Threshold of Freedom,* New York: Ronald Press, 1948.

Graham, Frank Jr., *Margaret Chase Smith: Woman of Courage,* New York: John Day, 1964.

Green, Arnold W., and Melnick, Eleanor, "What Has Happened to the Feminist Movement," in Alvin W. Gouldner, ed., *Studies in Leadership: Leadership and Democratic Action,* New York: Harper, 1950.

Green, Constance, *Washington: Capital City: 1879-1950,* Princeton: Princeton University Press, 1963.

Gusfield, Joseph R., *Symbolic Crusade: Status Politics and the American Temperance Movement,* Urbana: University of Illinois, 1963.

Harris, Louis, *Is There a Republican Majority?: Political Trends 1952-56,* New York: Harper, 1954.

Hunt, Morton M., *Her Infinite Variety,* New York-Evanston: Harper & Row, 1962.

Hyman, Herbert, *Political Socialization,* Glencoe, Ill.: The Free Press, 1959.

Irwin, Inez Haynes, *Angels and Amazons: A Hundred Years of American Women,* Garden City, N.Y.: Doubleday, Doran, 1933.

Jensen, Oliver, *The Revolt of American Women,* New York: Harcourt, Brace, 1952.

Kendall, Elaine, *The Upper Hand,* Boston-Toronto: Little, Brown, 1965.

Key, V. O. Jr., *American State Politics,* New York: Knopf, 1956.

Key, V. O. Jr., *Politics, Parties, and Pressure Groups,* 5th ed., New York: Crowell, 1964.

Komarovsky, Mirra, *Women in the Modern World: Their Education and Their Dilemmas,* Boston: Little, Brown, 1953.

Kruschke, Earl R., *The Woman Voter: An Analysis Based Upon Personal*

Interviews. Washington, D.C.: Public Affairs Press, 1955.

Lane, Robert E., *Political Life: Why People Get Involved in Politics,* Glencoe, Ill.: The Free Press, 1959.

Loth, David, *A Long Way Forward: The Biography of Congresswoman Frances P. Bolton,* New York-London-Toronto: Longmans, Green & Co., 1957.

Lundberg, George and Farnham, Marynia, *Modern Woman: The Lost Sex,* New York: Harper, 1947.

Luthin, Reinhard H., *American Demagogues: Twentieth Century,* Gloucester, (Mass.): Peter Smith, 1959.

LWV, *Facts About the League of Women Voters,* Washington, D.C.: Publication #221, 1964.

League of Women Voters, *Forty Years of a Great Idea,* Washington, D.C.: Publication #266, 1960.

League of Women Voters, *Handbook for Citizens,* Raleigh, North Carolina, 1963.

League of Women Voters, *It Makes a Difference,* Washington, D.C.: Publication #296, 1963

League of Women Voters, *Man and the River: The Story of the Delaware River Basin,* Delaware, New Jersey, New York, Pennsylvania, 1959.

League of Women Voters, *The Member and the League,* Washington, D.C.: Publication #264, 1960.

Marr, Jean, *Woman in Parliament,* London: Odhams Press, 1962.

Matthews, Donald R., *The Social Background of Political Decision-Makers,* New York: Random House, 1954.

Matthews, Donald R., *U. S. Senators and Their World,* Chapel Hill: University of North Carolina Press, 1960.

McGinley, Phyllis, *Sixpence in Her Shoe,* New York: Macmillan, 1964.

Mead, Margaret, *Male and Female: A Study of the Sexes in a Changing World,* New York: William Morrow, 1949.

Means, Marianna, *The Women in the White House: The Lives, Times, and Influence of Twelve Notable First Ladies,* New York: Random House, 1963.

Merriam, Charles E. and Gosnell, Harold F., *Non-Voting: Causes and Methods of Control,* Chicago: University of Chicago Press, 1924.

Mesta, Perle (with Robert Cahn), *Perle: My Story,* New York-Toronto-London: McGraw-Hill, 1960.

Monsen, R. Joseph, Jr., and Cannon, Mark W., *The Makers of Public Policy: American Power Groups and Their Ideologies,* New York-St. Louis-San Francisco-Toronto-London-Sydney: McGraw-Hill, 1965.

Montgomery, Ruth, *Mrs. LBJ,* New York-Chicago-San Francisco: Holt, Rinehart, and Winston, 1964.

Moore, Edmund A., *A Catholic Runs for President,* New York: Ronald Press, 1956.

Myrdal, Gunnar, *An American Dilemma: The Negro Problem and American Democracy,* New York-Evanston-London: Harper & Row, 1944.

Neuberger, Richard L., *Adventures in Politics,* New York: Oxford University Press, 1954.

Nye, F. Ivan and Hoffman, Lois Waldis ed., *The Employed Mother in America,* Chicago: Rand McNally, 1963.

Odegard, Peter H. and Baerwald, Hans H., *The American Republic: Its Government and Politics,* New York-Evanston-London: Harper & Row, 1964.

Park, Maud Wood, *Front Door Lobby,* Boston: Beacon Press, 1960.

Paxton, Annabel, *Women in Congress,* Richmond: Dietz Press, 1945.

Peck, Mary Gray, *Carrie Chapman Catt: A Biography,* New York: H. W. Wilson, 1944.

Pellet, Betty (with Alexander Klein), *"That Pellet Woman!"*, New York: Stein & Day, 1965.

Proxmire, Ellen, *One Foot in Washington: The Perilous Life of a Senator's Wife*, Washington, D.C.: Robert B. Luce, Inc., 1963.

Putnam, Mabel Raef, *The Winning of the First Bill of Rights for American Women*, Milwaukee: Privately Published, 1923.

Roe, Dorothy, *The Trouble With Women Is Men*, Englewood Cliffs, N. J.: Prentice-Hall, 1961.

Roosevelt, Eleanor and Hickok, Lorena A., *Ladies of Courage*, New York: Putnam's Sons, 1954.

Sanders, Marion K., *The Lady and the Vote*, Boston: Houghton Mifflin, 1956.

Sayre, Wallace S. and Kaufman, Herbert, *Governing New York City*, New York: Russell Sage Foundation, 1960.

Scott, Hugh D., Jr., *How to Go Into Politics*, New York: John Day, 1949.

Sinclair, Andrew, *The Better Half: The Emancipation of the American Woman*, New York: Harper & Row, 1965.

Smith, Eudochia Bell, *They Ask Me Why . . .*, Denver: World Press, 1945.

Smothers, Frank, ed., *The Book of the States 1964-1965*, Chicago: The Council of State Governments, 1964.

Stouffer, Samuel H., *Communism, Conformity and Civil Liberties*, Garden City, New York: Doubleday, 1955.

Strayer, Martha, *The D.A.R.: An Informal History*, Washington, D.C.: Public Affairs Press, 1958.

Tait, Marjorie, *The Education of Women for Citizenship: Some Practical Suggestions*, Basle: UNESCO, 1954.

Turner, Ralph H., *The Social Context of Ambition: A Study of High School Seniors in Los Angeles*, San Francisco: Chandler, 1964.

Upton, Harriet Taylor, *Random Recollections,* Committee for Preservation of Ohio Woman Suffrage Records, 1927.

Van Riper, Paul P., *Handbook of Practical Politics* 2nd ed., Evanston, Ill.: Row, Peterson, 1960.

Wahlke, John C., Eulau, Heinz, Buchanan, William, Ferguson, LeRoy C., *The Legislative System: Explorations in Legislative Behavior,* New York-London: Wiley, 1962.

Warner, W. Lloyd, Van Riper, Paul P., Martin, Norman H., and Collins, Orvis F., *The American Federal Executive,* New Haven and London: Yale University Press, 1963.

Weis, Jessica, in James M. Cannon, ed., *Politics U.S.A.,* Garden City, New York: Doubleday, 1960.

Wilson, James Q., *The Amateur Democrats: Club Politics in Three Cities,* Chicago: University of Chicago Press, 1962.

Wilson, Logan and Kolb, William L., ed., *Sociological Analysis,* New York: Harcourt, Brace, 1949.

Wolfle, Dael, *America's Resources of Specialized Talent,* New York: Harper, 1954.

Worrell, Dorothy, *The Woman's Municipal League of Boston: 1908-1943,* Boston: Privately Published, 1943.

Young, Louise M., *Understanding Politics,* New York: Pellegrini & Cudahy, 1950.

Young, Louise M., *The Political Role of Women in the United States,* Report to the International Political Science Association, The Hague, 1953.

Zeller, Belle, ed., *American State Legislatures,* New York: Crowell, 1954.

UNPUBLISHED Ph. D. DISSERTATIONS

Fletty, Valborg Esther, *Public Services of Women's Organizations,* Unpublished Ph. D. Dissertation, Syracuse University, 1952.

Johnson, Dorothy Elizabeth, *Organized Women and National Legislation: 1920-1941*, Unpublished Ph. D. Dissertation, Western Reserve University, 1960.

Kruschke, Earl R., *Female Politicals and Apoliticals: Some Measurements and Comparisons*, Unpublished Ph. D. Dissertation, University of Wisconsin 1963..

ARTICLES AND MAGAZINES

Adams, Grace, "Women Don't Like Themselves,"*North American Review*, June, 1939.

Addams, Jane, "Julia Lathrop at Hull House: Women and the Art of Government," *Survey Graphic*, Sept., 1935.

Barnard, Eunice Fuller, "Madame Arrives in Politics," *North American Review*, Nov., 1928.

Bettelheim, Bruno, "Women: Emancipation Is Still to Come," *New Republic*, Nov. 7, 1964.

Belmont, Mrs. O. H. P., "Women as Dictators," *Ladies' Home Journal*, Sept., 1922.

Blair, Emily Newell, "Men in Politics as a Woman Sees Them," *Harper's*, May, 1926.

Blair, Emily Newell, "New Styles in Feminine Beauty," *Outlook and Independent*, June 26, 1929.

Blair, Emily Newell, "Woman at the Conventions," *Current History Magazine*, Oct., 1920.

Booth, Mary, "If You're a Man," *This Week Magazine*, Jan. 10, 1965.

Broder, David S., "What Makes a Great Senator?", *New York Times Magazine*, June 14, 1964.

Brown, Nona B., "Inquiry Into the Feminine Mind," *New York Times Magazine*, April 12, 1964.

Brown, Nona B., "Women's Vote: The Bigger Half?", *New York Times Magazine*, Oct. 21, 1956.

Chomel, Marie Cecile, "Does the Wife Vote Like Her Husband?", *Ladies' Home Journal,* May, 1919.

Clarke, Ida Clyde "A Woman for the Senate," *Century Magazine,* June 1929.

Clarke, Ida Clyde, "A Woman in the White House," *Century Magazine,* March, 1927.

Coffin, Tris, "India Edwards: Queen-Maker of Washington," *Coronet,* April, 1951.

Cohen, Wilbur J., "Womanpower Policies for the 1970's," Seminar on Manpower Policy and Program, U.S. Department of Labor; 1967.

Colton, Olive A., "Adventures of a Woman Voter," *Survey,* Sept. 1, 1928.

Congressional Quarterly Weekly Reports, 1948-1965, *Passim.*

Connable, Roma, "Politics—A New Wide-Open World for Women," *Mademoiselle,* March, 1964.

Conway, Jill, "Jane Addams: An American Heroine," *Daedalus,* Spring, 1964.

Cortland, Ethel Wadsworth, "Kitchen Statesmen," *The Outlook,* March 17, 1926.

Current Biography, 1940-1965, *Passim.*

Davenport, Walter, "Where Men Go Wrong About Women," *Collier's,* Sept. 14, 1956.

Davis, Clare Ogden, "Politicians, Female," *North American Review,* June, 1930.

Degler, Carl, "The Changing Place of Women in America," *Daedalus,* Spring, 1964.

Democratic Campaign Manual, 1964.

Democratic Digest, 1926-1953, *Passim.*

Dodds, Harold W., "Women's Place in Politics," *Ladies' Home Journal,* Aug., 1952.

Dougherty, Page H., "It's a Man's Game, But Woman Is Learning," *New York Times Magazine,* Nov. 3, 1946.

Eddy, Edward D., Jr., "What's the Use of Educating Women?" *Saturday Review,* May 18, 1963.

Egan, Eleanor Franklin, "Women in Politics to the Aid of Their Party," *Saturday Evening Post,* March 22, 1920.

Erikson, Erik H., "Inner and Outer Space: Reflections of Womanhood," *Daedalus,* Spring, 1964.

Erikson, Joan M., "Notes on the Life of Eleanor Roosevelt," *Daedalus,* Spring, 1964.

Espy, Hilda Cole, "The League of Women Voters," *Woman's Day,* May, 1964.

Ethridge, Willie Snow, "The Lady from Georgia," *Good Housekeeping,* Jan., 1923.

Evans, Ernestine, "Woman in the Washington Scene," *Century Magazine,* Aug., 1923.

Evans, Wainwright, "When Lovely Woman Votes 'Thumbs Down!' ", *World's Work,* Feb., 1929.

Fisher, Marguerite J., "If Women Only Voted," *Christian Science Monitor Magazine,* Oct. 30, 1948.

Frazer, Alice, "You Are Losing Ground," *McCall's,* Aug., 1947.

French, Eleanor C., "Key Political Force—The Ladies," *New York Times Magazine,* March 11, 1956.

George, W. L., "Woman in Politics," *Harper's,* June, 1919.

Gerould, Katharine Fullerton, "Some American Women and the Vote," *Scribner's Magazine,* May, 1925.

Gorer, Geoffrey, "Political Behavior of the Human Female," *New York Times Magazine,* May 30, 1948.

Grafton, Samuel, "Women in Politics: The Coming Breakthrough," *McCall's,* Sept., 1962.

Graham, Lee, "Who's in Charge Here?", *New York Times Magazine,* Sept. 2, 1962.

Graham, Lee, "Women Don't Like To Look at Women," *New York Times Magazine,* May 24, 1964.

Green, Elizabeth, "I Resign From Female Politics," *New Republic,* April 22, 1925.

Greenstein, Fred I., "Sex-Related Political Differences in Childhood," *Journal of Politics,* May, 1961.

Hacker, Helen M., "Women as a Minority Group," *Journal of Social Forces,* Oct., 1951.

Hamill, Katherine, "Women as Bosses," *Fortune,* June, 1956.

Hard, Anne, "Are Women Making Good in Politics?" *Pictorial Review,* June, 1928.

Hard, Anne, "The Three Ruths in Congress," *Ladies' Home Journal,* March, 1929.

Harris, Corra, "Practical Politics for Gentlewomen," *Ladies' Home Journal,* Sept., 1921.

Hastings, Philip K., "Hows and Howevers of the Woman Voter," *New York Times Magazine,* June 12, 1960.

History of Democratic Women

Howard, George E., "Changing Ideas and Status of the Family and the Public Activities of Women," *The Annals,* Nov., 1914.

Independent Woman (Now called *National Business Woman),* 1920-1965. *Passim.*

Jordan, Elizabeth, "Women in the Presidential Campaign," *Ladies' Home Journal,* Oct., 1920.

Kenton, Edna, "Four Years of Equal Suffrage," *The Forum,* July, 1924.

Kenyon, Dorothy, "Case (by One of Them) for Women Lawyers," *New York Times Magazine,* Feb. 19, 1950.

Kerr, Barbara Wendell, "Don't Kid the Women," *Woman's Home Companion,* Oct., 1956.

Kinkead, Katharine T., "We Darn Near Killed Luella," *New Yorker,* May 5, 1956.

Kobler, John, "The First Tycoon and the Power of His Press," *Saturday Evening Post,* Jan. 16, 1965.

Kuhn, Irene Corbally, "Women Don't Belong in Politics," *American Mercury,* Aug., 1953.

LaCossitt, Henry, "The Mayor Wears Flowers in Her Hair," *Saturday Evening Post,* May 22, 1954.

Lape, Esther Evereth, "When Are Equal Suffragists Equal?", *Ladies' Home Journal,* July, 1920.

Lindsay, Malvina, "Mrs. Grundy's Vote," *North American Review,* June, 1932.

Lisagor, Peter and Higgins, Marguerite, "L.B.J.'s Hunt for Womanpower," *Saturday Evening Post,* June 27-July 4, 1964.

Literary Digest, 1920-1937, *Passim.*

Low, A. Maurice, "Women in the Election," *Yale Review,* Jan., 1921.

Lynch, Denis Tilden, "Friends of the Governor, " *North American Review,* Oct., 1928.

March, James G., "Husband-Wife Interaction over Political Issues," *Public Opinion Quarterly,* Winter, 1953-54.

Markel, Helen, "Twenty-Four Hours in the Life of Margaret Chase Smith," *McCall's*, May, 1964.

Martin, Anne, "Woman's Vote and Woman's Chains," *Sunset Magazine*, April, 1922.

Martin, George Madden, "The American Woman and Representative Government," *Atlantic*, March, 1925.

McGill, Helen Gregory, "These Women in Politics," *Canadian Magazine*, May, 1934.

McLaughlin, Kathleen, "Women's Impact on Public Opinion," *The Annals*, May, 1947.

Mead, Margaret, "Must Women Be Bored With Politics?", *Redbook*, Oct., 1964.

Merriam, Charles E., "The Chicago Citizenship School," *Journal of Social Forces*, Sept., 1923.

Miller, J., "She Chose to Run," *Christian Science Monitor Magazine*, Nov. 2, 1940.

Moncure, Dorothy A., "Women in Political Life," *Current History Magazine*, Jan., 1929.

Moyer-Wing, Alice Curtice, "Men Only," *Scribner's Magazine*, Sept., 1926.

Moyer-Wing, Alice Curtice, "The Vote: Our First Comeback," *Scribner's Magazine*, Sept., 1928.

National Council of Women Bulletin.

Neuberger, Maurine, "Footnotes on Politics by a Lady Legislator," *New York Times Magazine*, May 27, 1951.

Neuberger, Richard, "My Wife Put Me in the Senate," *Harper's*, June, 1955.

Newell, Margaretta, "Must Women Fight in Politics?", *The Woman's Journal*, Jan., 1930.

Norris, Kathleen, "If I Were President," *Delineator*, Jan., 1929.

O'Brien, John C., "Women's Bid for Politics," *The Sign,* Jan., 1959.

Perkins, Frances, "Eight Years as Madame Secretary," *Fortune,* Sept., 1941.

Peterson, Esther, "Working Women," *Daedalus,* Spring, 1964.

Pratt, Ruth, "Men Are Bad Housekeepers," *Harper's,* May, 1927.

Pratt, Ruth, "The Lady or the Tiger," *Ladies' Home Journal,* May, 1928.

Rice, Stuart A. and Willy, Malcolm M., "American Women's Ineffective Use of the Vote," *Current History Magazine,* July, 1924.

Richardson, Eudora Ramsay, "The Ladies of the Lobby," *North American Review,* June, 1929.

Riencourt, Amaury De, "Will Success Spoil American Women?" *New York Times Magazine,* Nov. 10, 1957.

Roberts, Steven V., "Another First for Nancy," *New York Times,* Jan. 3, 1965.

Roosevelt, Eleanor, "The Wisdom of Eleanor Roosevelt," *McCall's,* 1962.

Roosevelt, Eleanor, "Women in Politics," *Good Housekeeping,* Jan., 1940.

Rose, Arnold M., "The Role of Voluntary Associations in American Democracy," *The American Review,* Dec., 1961.

Rossi, Alice S., "Equality Between the Sexes: An Immodest Proposal," *Daedalus,* Spring, 1964.

Ross, John Gordon, "Ladies in Politics," *The Forum,* Nov., 1936.

Samuels, Gertrude, "Really a Man's World—Politics," *New York Times Magazine,* Oct. 15, 1950.

Sanders, Marion K., "Issues Girls, Club Ladies, Camp Followers," *New York Times Magazine,* Dec. 1, 1963.

Sanders, Marion, "Women in Politics," *Harper's,* Aug., 1955.

Scott, Anne F., "After Suffrage: Southern Women in the Twenties," *Journal of Southern History,* Aug., 1964.

Selden, Charles A., "The Most Powerful Lobby in Washington," *Ladies' Home Journal,* April, 1922.

Sessions, Jack, "Who Runs the Public Schools?", *The American Teacher,* Jan., 1964.

Shaffer, Helen B., "Women in Politics," *Editorial Research Reports,* Feb. 20, 1956.

Shalett, Sidney, "Is There a 'Women's Vote'?", *Saturday Evening Post,* Sept. 17, 1960.

Shannon, William V., "Reforming the House—A Four-Year Term?", *New York Times Magazine,* Jan. 10, 1965.

Shuler, Marjorie, "Teaching Women Politics," *Review of Reviews,* Sept., 1921.

Smith, Helena Huntington, "Mrs. Willebrandt," *Outlook and Independent,* Oct. 24, 1928.

Stanford, Neal, "The Woman's Vote," *Christian Science Monitor Magazine,* Nov. 16, 1964.

Stern, Lynn, "Housewife in Politics," *American City,* Oct., 1954.

Stewart, Al, "Feminine City Managers," *American City,* May, 1964.

Stewart, Ella S., "Woman Suffrage and the Liquor Traffic," *The Annals,* Nov., 1914.

Stolberg, Benjamin, "Madame Secretary: A Study in Bewilderment," *Saturday Evening Post,* July 27, 1940.

Stuart, Mrs. Robert J., "The New Political Power of Women," *Ladies' Home Journal,* Sept., 1964.

Tucker, Ray, "Fearless Frances," *Collier's,* July 28, 1934.

Wakefield, Dan, "The Outriders," *Esquire,* July, 1962.

Weston, Marybeth, "Ladies' Day on the Hustings," *New York Times Magazine,* Oct. 19, 1958.

White, William S., "Public Women," *Harper's,* Jan., 1960.

Worden, Helen, "Pretty Good Politicians," *Collier's,* Jan. 14, 1950.

Young, Louise M., "The American Woman at Mid-Century," *The American Review,* Dec., 1961.

GOVERNMENT PUBLICATIONS

American Women: Report of the President's Commission on the Status of Women.

Clarenbach, Kathryn F., "University Education of Women," Annual Report University of Wisconsin, Oct., 1964.

Employment Opportunities for Women in Legal Work, Women's Bureau Bulletin, No. 265, 1958.

1962 Handbook on Women Workers, Women's Bureau Bulletin, No. 285, 1963.

House Foreign Affairs Committee Hearings on the Foreign Assistance Act of 1964.

Job Horizons for College Women in the 1960's, Women's Bureau Bulletin, No. 288, 1964.

New York Women and Their Changing World, (Report of the Governor's Committee on the Education and Employment of Women), 1964.

Oettinger, Katherine B., "The Role of Women in Government," Address before the Boston Council of Club Presidents, March 23, 1963.

Peterson, Esther, "Women and Policy Politics," Address to Sixth Annual Alumnae Forum of Boston, April 4, 1964.

Report of the First Governor's Conference on the Changing Status of Women, Madison, Wisconsin, Jan., 1963.

Report on Four Consultations of the President's Commission on the Status of Women, Washington, D.C., Oct., 1963.

Second Governor's Conference on the Status of Women, Madison, Wisconsin, March 6, 1965.

Women in the World Today: Women in High-Level Elective and Appointive Positions in National Governments, Feb., 1963, Women's Bureau of U.S. Department of Labor.

Reports of about 20 of the 45 Governors' Commissions on the Status of Women.

Report on Progress in 1966 on the Status of Women, Third Annual Report of Interdepartmental Committee and Citizens' Advisory Council on the Status of Women, Washington, D.C., December 31, 1966.